WHY WE WORRY

Something must have changed in society. We weren't always this worried. Not always caught up in disastrous scenarios in our minds. What is this nagging voice in our head? Why won't it stop, and why are we so fixated on it?

In *Why We Worry*, Roland Paulsen paints a broad picture of the cultural variations and historical evolution of anxiety. Through this lens, he invites readers to explore the paradox of how material wealth has enriched our lives in every aspect except one: our mental well-being.

This book offers empirically grounded insights into the sociological underpinnings of issues relating to worry. As such, it is suitable for undergraduate students in psychology, sociology, and medicine – and anyone who has ever been trapped in rumination.

Roland Paulsen is an Associate Professor of Sociology at Lund University. His research focuses on medical sociology, cultural studies, and the sociology of work. The meaning of work, and also the meaninglessness of work, are the subjects of two of his books: *Empty Labor: Idleness and Workplace Resistance* (2014) and *Return to Meaning: A Social Science with Something to Say* (with Mats Alvesson and Yiannis Gabriel, 2017).

"Paulsen's book is a fascinating and penetrating analysis of our late-modern anxieties when we are confronted with the basic uncontrollability of the world – and a passionate plea for regaining a robust trust in life that does not depend on control and domination."

Hartmut Rosa, *Friedrich Schiller University Jena, Germany*

WHY WE WORRY

A Sociological Explanation

Roland Paulsen

Routledge
Taylor & Francis Group
LONDON AND NEW YORK

Designed cover image: Fredrik Wenzel

First published in English 2025
by Routledge
4 Park Square, Milton Park, Abingdon, Oxon OX14 4RN

and by Routledge
605 Third Avenue, New York, NY 10158

Routledge is an imprint of the Taylor & Francis Group, an informa business

Published in Swedish by Albert Bonniers Förlag, July 2020
Original Title: *TÄNK OM - EN STUDIE I ORO*
Translated by Alice Menzies

British Library Cataloguing-in-Publication Data
A catalogue record for this book is available from the British Library

ISBN: 978-1-032-84779-5 (hbk)
ISBN: 978-1-032-84777-1 (pbk)
ISBN: 978-1-003-51493-0 (ebk)

DOI: 10.4324/9781003514930

Typeset in Sabon
by Deanta Global Publishing Services, Chennai, India

To Anna

CONTENTS

1 A Window onto Our Thoughts 1

PART 1
Worry in Our Time **15**

2 How We Feel 17

3 The Nature of Worry 37

4 In Thought's Clutches 53

PART 2
Trickles of History **69**

5 Time Horizons 71

6 Disenchantments 90

7 An Appendage of the Machine 104

8 The World as Risk 121

9 The Self as Risk 141

10 Self-Suspicions 162

PART 3
Action in Our Time **193**

11 Quieting Worry 195

12 Living with Worry 214

13 Beyond Treatment 227

Index *239*

Think of the old cliché about the mind being an excellent servant but a terrible master. This, like many clichés, so lame and unexciting on the surface, actually expresses a great and terrible truth. It is not the least bit coincidental that adults who commit suicide with firearms almost always shoot themselves in the head.

– David Foster Wallace

1

A WINDOW ONTO OUR THOUGHTS

According to Greek mythology, Poseidon created a bull, Athena a house, and Zeus a man. It was meant as a competition of sorts, and they called on Momus, the god of satire and criticism, to decide the winner. Momus began by rejecting the placement of the bull's eyes. Poseidon should have placed them beneath its horns so that the bull could better take aim when it charged. Athena's house was similarly flawed. Without wheels, its owner would be unable to take it with them when they moved. The issue with Zeus's creation was that his mind was closed to the outside world. The man lacked a window in his chest, meaning no one could see what he was thinking.

Zeus was reportedly so enraged with Momus' criticism that he banished him from Mount Olympus and that is more or less all we know about the god of criticism.

In Aesop's Fables, the oldest written source of the myth, Momus doesn't explain why he wanted an insight into man's mind; the reader is left to work that out for themselves. Yet another version of the myth, dating from late Antiquity, claims that Momus wanted to make it easier to determine whether or not a person was telling the truth. That seems like a good enough reason, but it isn't hard to imagine other, less cynical reasons for wanting a window onto our thoughts – not least because such a window would help us to feel less alone.[1]

The fact that we underestimate other people's problems is a well-established phenomenon. In studies where participants are asked both to share their problems and describe the problems they believe others face, the comparison is a simple one: We assume that other people have things easier than they really do. This applies to both strangers and people we know, and those who most underestimate the suffering of others also happen to be those who

DOI: 10.4324/9781003514930-1

are suffering most themselves. Our notions of other people's happy lives become an anxiety in and of themselves, a source of dejection. This may look like envy, but perhaps it is more that our suffering becomes less of a failure if we know that others are suffering too.[2]

How scared of our own minds would we really be if we knew what was going on inside other people?

100-Decibel Thoughts

Daniel is a musician. He has a thick mop of fuzzy brown hair, and it is easy to picture his head bobbing over his cello as he plays a sonata. Although I know that Daniel has his problems – that is why we arranged to chat, after all – I still find myself imagining a happy existence the first time we meet. I picture a childhood full of healthy food, loving parents, tennis camps, and never-ending summers at the family's place in the country. A childhood shaped by his love for the cello, which he has been mastering since he was a boy. A sublime existence shared with like-minded peers at the conservatoire, going on school exchanges abroad to Paris and Strasbourg.

And the truth is that Daniel did enjoy many of these things. Music has always been a source of light to him, a form of sanctuary, even during the most monotonous practice sessions. Looking back now, Daniel regrets not making more of an effort to devote himself to it. Perhaps, it could have saved him from everything else, not least his devastating quest to be a good person through and through.

It isn't that he thinks there is anything wrong with being good – the ambition itself is a noble one. The question is what it *means* to be good. For Daniel, taking responsibility for one's actions is a minimum requirement. But what does that really entail?

In the town where Daniel grew up, there is a river. The children used to swim in it during the summer, and in winter, they would take shortcuts across the ice. Leaning over the railings on the bridge to watch the river flow by was a peaceful activity. As was throwing rocks into it, seeing them swallowed up by the dark water below. On his way home from school one day, Daniel decided to indulge in this simple pleasure. He grabbed a few stones from the side of the road, threw them from the bridge, and went on his way.

But later that night, as he lay in bed, it struck him that he might have done something stupid. He remembered hearing that someone had thrown a bicycle into the river a few years earlier, and since no one had bothered to rescue it, it had been there ever since. Just the thought of the bicycle lying on the bottom of the river made him uneasy. Rusty junk, buried in the mud ...

What if.

Daniel remembers that when the thought first came to him, it felt more like a joke than anything. It was impossible to take seriously, both surreal and unlikely. Not *entirely* unlikely, of course. No, there was always a risk. But it was a ridiculous risk. Illusory. Still, it *could* be that one of the rocks he threw into the river had hit the bicycle on the bottom. Unlikely, yes, but it could have happened. In addition to that – though this was incredibly unlikely – there was a small risk that the rock could have caused some of the rust to come loose from the bicycle.

A small risk? Minimal. But a risk all the same. Roughly the same as the risk of a plane crashing, he thought. Or maybe more like the Earth being hit by an asteroid. Small, small risks that sometimes lead to catastrophe. There was also a risk that any rust that came loose would spread through the water and ... No, we're talking vanishingly small risks here, impossibly small risks.

But still.

The thought did come to him.

What if the rust, which might have been dislodged by him throwing a rock that might have hit the bicycle, poisoned the fish in the river?

It was a crazy thought, he knew that the moment he thought it, and yet: The risk was still there. And if there was a risk that he had caused such a catastrophe, shouldn't he take responsibility for it?

Daniel twisted and turned in bed that night. He couldn't take the thought seriously, but he felt it weighing on him. Putting pressure on him. And the more he thought about it, the heavier it seemed to become, not least when he began to embellish the thought. In his mind's eye, he saw images of dead fish on the front of the local paper. A police officer saying that they didn't yet have any suspects but that they had received reports of a boy throwing rocks from the bridge. Perhaps they would bring in an expert to say that of course people couldn't go around throwing rocks into the river when there was junk on the bottom, not considering the implications for the "fauna" and the "biotope" and the "ecosystem."

Daniel reflected on the thought. Madness! But it overwhelmed him again a moment later. Why had he thrown *multiple* rocks into the river? And why the big one?

The thought kept him awake. Should he do something? Tell an adult? But the thought was crazy. He *knew* it wasn't true, so why did he keep thinking it? What if it *was* true? The images of the dead fish floating among the reeds came back to him. The rest of the house was asleep, but Daniel was wide awake. He stayed that way for quite some time. And the next morning, he searched for the thought the moment he opened his eyes.

Was it still there?

It was. For several days, it continued to weigh on him.

He debated back and forth with himself. Maybe he should turn himself in, simply confess, and take his punishment? But they would laugh at him! That was the worst part. He was afraid of what he might have done, but he was also afraid that he was actually this afraid that he seemed to be taking the thought so seriously. Something wasn't right, something had happened *to him*.

In the end, he decided to take responsibility and confess to his mother. When she failed to grasp the problem, he had to take her through every single risk moment as carefully as he could, really emphasising the gravity of what he had done. Even now, he isn't convinced she fully understood what he was saying, but this marked the beginning of a long line of confessions and reassurances between the two.

It could be about anything, from a fear of dying – not least in relation to things he had done that might have caused cancer – to a vague sense of unease in which the catastrophe was less defined. Daniel often worried about having left his school books at home, for example. Or the key to his locker. Shouldn't he check one last time? Even if his mother reassured him that he had just checked his rucksack, he would unzip it to make sure everything was there another ten times on the way to school. From a purely theoretical point of view, there was a risk he had been wrong earlier. And when he finally got to his locker, he might spend twenty minutes making sure it really was locked.

"Why was that so important to you?" I ask him.

"I can't tell you the exact reason, but it was important to do well in school. I stayed up late for weeks preparing for exams. Don't know if it was an identity thing or what it was. I think I had some sense that if I didn't do well, everything would go to shit. Though what 'go to shit' means was probably pretty hazy."

Daniel's worry underwent several metamorphoses and became a worry in and of itself. What exactly had he done wrong? Whenever he confessed to his mother, he already knew what she was going to say to reassure him, and he knew she would be right. Despite that, the doubt followed him around like a constant murmur in his head, and physical exercise and intense musical practice were the only things that could bring him any respite.

When Daniel eventually left home to begin an engineering degree, he continued to call his mother so that she could reassure him. After he handed in his dissertation, he experienced an extended period of doubt over whether he might be guilty of plagiarism. One of his classmates had given him a few suggestions about what to write in the theory section, and though he knew, deep down, that that wasn't enough to count as plagiarism, he started to google the criteria. The various debates over what fell into the grey zone and what was out-and-out plagiarism bore no relation to what he had actually done. And yet on some abstract level, it felt like they applied to him.

He worried that he might have misinterpreted the law. He read up on precedent and wrote lists of arguments that a prosecutor might use against him. In another column, he made a list of the arguments his defence lawyer might use. He fantasised about being kicked out of university, what the student paper might write about him. His mother reassured him as best she could, but in his head, the trial went on for hours. Before long, he had advanced to propositional logic and become something of an expert in copyright law.

It wasn't until he had rushed into the next set of worries that his plagiarism concerns gave way, but his new worry would make all his previous worries seem like a meditative state of mind in comparison.

Watching porn online had always been a conflicting activity for Daniel. Even as a young man, it often made his mind race. Why, for example, did he find it arousing to watch a woman suck off a man? What if it wasn't the woman he was aroused by, but the man's erection? Would that mean he was gay? That wouldn't be a problem in and of itself, it was just that he had never thought of himself as gay. He was attracted to women, not men, but what if that was because he was lying to himself? What if, deep down, he simply didn't know he was gay? Maybe he was actually a homophobe, like one of those priests who talk about homosexuality being the devil's work only to be caught in the act with another man, pants around his ankles?

This time, his mother took his concerns much more seriously than usual. If her son was gay, she didn't want him to feel any shame, and she tried to keep the topic open.

But when Daniel began to suspect that he might actually be a paedophile, he could no longer turn to his mother for help. He had just been accepted onto an exchange programme in Strasbourg, where he had also made contact with an ensemble. On a porn site one day, his screen suddenly filled with pop-ups. As he was closing them, he saw one filled with what he thought might be child porn. For a few seconds, the blood seemed to pound in his ears. He panicked and desperately tried to shut down his computer.

"I was so scared that I had to go and hide under the bed."

Was child porn really something that could just pop up on your screen like that? Didn't you have to search for it on the "dark web" or whatever it was called? Had his computer been infected with a virus of some kind, and had Google reacted to that? Though didn't Google actively work to prevent the spread of that very kind of material?

He started googling.

Questions he had never thought he would have to grapple with suddenly dominated his thoughts. A new trial got underway. *What if* after *what if* took hold, in a series of circular stories which, the more he thought about them, seemed as true as they were surreal.

What if no. 1: What if he really was guilty of possessing images of child pornography? He read online that it was enough for a computer to have downloaded that type of content for a person to be considered guilty.

What if no. 2: What if he became a police suspect and they found some kind of digital evidence on his computer? But why would the police be interested in *his* computer?

What if no. 3: What if his computer had been flagged up by some online crime unit while he was trying to google whether it was possible that he had seen child porn? Jesus Christ, he had searched the most suspect thing of all: How to find child porn. If that didn't set alarm bells ringing, the security services weren't worthy of their name.

What if no. 4: What if the police had put him under surveillance and he was now being investigated? But wouldn't that be a good thing? They would see that there was no suspect traffic on his computer. Well, except ... see *What if no. 1.*

What if no. 5: What if a prosecutor took charge of the case? How pathetic would his excuses sound? But surely a prosecutor could understand that? He hadn't done anything wrong; surely they would be able to see that? Even if there was an investigation, the prosecutor might decide there wasn't enough evidence to go to trial – he knew that from before.

What if no. 6: What if there *was* a trial and he had to find a defence lawyer? Would he even manage that process?

What if no. 7: What if there was a trial and he was acquitted? That would be better than being convicted, of course, but would he be able to live with having been a suspect? What if that information was kept in some kind of register, and he was tarred with the "no smoke without fire" brush for the rest of his life?

What if no. 8: What if he was convicted?

Daniel tells me that every layer of *what if* made his anxiety grow.

"It's the same today. It doesn't make me any calmer to know that the chances of me being sent down are miniscule. Just the fact that there's a risk is enough to make me focus everything on it. It got to the point where I started planning what I would do if I really was sent down and all my friends distanced themselves from me."

"What would you do?"

"I'd become a monk somewhere, live a life of solitude."

In parallel to the legal questions, Daniel's anxieties about his sexuality also re-emerged – this time with a charge that felt unmanageable. What exactly was it that upset him so much about all of this? Was it purely the fear of being sent to prison, or was it down to something else? He had spent weeks wondering how to get hold of child porn – wasn't that strange behaviour? Yes, he was doing it in an attempt to reassure himself that he hadn't committed any crimes, but what if there was also a hidden motive? What if, *unbeknownst to him*, he was actually a paedophile? What if *that* was the source of all his previous problems?

These thoughts seemed to be thundering through his head at 100 decibels. Daniel shared the paedophile's guilt, the paedophile's shame, without also sharing the paedophile's arousal. That was his one consolation, the straw he clung onto as proof that it was all in his mind: the fact that paedophilia filled him with nothing but disgust. But what if that disgust was itself a sign of arousal? Could he really be sure that what he felt wasn't arousal?

During his exchange year in Strasbourg, he began to test himself.

"It got to the stage where I struggled even to look at children, because every time I did, I had to check I wasn't sexually attracted to them. And that in itself is pretty suspect, isn't it, because why are you looking if you're not sexually attracted?"

Daniel was in a situation where it had become impossible to prove to himself that he wasn't a paedophile. In the court of his mind, he lost appeal after appeal. If he decided it was all in his head, he was repressing his true feelings. If he checked whether he was sexually aroused, he was acting like a paedophile. If he decided not to think about it, the thoughts came to him anyway. And surely that, if anything, was proof – not being able to stop thinking about paedophilia.

Time didn't help. In fact, his anxieties seemed to grow the longer he was trapped inside them. He went to the student health centre, told them about the way his mind kept racing. But he couldn't tell them everything, not what was really on his mind. When he got back to Sweden, however, he went to see a psychiatrist who insisted on knowing.

Once Daniel had told her, the psychiatrist said something that saved his life. She said that if she was ever afraid that her children might be at risk of abuse, she would turn to Daniel to babysit. Because Daniel was not a paedophile. In fact, if it weren't for his aversion to paedophilia, it never would have developed into an obsessive thought.[3]

Living with Uncertainty

Daniel suffered from obsessive-compulsive disorder, specifically the form sometimes known as Pure O, where unwanted ideas such as "what if I'm a paedophile?" intrude and dominate a person's thoughts. Anyone can experience this type of unwanted thought, but what causes problems for certain people is that they do not allow themselves to think them. The thought has to be "neutralised" – condemned or disproven – at which point, paradoxically, it gains meaning and grows stronger.

Why this issue arises is unclear, but a number of theories have been proposed over the years. From a medical perspective, the following approaches have been particularly influential:

1. Daniel's problems stem from a dysfunctional connection in the brain, likely between the orbitofrontal cortex, the basal ganglia, and the thalamus. In very basic terms, the orbitofrontal cortex processes sensory information in order to send signals to the basal ganglia, which, in turn, send signals to the thalamus, which controls the motor system and, in all likelihood, any attempts to neutralise unwanted thoughts. The thalamus then sends information back to the orbitofrontal cortex – all in a never-ending loop. The problem arises when the thalamus sends faulty warning signals back to the orbitofrontal cortex, thereby – because the sensory information tells it there is no danger – leading to a mismatch between the expected and actual outcome of the neutralised thought. This creates a sense that the thought needs to be neutralised again – a spiral of "do it again, and do it right."[4]
2. Daniel has developed a kind of hypermorality in an attempt to hide and compensate for unpleasant truths about himself. This not only covers unconscious feelings of guilt over masturbating at a young age but aggressive impulses that, as a result of his hyper-morality, are forced out of his consciousness and return as obsessions. In one infamous case (given the name "Rat Man" by Sigmund Freud), a man worried that his father and future wife would be subjected to a method of torture in which a starved rat ate its way out through their rectums. The thought, which was fraught with anguish and disgust, became an obsession, and Freud came to the conclusion that it was an expression of repressed anal erotic fantasies. By focusing on the rat in his father's anus, the man was able to avoid acknowledging his own anal erotic orientation. Daniel's obsessive thoughts, however awful they may seem, help him to hide an even more unpleasant truth about himself.[5]

It may be the case that both theories are correct – one does not rule out the other – but both also have their shortcomings. One such shortcoming is that they only partly answer the question of *why* the problem emerged in the first place. If obsessive thoughts are the result of dysfunctional connections in the brain, why does this dysfunctional connection arise? And if obsessive thoughts stem from a hypermorality in which shameful desires cannot be admitted, why does such a hypermorality develop? What might have preceded these issues?

In this book, I aim to explore a third theory. What I propose is that Daniel's problems represent an extreme of a learned inability. The majority of us suffer from this inability to some degree, but over the past two centuries, the problem has worsened dramatically. The inability manifests itself not just in people's actions, but in society, politics, law making, technology, and work. To the extent that this is a disease, it is therefore not simply an individual pathology. Humanity has, on a collective level, developed an *inability to live with uncertainty.*

What if questions are our mind's way of dealing with uncertainty. We imagine things that may have happened or may still happen. We calculate likelihoods and weigh risks against one another. In the course of writing this book, the public debate was for a while almost entirely dominated by various *what ifs* on the theme of Covid-19.

What if we do too little to halt the spread of the coronavirus pandemic? What if we do too much? What if the measures cause a global financial downturn? What if this downturn means that even more people die as a result of unemployment and poverty than from Covid-19?

Fortunately, there was plenty of information against which to position these *what ifs*. Since the pandemic first began to dominate our news feeds, levels of online traffic to many major news sites doubled. We had access to statistics, scientific reports, and hundreds of experts who had devoted their entire working lives to studying exactly this type of epidemiological question. And yet the future seemed uncertain, every decision risky. The experts couldn't agree. The differences of opinion were plain to see, not least in the various strategies the world's governments implemented with regards to measures like travel bans; lockdowns; the closure of schools, universities, and restaurants; and the banning of large public gatherings. In every country, there were debates about whether the measures have been too soft or too draconian.[6]

When an individual is faced with similar *what if* questions in their personal life, things can get extremely complicated.

Over the course of history, we have become increasingly preoccupied with *what if* questions. Researchers in the 1970s estimated that between 0.005 and 0.05 percent of the U.S. population suffered from obsessive thoughts. As a practicing psychologist, it was unlikely you would ever encounter a patient with obsessive-compulsive disorder. In fact, in 1973, one American researcher wrote that obsessive-compulsive disorder is "without doubt, one of the most uncommon forms of psychiatric disorder."[7]

Today, however, the World Health Organization lists obsessive-compulsive thoughts as one of the most widespread psychiatric problems globally. The majority of studies estimate that around two to three percent of the Western World meets the criteria for the diagnosis, yet obsessive-compulsive thoughts are just one of many expressions of the same pattern of thoughts. The worry that arises with *what if* also belongs here, resulting in a risk analysis of what might be lurking in the unknown. Many of these *what ifs* have, over the years, been assigned specific diagnoses.[8]

"What if my headache is a sign of meningitis?" We call this hypochondria.

"What if those silences are a sign that they don't really like me?" We call this social anxiety.

"What if I die right now?" We call this panic disorder.

The number of diagnoses has multiplied, illuminating variations on the same theme, and if we bring together all the so-called anxiety disorders where *what if* forms the cognitive hub, then around a third of all Europeans are estimated to have suffered at some point in their lives. Globally, anxiety disorders represent the most widespread form of mental illness.[9]

Calling this type of anxiety a "disorder" does, however, require a corrective. The "disorder" manifests primarily in the person in question *suffering* as a result of their *what ifs*. A person might think, "what if there's a zombie apocalypse" and dig a bunker in their back garden, for example, but they do not, in the diagnostic sense, have a disorder unless this behaviour also disrupts their life. In fact, they could even gain social recognition from it and build an identity around their aversion to risk.

In the same way, a programmer developing a monitoring system to register performance, client interactions, and sales is simply doing their job; no risk is too small when it comes to measuring performance or maximising profit. A politician can win votes if they promise to be tougher on crime, regardless of whether crime levels in society are actually rising or not. Politics has taken on a guarding function in that sense, its purpose to manage risks – the risk of financial crisis, of increased unemployment, lower competitiveness, reduced growth, and poorer health. Nowadays, a focus on risk even permeates more radical politics. Building a political platform based on the need to tackle climate change, for example, takes a calculation of risk as its starting point. It may be a reasonable policy, but it stems from the same basic principle.

It wasn't always this way.

Anxiety contains its own enlightenment. Being aware of risks is not an illusion – it could just as easily be called insight. And inherent in all anxiety is an insight into uncertainty. Just as there is a risk that the sun will not rise tomorrow, there was a risk that the stones Daniel threw into the river could, through a series of incredibly unfortunate butterfly effects, have poisoned at least one fish. Catastrophe can strike at any moment, and the fact that a hypochondriac has already sought medical attention for what they suspect to be cancer seventy-five times does not mean they won't discover it on the seventy-sixth. If we include the less fantastical risks of death, illness, and accident, then statistically speaking something terrible is likely to happen to each of us at some point in our lives. The real delusion is to perceive the world as safe.

Yet anxiety does not simply contain an insight into the myriad risk moments surrounding us. It is also linked to our own actions and what we do with those risks. It is here that anxiety differs from fear.

The Danish philosopher Søren Kierkegaard identified fear as the feeling we get when looking over the edge of a precipice. The risk is a simple one: What if I fall? Anxiety, on the other hand, arises from the thought that it is *me* standing here, looking down; that it is *me* exposing myself to this sight, and that it is *up to me* whether I keep looking down – or possibly even take a step forward and jump.

Anxiety is not simply about the risk that something might happen; it also contains a note of self-reflection. What should I do? Why am I thinking this? Am I going crazy? These introspective questions wake what Kierkegaard called the "dizziness of freedom."[10]

A similar line of thought can also be found in Buddhist teachings about our impotence in the face of *anicca* – the simple fact that everything in the world is impermanent and that there will eventually be a catastrophe in the form of our own death. Anxiety lacks acceptance of this impermanence. We see a danger and enter a self-fulfilling spiral of being upset by our own upset, while at the same time trying to find ways of neutralising the danger. In this sense, all anxiety oscillates between *obsession* (fixating on discomfort) and *compulsion* (attempting to neutralise the discomfort).

Scholars influenced by Buddhism have long pointed out that this oscillation is not pathological in the sense of being abnormal. On the contrary, the majority of our thoughts, even among strictly "healthy" people, swing between seeing problems in the future and neutralising these problems. We live with this back and forth as a kind of non-stop noise in our heads, and the noise is often so loud that it can negate the importance of all external conditions. It makes no difference where we are – whether we're lying between the soft sheets in our beds, listening to ourselves breathing; whether we're meeting friends in the most merry of contexts; or whether we're watching the northern lights dance across the sky. The noise can make anything seem like a nightmare.

And yet, it continues. The fact that we have repeated a particular cycle of thought countless times before does not stop us from dwelling on something one more time – as though doing so were more responsible than refraining. This mental rumination merges together with what we consider our "self." Our stream of thoughts – which is difficult to control and varies on the basis of uncontrollable impressions in the past and the present – becomes our centre point. We identify with the voice in our head as though it was coming from some kind of cerebral control room, and we use it to build stories about who we are.

This headache has followed us for so long that we – Buddhists, Stoics, existential philosophers, psychoanalysts, and behaviourists alike – have come to consider it existential.

In this book, I will argue that it is not, in fact, existential. We have not always lived with questions about who we "really" are and what might happen in the future. Our inner critics and eternal self-suspicions are, from a historical perspective, relatively young phenomena. The same applies to our obsession with future catastrophes.

Consider the two hundred thousand or so years in which humans lived as nomads, the long, long period in which we had to gather the food we needed every day. Without any crops to tend to, and without any harvests to store, not only was it difficult to plan more than a few days ahead, it was also pointless. Loose social ties with multiple regroupings and vague or non-existent hierarchies also meant that any advanced notions of the self had little to build on. Among the few people who continued to live this way into the twentieth century, there seems to have been no great need for ritualised meditation practice or psychedelic ego transcendence. They already lived in the present.[11]

This book is about the erosion of the social foundations of being present. About how the future was stretched to incomprehensibility through thousand-year plans for radioactive waste and savings accounts for unborn children. About how the individual was equipped with a "self," with a family name and a personal identification number, twelve years of being filtered through the education system, thousands of possible career paths, and a ranking system of material living standards – from less than two dollars a day to millions of dollars a day – to fit into. About how choice and the mass production of culture and technology has infiltrated our lives to such an extent that the most affluent of us now face over 200 daily choices relating to our eating habits alone. About how every decision – even around the most complex of subjects, such as whether we would rather live in a single-family household, as a couple, in a polyamorous relationship, in a nuclear family, or in a rainbow family with multiple children – has been burdened with the expectation of rationality. And about how choice has created the risk of making the wrong decision, of taking a misstep and careening into the abyss in an increasingly distinct division between winners and losers.[12]

Certain threads in this depiction will be freer than others, but on the whole the research I touch upon will be enough to sketch the outline of a sociology of worry. The colour comes from the many interview subjects who wanted to talk about everything from the most mundane of concerns to the most shameful of obsessive thoughts. If this book manages to succeed in fulfilling the great promise of literature – functioning like Momus' window onto the thoughts we all have, but which only the bravest of us choose to share – then the credit is all theirs.

Notes

1 Laura Gibbs, *Aesop's Fables,* Oxford: Oxford University Press, 2002, p. 518.
2 For summary, see Alexander H. Jordan et al., "Misery has more company than people think: Underestimating the prevalence of others' negative emotions", *Personality and Social Psychology Bulletin*, vol. 37, nr. 1, 2011. Studies also show that people experience fewer negative emotions when they are in the company of others and can observe their emotions more directly, see Ed Diener, Randy J. Larsen and Robert A. Emmons, "Person situation interactions: Choice of situations and congruence response models", *Journal of Personality and Social Psychology*, vol. 47, nr. 3, 1984; Reed Larson, Mihaly Csikszentmihalyi and Ronald Graef, "Time alone in daily experience: Loneliness or renewal", *Loneliness: A Sourcebook of Current Theory, Research and Therapy*, 1982. One factor that comes into play is that people seem to communicate more positive emotions to their surroundings than negative, see James J. Gross, Jane M. Richards and Oliver P. John, "Emotion regulation in everyday life" in *Emotion Regulation in Couples and Families: Pathways to Dysfunction and Health*, vol. 2006, 2006.
3 The name Daniel is a pseudonym. This applies to all interview subjects, numbering fifty-four in total. Certain biographical details have also been changed, for example where the people live and work.
4 See, e.g. David Mataix-Cols and Odile van den Heuvel, "Neuroanatomy of obsessive compulsive and related disorders" in *The Oxford Handbook of Obsessive Compulsive and Spectrum Disorders*, ed. Gail Steketee, Oxford: Oxford University Press, 2011.
5 Sigmund Freud, *Three Case Histories*, New York: Simon and Schuster, 2008, pp. 41–65.
6 See Ella Koeze and Nathaniel Popper, "The virus has changed the way we internet", *The New York Times*, 7/4, 2000.
7 See Lee Baer and William E. Minichiello, *Obsessive-Compulsive Disorders: Practical Management*, New York: Mosby Incorporated, 1998, p. 4. I can already hear the protests at this point: can these historical frequencies really be compared with today's? They are not fully comparable, because the data does not come from standardised surveys. Medicalisation and awareness of the diagnosis likely has an impact here. But it does give us a rough idea of the historical changes in the prevalence of OCD, as discussed in Lennard J. Davis, *Obsession: A History*, Chicago: University of Chicago Press, 2009, above all pp. 220–229. See also the chapter "Self-Suspicions" in this book. For comparable longitudinal statistics covering anxiety disorders more generally, see the chapters "How We Are" and "In Thought's Clutches".
8 It is also worth mentioning that if we expand the diagnosis of OCD to anyone who has ever suffered the same type of issue for a period of two weeks or more, then we are – at least with regards to the U.S. population – looking at closer to thirty percent. See Ayelet M. Ruscio et al., "The epidemiology of obsessive-compulsive disorder in the National Comorbidity Survey Replication", *Molecular Psychiatry*, vol. 15, nr. 1, 2010. See also Ayelet Meron Ruscio et al., "Cross-sectional comparison of the epidemiology of DSM-5 generalized anxiety disorder across the globe", *JAMA Psychiatry*, vol. 74, nr. 5, 2017.
9 On the proportion of Europeans with anxiety disorder: Borwin Bandelow and Sophie Michaelis, "Epidemiology of anxiety disorders in the 21st century", *Dialogues in Clinical Neuroscience*, vol. 17, nr. 3, 2015. On anxiety disorder as the most widespread disorder: Dan J. Stein et al., "Epidemiology of anxiety disorders: From surveys to nosology and back", *Dialogues in Clinical Neuroscience*,

vol. 19, nr. 2, 2017. Note that the diagnoses that are classified as anxiety disorders have varied over time. Prior to DSM-5, for example, obsessive-compulsive disorder and post-traumatic stress disorder were both included.

10 Søren Kierkegaard, *Begreppet ångest*, Stockholm: Wahlström & Widstrand, 1965, p. 42.

11 See e.g. Morris Berman, *Wandering God: A Study in Nomadic Spirituality*, New York: SUNY Press, 2000. The question is investigated in more detail in the chapter

12 On the daily number of decisions relating to food: Brian Wansink and Jeffery Sobal: "Mindless eating: The 200 daily food decisions we overlook", *Environment and Behavior*, vol. 39, nr. 1, 2007. On the highest wage, at time of writing: Hillary Hoffower, "We did the math to calculate how much money Jeff Bezos makes in a year, month, week, day, hour, minute, and second", *Business Insider*, 9/1, 2019.

PART 1

Worry in Our Time

2

HOW WE FEEL

I ASKED FOR A SIGN NOT TO DO THIS. THERE WAS NOTHING.

-Unnamed man [1]

Suicide was the subject of one of the first sociological studies in history, and it also happens to be the subject that led me to rediscover the sociology in which I once earned my doctorate. It happened when I stumbled across the type of dense academic study that isn't typically read by more than a handful of researchers. The book reproduced hundreds of suicide notes, and I read them as though a window had opened up onto our minds and I had been invited to peer in.

It is conceivable that suicidology (the study of suicide) could engross the media on a daily basis, much like the economy does. With their graphs and macro-theories, the two disciplines actually resemble one another in many ways. Sadly, they are also similar in the sense that they focus largely on the abstract, with statistical measures and correlation tests making any analysis opaque to the general public.

When the French sociologist Émile Durkheim cleared the way for suicidology a little over a century ago, he argued that an individual's motive for committing suicide was irrelevant; science could understand what was going on inside a person's mind far better than the individual themselves ever could. This nineteenth-century approach proved tenacious, and little by little, it also cloaked itself in medical terminology: Those who take their own lives are mentally ill and therefore have no grasp of their own motives.

One problem with the research stemming from this approach is that it does not offer a Momus window onto what is going on inside the individual.

DOI: 10.4324/9781003514930-3

It provides no answers to the most pressing question of all: What those who take their own lives are thinking and feeling.

> I decided in Sept.2007 life was no longer worth living. I liquidated all my assets and decided to end it when they ran out. They ran out.[2]

Because the fact is that motives are multifaceted. For every answer they give us, new questions arise. Take the quotation above, for example. What could have driven this man, born in one of the world's wealthiest countries, and evidently with a decent level of personal wealth, to want to end his own life? Are rationally acceptable reasons really possible, or are we looking at fabricated explanations that simply float on the surface of a much deeper bog?

We know that suicide is not simply a case of individual deviation. It is no coincidence, for example, that suicide rates in Russia have for decades been between twenty to sixty times higher than in Barbados. Something in Russia has a comparatively more negative effect on people's will to live, but what? What part of society can explain the despair inherent in suicide?[3]

It is difficult to bring order to this question, not least against the background of the powerful belief that we have never had it so good. It seems reasonable to think that the average fourteenth-century European might have found life tough. Between a third and half of the population dying of the plague – we understand that. We shudder at the thought of bygone eras of crop failure, epidemics of tuberculosis, smallpox, dysentery, and mumps. We can barely even imagine what life must have been like when twenty to thirty percent of all children, rich and poor alike, died within just a few years of being born.[4]

But as this type of suffering decreased, it can seem hard to understand why anyone would have reason to complain. Nowadays, murder rates in Europe are forty times lower than they were in the Middle Ages. We have developed food production techniques that enable us to cope with weather conditions that, just a few centuries ago, would have led to famine, and considerably, more people are now overweight than starving. Having plagued humanity for thousands of years, smallpox has been eradicated. Even polio is close to being wiped out, and having children should – with global infant mortality rates having undergone a fivefold reduction – no longer be anywhere near as troubling.[5]

It simply cannot be emphasised enough: We are currently surfing a wave of financial and technological development on a scale never before seen. In terms of diet, technology, household conditions, and access to healthcare, many low-income individuals now enjoy higher standards of living than a medieval king. The mobile phones in our pockets have a memory seven million times larger, and a processing power 100,000 times greater than the computer on Apollo 11, which took man to the moon.[6]

So why on earth would anyone have reason to feel bad?

The Whims of Happiness

There is a common belief that the constant march of progress also applies to our well-being. We know that people tend to rate their own happiness – or "life satisfaction" as it is also known – higher the more economic growth a country experiences. Since every country now produces and consumes more than ever, this seems like good news. If the wheels of the economy are allowed to keep turning at a faster and faster pace, we might assume that our collective happiness will also continue to rise. This is reassuring; nothing to criticise or worry about here. All that matters is that we continue down this path.

But if we take a closer look at the research into happiness, we quickly see several reasons to question this view of the world. After a certain level (equivalent to that reached by Sweden in the 1950s), the link between a country's economic growth and the number of people who rate their life satisfaction as good flattens out. Above that level, it becomes increasingly difficult to see any pattern whatsoever. Happiness rates in an immensely wealthy city state like Singapore, for example, are no higher than they are in a much poorer country like Panama. And a moderately wealthy country like Finland outclasses considerably richer countries like Luxembourg and Kuwait.[7]

Historically, this flattening out is clearest in the richest countries. In Japan, the United States, and the United Kingdom, happiness levels have been stagnant for so long that economic growth has had time to double. In fact, surveys from the early 1970s to the present day show that Americans have actually become slightly less satisfied with their lives, despite the fact that their country has doubled its wealth.[8]

These measurements of happiness are, in other words, open to interpretation. The way the surveys are carried out is another widely debated area of concern. As a rule, a ten-point scale (known as the Cantril Ladder) is used, asking respondents to choose between 0 for "the worst possible life for you" and 10 for "the best possible life for you." But what does this really mean? How should we understand best "*possible life*" and "*for you*"?

Many have argued over this very issue. One concerning result repeated in several studies is that parents in the majority of countries tend to rate their happiness levels lower than those who do not have children. Parents seem less satisfied with their lives – particularly during the periods in which they are taking care of their children.[9]

But if we dig even a millimetre deeper into the data, a different picture of parenthood emerges. When asked whether they believe their lives to have a purpose – whether they consider their lives to be meaningful, in other words – parents answer yes to a much higher degree than non-parents.[10]

The distinction between "happiness" and "purpose" demonstrates a different aspect of what it means to be human and "feel good." There are parts of us that may be satisfied or dissatisfied, happy or sad, fortunate or misfortunate, but there is also something inside us that wants more: to know what the point is, whether our life is part of some bigger picture, whether we are living a morally defensible life, whether we are contributing to making the world a better place.

And when we take these questions into consideration, the idea of the world forever becoming a better place becomes unsustainable.

Despite 200 years of economic and social progress on a scale never before seen, today's generation says something new: *This is the turning point.* Those growing up now will be worse off than their parents. In terms of material living standards in particular, faith in the future has collapsed. In both high- and low-income countries, the majority think that today's children will be financially worse off than their parents. In certain countries such as France and Japan, only fifteen percent of people believe that children will be better off. Even when you ask younger people (those born after 1982), the majority answer that not only will they be financially worse off, but they will also lead less happy lives than their parents.[11]

The importance of this shift cannot be overestimated. Things used to be the other way around. Younger generations said: We don't want to live the same lives as our parents, we want to find new ways of living. As the wave of student protests swept across the Western world in the 1960s, the revolution was aimed squarely at the society their parents had left behind. "In a society that has abolished every kind of adventure, the only adventure that remains is to abolish society," read the graffiti on the streets of Paris. Being forced to repeat their parents' humdrum existence, struggling through yet another life torn between their duties at home and at work, was precisely what the revolution was fighting against.

Today, the very opposite is true. The younger generation – often accused of being selfish and narcissistic – worries that their parents' humdrum lives are beyond the realms of possibility.[12] Even for those who manage to get the hamster wheel spinning, there is no guarantee they will ever feel a sense of context. When asked whether their job makes a positive difference to the world, almost half of respondents answer no. In response to another question that has been asked since the 1950s – what would you do if you won enough money never to have to work again? – around two thirds reply that they would resign from their current job.[13]

These surveys have primarily been deployed in Europe and North America, but the perceived lack of meaning is striking even on a global level. The analytics company Gallup recently conducted a worldwide study of how people view their jobs. Just thirteen percent classed themselves as "engaged" in their work. The majority, sixty-three percent, were "not engaged"; they had "mentally checked out" and primarily went to work because they got paid. Another twenty-four percent were "actively disengaged." Not only were they unhappy, they had also adopted a hostile attitude toward their respective companies. While the majority broadly endured their jobs, there were almost twice as many who hated going to work as enjoyed it.[14]

The surprising thing about the experience of meaningfulness is that, globally, it follows the opposite pattern to happiness. While happiness rises the richer a country becomes, the perception of meaningfulness shows the inverse. It falls.

In a compilation of Gallup data from 132 countries, the trend is as strong as it is clear: The higher the GDP per capita, the fewer people who reply that life has real meaning. It isn't the case that a higher GDP necessarily *causes* this lack of meaning – we don't know that. What we do know is that industrialisation and the mass production of goods and services do not solve the problem.[15]

Another thing that growth does not solve is the fact that some people choose to take their own lives. Here, again, we see an inverted – albeit slightly weaker – pattern: the richer a country, the higher the incidence of suicide.[16]

Lost to Unhappiness

If I were to go to a Swedish train station and watch the people passing by, I could be confident that every tenth person is either taking or has taken some form of antidepressant over the past year. According to OECD data, the number has doubled since 2001, and if we include anti-anxiety medication and other types of psychopharmacological drugs, then – per the Swedish National Board of Health and Medicine – we are looking at every sixth person. The figures are roughly the same in other Western countries, subject to slight variation. In the United States, for example, one in four middle-aged women is taking some form of antidepressant.[17]

But why do so many people feel the need for chemical assistance?

By asking this type of question, we have flipped the perspective: rather than asking how *well* people are feeling, we are instead asking how *bad* they feel. There are numerous advantages to this approach.

"Happy families are all alike; every unhappy family is unhappy in its own way." This is the opening line from Leo Tolstoy's *Anna Karenina,* but the words could equally be applied to unhappiness in general. Unhappiness can be sorted and made concrete in countless sub-categories and survey questions. Since a *happy life* is seen in many parts of the world as a *successful life*, it is possible, by drawing attention to all of the ways in which we are unhappy, to reduce the influence of what is known in survey methodology as social desirability: the fact that many respond in accordance with what they *think* signals a good life.[18]

Investigating how bad we are feeling is, however, associated with another problem: the studies in this area are often conducted on the basis of medical grounds, where a person's unhappiness is seen as some kind of illness. This problem links to the longstanding debate as to whether human concerns are being *medicalised* – made the subject of medical treatment, in other words.

Where, for example, should we draw the line between shyness and social anxiety? Between feeling down and depression? Between worry and a generalised anxiety disorder?

Much of what was once considered perfectly normal has, today, been declared an illness. This is particularly evident in the increased number of diagnoses and in the way the criteria for diagnosis have become much more inclusive. An example of this can be seen in the latest edition of the American Diagnostic and Statistical Manual of Mental Disorders, which removed the "bereavement" exception from the criteria used to diagnose depression. In previous editions, a diagnosis of depression could not be made if the patient had lost a close relative within the past two months. Following the change, what was previously seen as grief could now be labelled depression.[19]

This type of medicalisation makes it difficult to draw any firm conclusions from the number of people currently receiving psychiatric care.

Medicalisation also raises issues of over-medication. Unfortunately, there is a risk that the critique of medicalisation may warp the question of how we are really feeling today. Many of those now prescribed psychopharmacological drugs would not have been given them fifty years ago, but that doesn't mean that the increased consumption of medication is entirely down to medicalisation. After all, the person taking the drugs is someone who does not feel well. They aren't lazy, they are no less authentic; they are someone who has sought professional help. The statistics for the consumption of psychopharmacological drugs is one of several indicators of just how many believe they need help.

In terms of diagnoses, the global studies into mental illness provide a valuable empirical database, and the fact that medicalisation takes place is no reason to ignore this data. I personally have little time for the idea that a diagnosis implies an *illness*, but that does not prevent me from seeing a diagnosis as an indication of *mental suffering* – if for no other reason than because "clinically significant suffering" is a criterion in all psychiatric diagnosis.[20]

A bigger problem is if the diagnoses are made on shaky foundations.

In a now-classic study published in the journal *Science* in 1973, the American psychologist David Rosenhan sent out twelve postgraduate students to twelve different emergency mental health units. Their only instruction was to claim they could hear a voice saying the word "thud." Though the students largely behaved in an entirely normal manner, almost all were diagnosed with schizophrenia and admitted for treatment. In another stage of the experiment, Rosenhan came to an agreement with a psychiatric hospital that he would continue to send them pseudo-patients for another three months. Once the three months were up, the hospital reported that they had seen 193 patients, forty-one of whom had raised suspicions and twenty-three of whom were highly likely to be faking. This time, however, Rosenhan had not sent any pseudo patients at all.[21]

The Rosenhan study faced a lot of criticism, but it also created a crisis within the field of psychiatry that ultimately led to the diagnostic criteria being clarified in later editions of the Diagnostic and Statistical Manual. Despite this, the issue of over- and underdiagnosis has lingered ever since. There is, for example, no medically sound explanation as to why two percent of children in Nevada are on medication for ADHD, while the number in Louisiana is over five times higher. In some places, doctors are simply more inclined to make diagnoses than in others. This is why data on psychiatric patients is of little use when it comes to estimating just how widespread a particular diagnosis might be.[22]

In order to be able to measure the true spread of a diagnosis, the World Health Organization (WHO) has developed diagnostic questionnaires for use on representative selections of hundreds of thousands of people around the world. Since the 1970s, these questionnaires have been refined with huge batteries of questions, and simply conducting an interview can take hours, requiring the interviewer to visit the interviewee on several occasions. The purpose is to enable a uniform evaluation of global mental health, and the surveys are now conducted routinely as part of the WHO's *World Mental Health Survey Initiative*. The results have been eye opening.[23]

In 1990, depression was the fourth biggest cause of ill health globally, after respiratory disease, diarrheal diseases, and antenatal disorders. A decade later, in 2000, it was the third biggest cause, and by 2010 depression had climbed to second place. In 2017, the WHO reported that what they had long feared – and which, just a few years earlier, they had predicted would happen around 2030 – had already happened: The leading cause of ill health globally was no longer a somatic illness, but depression. In just ten years, the number of people with depression globally had increased by close to twenty percent.[24]

If we look at the most common psychiatric diagnoses and the number of people who, during any given year, meet the diagnostic criteria, the figures for the world's richest countries are astounding. One in four Americans now qualifies for at least one of the most common diagnoses. The United Kingdom and Australia are not far behind, and in France and Canada, one in five qualify.[25]

This warrants returning to the question of exactly what is considered normal. If a quarter of the population has some kind of mental "illness," we must conclude that it is relatively normal to be unwell. And if we ask how many people have, at some point in their lives, experienced periods that fulfil the criteria for the most common depression and anxiety disorders, then the question of normality becomes even more pressing. Yet again, there are variations in the results: From twelve percent in Nigeria to forty-seven percent in the United States. That is approaching every other person.[26]

The fact that the WHO has observed a rapid increase in certain diagnoses (not least those related to depression and anxiety) should be balanced against the fact that there are no long-term data on this global development. For some countries, however – particularly the United States – it is possible to speak of historic trends. As early as 1985, two epidemiological studies documented that the risk of an American becoming depressed had increased tenfold over just two generations.[27]

But one complication of making historical comparisons is that the diagnostic criteria have shifted over the years. To circumvent this, we can instead ask about physical issues such as sleeping problems, dizziness, shortness of breath, difficulty concentrating, and headaches – the idea being that the experience of these issues is less affected by how we talk about them.

One person who has taken this approach particularly far is the American psychologist Jean Twenge. Her summaries show that anxiety has become a normalised part of modern life. Comparing 269 studies carried out between 1952 and 1993, she found that the average North American child in the early 1990s was more anxious than the typical patient within the child psychiatric system in the 1950s.[28]

According to Twenge and her fellow American psychologist Jonathan Haidt, the well-being of young people in the 2010s has worsened at a pace never before seen. They give a range of explanations for this.

One concerning detail is that the increase in depression and anxiety seems to correspond with an historic sense of cautiousness among the young. Eighteen-year-old Americans drink roughly half as much alcohol as their counterparts in the 1970s. Casual sexual interactions have also decreased markedly, and the number of high school students who have been in a fight has halved since 1991. In parallel to this, between 2012 and 2015 – in just *three years* – the symptoms of depression increased by twenty-one percent among young men and fifty percent among young women.[29]

These figures have attracted attention around the world, and many have come to the conclusion that the U.S. currently excels in mental illness, a development that also manifests in the broader wave of "death from despair" (in other words, death caused by suicide, alcohol or overdose) that has increased so much that average life expectancy has fallen for several years in a row.[30]

But in terms of childhood mental health, there is at least one country that has long collected data beyond the psychiatric diagnoses: Sweden.

Even here, the picture is far from rosy. Among the children calling BRIS (a Swedish non-profit championing children's rights) to ask for help, mental health issues are the most common topic of conversation today. This is new and is reflected in the data collected by the National Public Health Agency since 1985. The incidence of psychosomatic problems has increased dramatically among eleven-year-olds in Sweden. Among thirteen- and fifteen-year-olds, the proportion with problems has doubled. In terms of trouble sleeping, nervousness, and feeling low, roughly four in ten fifteen-year-old girls report serious issues. With respect to Twenge and Haidt's emphasis on the effects of "screen time," it should be noted that these steep increases started in the 1990s, long before children had exposure to social media.[31]

The same general developments can be seen across high-income countries. Even in Statistics Sweden's annual survey of living standards, the proportion of young adults who report serious problems with anxiety, anxiousness, and worries has doubled over the past ten years – with twice as many women suffering problems as men.[32]

Whenever this development enters the public debate, it is almost always in relation to one thing: the need for increased access to psychiatric care. But there are other things worth considering here – for example, how on earth so many people can be feeling so much less happy in such a short space of time.

Explanations involving some kind of chemical imbalance in the brain seem unlikely, as this would require something to have preceded the "imbalance," given the synchronicity in the numbers affected. Similarly, genetics should be given only limited relevance, as the collective gene pool typically takes thousands of years to change. Medicine's now-dominant explanatory models into why people feel bad are therefore not applicable, making it rare to hear psychiatrists talk about the increasing deterioration of our well-being over time.

One complicating factor is that it is so difficult to pinpoint any single variable that improves or worsens how we are feeling. We cannot be sure whether more education, more work or even more democracy would solve the problem. As with the experience of meaninglessness, there does not seem to be anything in economic growth that lessens the burden. If anything, a *lower* GDP corresponds surprisingly consistently with higher well-being.

Looking at WHO data for the most common diagnoses, the global pattern is clear: The richer a country is, the higher the percentage of its inhabitants who meet the criteria for the various diagnoses. Indeed, for diagnoses such as generalised anxiety disorder, panic disorder, agoraphobia, post-traumatic stress disorder, substance abuse, and psychotic episodes, the frequencies are more than twice as high in rich countries as in low-income countries.[33]

This pattern reappears in the *Global Burden of Disease Study*, despite the fact that this annual study uses different measures and methods to gather and analyse data.[34]

Yet again, this does not necessarily mean that a higher income makes us unhappy. In fact, it appears that those with the lowest incomes tend to feel worst *within* a country. But viewed in the context of the wider country's material living standards, it is, as the WHO research team behind the *World Mental Health Survey* writes, "striking" that there is "a consistent pattern in 17/18 disorders (SepAd being the exception) of prevalence being lower in the low/lower-middle-income countries than in the high-income countries."[35]

No part of global development acts as a brake, in other words. On this point – how we feel – it does not seem as though growth is the answer.

The variation between countries demonstrates that social circumstances play a greater role than previously thought. Today, this is not a controversial statement. In another WHO report, the state of the research is summarised as follows:

> Mental health is produced socially: The presence or absence of mental health is above all a social indicator and therefore requires social, as well as individual solutions. A focus on collective efficacy, as well as personal efficacy is required. A preoccupation with individual symptoms may lead to a "disembodied psychology" which separates what goes on inside people's heads from social structure and context.[36]

In an official statement made on World Health Day 2017, the United Nations pointed out that while the medical treatment of mental health problems will continue to be necessary, "recent decades have been marked with excessive medicalization of mental health and the overuse of biomedical interventions." The diagnosis is clear: "The longstanding biomedical tradition of medicalizing various forms of psychosocial distress and human suffering has cast a long shadow over the importance of addressing the social and underlying determinants of health."[37]

But what are these social and underlying determinants? In few areas does social science grapple with such uncertainty.

The Suicide Notes

Only a fraction of those suffering mental health issues commit suicide, and whether or not that percentage has increased or decreased in the long run is impossible to say. Some studies suggest a global increase during the second half of the twentieth century, but in large parts of the world the number of suicides has fallen in recent years, which is obviously something to celebrate. Other tendencies are more concerning, not least the fact that an increasing number of men shoot others before killing themselves (in the United States in particular, the number of fatal mass shootings has risen at an alarming rate). Seventy years ago, this was a largely unheard of phenomenon.[38]

At present, around one million people die by suicide every year, making it the fourteenth most common cause of death globally – more common than the sum total of those dying in wars or through other forms of violence. A person is, in other words, more likely to die by their own hand than someone else's.[39]

For every person who dies, a further twenty attempted suicides are thought to take place – roughly one every other second. If we add to this the number of people who have ever considered suicide, then anyone who has read this far should be able to glimpse the hidden world of suffering upon which this book focuses.

Two researchers who have devoted countless studies and hours of data collection to the issue are John Chiles and Kirk Strosahl. In one of their population studies from the United States, ten to twelve percent of participants reported having attempted to take their own life on at least one occasion. In another, twenty percent reported having had serious suicidal thoughts (meaning thoughts that persisted for at least two weeks and involved the creation of a plan and decisions on the means) at some stage. Another twenty percent said that they had seriously considered suicide without ever having come up with a plan.[40]

Twenty percent plus twenty percent? We're approaching half here.

Since not everyone who takes their own life leaves a note (the figure is around one in three), researchers have discussed just how much the letter writers can really help us understand suicide. Perhaps those who leave a note behind differ from those who do not? But aside from the fact that the writers tend to live alone more often than non-writers, the differences seem negligible.[41]

In the most rigorous study of the issue, a group of American researchers collected 1,280 suicide notes from the state of Ohio. Some of the letters were difficult to read as a result of spelling mistakes, illegible handwriting, blood stains and other issues – in one case, for example, the author was found to have drunk a litre and a half of vodka, and the note became increasingly incoherent before ending mid-sentence – but the researchers transcribed and categorised them by the type of message, motive and overarching theme.[42]

What was most striking was that the note writers were generally more concerned about declaring their love for those they were leaving behind than explaining their motives. The most frequent message in the notes was "love for others" – this applied to more than three quarters of the letters. One woman who had been sexually abused as a child wrote the following to her husband:

> *You* loved me *well. So* well. In the end, I couldn't love *myself.*[43]

Another dominant theme was apologising. One man who had struggled with alcoholism wrote:

> I am sorry, I know sorry doesn't seem to have meaning anymore, but I am sorry I could not have been a better person.[44]

Many were also keen to stress that those left behind should not feel any guilt. One woman wrote:

> Please make sure everyone knows it was NOT THEIR FAULT!!! I was loved and I know it. You were all there for me but I guess I needed more than any human being could be asked to give. I honestly and truly love you all.[45]

Others carefully detailed the guilt they believed the wider world held, such as this twenty-three-year-old man:

> I can't hold you and mom responsible all the way, just 25/25, and the other 50 was my fault.[46]

Only thirteen percent of people expressed this type of sentiment, placing the blame elsewhere. Some were more explicit than others. One woman wrote her own obituary, for example, with instructions to publish it without amendment. After her name and the date, the text read:

> She leaves behind a living hell to go be with God. I want to thank my family for helping a weak mind and body to get to this point. You took so much and gave so little. I reached out to all of you, where were you?[47]

Only four percent of note writers expressed this type of anger, however. The angriest letter in the study was penned by a middle-aged nurse who hanged herself in the garage one afternoon:

> I wish I would have left you years ago … I told you I wish I was dead – I chose the time & place. HAPPY ANNIVERSARY … DO NOT TAKE THIS OUT ON THE KIDS … I guess now you'll have to get off your ass, stop drinking & smoking your weed and stop being a loser. GET A JOB. You act like an old man – try living – I wish I had…[48]

If we take a closer look at this particular note, we see a common motivation for suicide: relationships. After "painful life circumstances," "interpersonal problems" was the second most common motivation. This is also borne out by the fact that twelve percent of those who took their own lives did so in front of other people – sometimes without warning, for example with a fire-arm in the middle of an argument.[49]

In contrast to the quotation above, the majority of suicide notes referencing relationships focus almost exclusively on failings in love. A forty-year-old man who hanged himself wrote the following to his wife:

> I have let you down; I have done this in such a way that I can't even look at myself in the mirror. I didn't do my job taking care of you – and for that I am so very very sorry.[50]

Another man wrote to his girlfriend:

> I just couldn't believe I hurt someone I love as bad as I hurt you. I'm truly sorry. It was not me that did that. That is why I cannot live with myself. Because I know I could not hurt you & I still did.[51]

The sense of having failed in life was another theme that appeared in seventeen percent of notes. A twenty-two-year-old man wrote the following on the back of an anti-suicide contract given to him by his therapist:

> I am a disappointment ... I have been a failure in my own eyes my entire life. There is nothing that I excel at. There is nothing where I am the best. I have not ever completed anything of any importance. I am not a good friend. I am selfish. No one ever seems to care about me and if they do it seems self-fulfilling. That is how I treat people so that is how I should be treated in return... Why should I hang around and continue to make myself miserable? I HATE MYSELF. Fuck it I'm out.[52]

Aside from the feeling of failure, the majority of emotions are represented in the notes: weariness (twelve percent), loneliness (eleven percent), grief (nine percent), guilt (seven percent) and shame (five percent).

The only type of suicide not included was, funnily enough, one of Durkheim's key categories of suicide, what he called "altruistic suicide" – when death is seen as an honourable duty. If Durkheim had paid more attention to what people actually thought, rather than speculating about their subconscious motivations, his theories of suicide would likely have looked rather different.

The Master in Our Head

This book opens with a quote by David Foster Wallace, reflecting on the fact that almost everyone who shoots themselves does so with the barrel of the gun to their head. The old cliché is true, Wallace writes: the mind is an excellent servant but a terrible master. We want to escape our thoughts, and that is why we take aim at our heads.

There are two problems with this argument. One is that Wallace is writing from an American perspective in which firearms are widespread. Globally, the majority of those who take their own lives do not do so by shooting themselves. In Europe, the figure is just a few percent, and the most common method of suicide is actually hanging – in some countries, not least in Eastern Europe, it represents 90 percent of cases.

In the United States, however, only fifteen percent (including Wallace himself, sadly) choose hanging. There, the majority use firearms instead. Three studies have taken a closer look at this particular subject, and the results indicate that Wallace was right: the majority of those who shoot themselves – around eighty percent, to be precise – do so in the head.[53]

The second problem with Wallace's analysis is that there could be more reasons to aim for the head than to escape our thoughts. Perhaps it is simply seen as a more effective way of dying?

Despite these issues, Wallace's intuition was likely correct, and the strongest evidence of this is right there in the suicide notes:

> I can't fight anymore, too much on the head.[54]

If there is one thing that emerges as an overarching theme, it is the desire to get rid of the "pain in my head," the "crap in my head," the "voices in my head," or whatever the deceased chose to call it. Finally achieving "peace of mind" is a motivation that crops up in virtually every other note.

This desire to still one's thoughts is plain, and particularly evident in the following letter:

> I simply abhor my very being – my tortured, twisted, weird, unfulfilling existence; and so I can be no more. I just have to turn off my thoughts – I have to. This is euthanasia, pure and simple. They shoot horses, don't they? (...) My thoughts have become completely unbearable and I can't think of any other way to escape them.[55]

The problems these thoughts revolve around vary wildly. One person describes how their thoughts *about suicide* had become unbearable:

> It is the one consistency in my everyday activities. I think about it all the time. You know how men think about sex like every minute, or something like that? Well, I think of suicide and killing myself the same way.[56]

The striking thing about these notes is how the thoughts themselves have grown into something more troubling than the subject of the thoughts. We have to wonder: if there were a stop button, how hard would it have been to endure the loneliness, the failure, the guilt or the grief?

One man who had separated from his wife and was living alone described the process in detail. He had recently lost his job and was struggling financially. He couldn't afford the alimony payments to his ex-wife and their daughter, and that left him shaken. For several days, he couldn't sleep. One night, he decided to take his own life.

In his final letter, he carefully details his concerns. One by one, he sets them out, forming a swirling vortex of thoughts that he also adds to the list:

> I AM FULLY MEDICATED, SO MY BIOLOGICAL ISSUES ARE NOT TO BLAME FOR THIS. HOWEVER, BEING MEDICATED DOES NOT ALTER THE FOLLOWING, INESCAPABLE FACTS:
>
> I CAN'T even pay my rent in full at the start of any given month.
>
> I CAN'T meet my moral responsibility to give Cindy ample financial help.
>
> I CAN'T even really afford this shithole of an apartment, much less a decent place.
>
> I CAN'T afford a decent car.
>
> I CAN'T afford a decent, normal social/dating life.
>
> I CAN'T offer a woman an acceptable explanation for my lowly circumstances.
>
> I CAN'T be a worthy half of a real relationship.
>
> I CAN'T sleep through the night and so...
>
> I CAN'T escape my tortured thoughts which ricochet incessantly off the walls of my brain.
>
> I CAN'T get a grasp on my swirling, slippery thoughts.[57]

Every single point here is anything but an imagined pain. Not being able to afford the rent or a normal social life are undeniably heavy burdens. But these facts alone do not offer a full explanation. Many other people have been in similar situations without committing suicide. This note not only details the problems, but also floats the idea that there is no room for problems of this kind in a life worth living.

Ultimately, it is difficult to reach any certainty on the matter. The thoughts continue to ricochet off the walls of the brain. The master of thought that Wallace feared doesn't seem to be able to make up his mind. Perhaps that is also the reason these thoughts demand our attention. They may be monotonous in their brooding, but in the doubt that gives them their power, they remain ambiguous. The exhortation asks us to do nothing more than straighten things out, tying up the trains of thought sprawling towards how things are on the one hand, and how things could be on the other.

Solve the problem, demands the mind. That is what the mind does.

Notes

1 Cheryl L Meyer et al., *Explaining Suicide: Patterns, Motivations, and What Notes Reveal*, London: Academic Press, 2017, p. 194.

2 Meyer et al., *Explaining Suicide: Patterns, Motivations, and What Notes Reveal*, p. 45

3 World Health Organization, "Suicide rate estimates, age-standardized: Estimates by country", *Global Health Observatory Data Repository*, 2019-05-15, 2019.

4 See e.g. Katharine Olson, "10 dangers of the medieval period," *BBC History Magazine*, vol. 5, 2015.

5 On Murder frequency: Manuel Eisner, "Long-term historical trends in violent crime", *Crime and Justice*, vol. 30, 2003. On the spread of disease: E. Norrby et al., "Polio närmar sig utrotning," *Läkartidningen*, vol. 114, 2017. On more people being overweight than going hungry: World Health Organization, "Obesity and overweight", 2018. On child mortality: Max Roser, "Child mortality," OurWorldInData.org, 2018.

6 For mobile phones and Apollo 11, see Graham Kendall, "Would your mobile phone be powerful enough to get you to the moon?" *The Conversation*, 1/6, 2019.

7 Only if one looks at a logarithmic income scale is there any consistent relationship between income levels and happiness. What this means is that an increase in income from 100,000 to 1 million dollars sees roughly the same increase in happiness as 1 million to 10 million. The richer we become, the more wealth we need to increase our happiness. With enough will, it is possible to interpret this as meaning that the relationship between growth and happiness is eternally positive, despite the fact that the relationship is becoming weaker and weaker. See John F. Helliwell, Jeffrey D. Sachs and Richard Layard, "World Happiness Report 2019", 2019; World Development Indicators, The World Bank, 2019; Christer Sanne, *Keynes barnbarn: En bättre framtid med arbete och välfärd*, Stockholm: Formas, 2007, pp. 40–45.

8 See Jeffrey D. Sachs, "America's health crisis and the Easterlin paradox" in *World Happiness Report 2018*, ed. Jeffrey D. Sachs, Richard Layard and John F. Helliwell, 2018, and Richard Wilkinson and Kate Pickett, *The Spirit Level: Why Equality is Better for Everyone*, New York: Bloomsbury Press, 2010.

9 Jennifer Glass, Robin W. Simon and Matthew A. Andersson, "Parenthood and happiness: Effects of work-family reconciliation policies in 22 OECD countries", *American Journal of Sociology*, vol. 122, nr. 3, 2016. Daniel Kahneman et al., "A survey method for characterizing daily life experience: The day reconstruction method," *Science*, vol. 306, nr. 5702, 2004.

10 This applies to the average, of course – there are also parents who perceive less meaning in life and those who, however unbelievable it may sound, become happier after having children. See Shigehiro Oishi and Ed Diener, "Residents of poor nations have a greater sense of meaning in life than residents of wealthy nations", *Psychological Science*, vol. 25, nr. 2, 2014; Glass et al., "Parenthood and happiness: Effects of work-family reconciliation policies in 22 OECD countries".

11 Deloitte, "The 2017 Deloitte Millennial Survey: Apprehensive Millennials: Seeking stability and opportunities in an uncertain world," 2017, p. 5; Bruce Stokes, "A decade after the financial crisis, economic confidence rebounds in many countries", Pew Research Center, 2018, p. 12.

12 See Carl Cederström, *The Happiness Fantasy,* Cambridge: Polity, 2018.
13 This question has been asked in the UK, the Netherlands and Sweden. In Sweden, those who did not believe that their job improved the world were unusually few in number. See David Graeber, *Bullshit Jobs: A Theory,* New York: Simon and Shuster, 2018, and Carl Johan von Seth: DN/Ipsos: "Två av tre anser att deras arbete gör världen bättre", *Dagens Nyheter,* 28/12, 2018. For a summary of how many people would continue to work if they won the lottery, see Roland Paulsen, "Economically force to work: A critical reconsideration of the lottery question", *Basic Income Studies,* vol. 3, nr. 2, 2008.
14 Gallup, "State of the global workplace", Gallup, 2013.
15 Oishi and Diener, "Residents of poor nations have a greater sense of meaning in life than residents of wealthy nations".
16 Oishi and Diener, "Residents of poor nations have a greater sense of meaning in life than residents of wealthy nations". See also Alison Brunier and Fadela Chaib, "Suicide: One person dies every 40 seconds," 9/9, 2019.
17 OECD, "Pharmaceutical market," 2019; The Swedish National Board of Health and Welfare, "Statistikdatabas för läkemedel," 2019. For a discussion of the total consumption of psychopharmaceuticals, see Isabelle Hedander, "1,6 miljoner svenskar äter läkemedel för att förbättra sin psykiska hälsa," *Kurera,* 11/11, 2016. For the use of antidepressants among middle aged American women, see Laura A. Pratt, Debra J. Brody and Quiping Gu, *Antidepressant Use in Persons Aged 12 and Over: United States, 2005-2008,* US Department of Health and Human Services, Centers for Disease Control, 2011. In the United States, the figures are as follows: twelve percent take antidepressants, eight percent take sedatives and close to two percent take antipsychotics. That the total number consuming psychopharmaceuticals is lower is likely down to the fact that certain individuals take several types, see Thomas J. Moore and Donald R. Mattison, "Adult utilization of psychiatric drugs and differences by sex, age, and race", *JAMA Internal Medicine,* vol. 177, nr. 2, 2017.
18 For a discussion of social desirability, see e.g. ZiaoChi Zhang et al., "Survey method matters: Online/offline questionnaires and face-to-face or telephone interviews differ", *Computers in Human Behavior,* vol. 71, 2017.
19 Gary Greenberg, *The Book of Woe: The DSM and the Unmaking of Psychiatry,* New York: Blue Rider Press, 2013.
20 Even for obviously destructive behaviours, "clinically significant suffering" is used as a diagnostic criterium, see Gary Greenberg, *The Book of Woe: The DSM and the Unmaking of Psychiatry,* pp. 290–294.
21 David L. Rosenhan, "On Being Sane in Insane Places," *Science,* vol. 179, nr. 4070, 1973. It should be stressed that although a number of shortcomings have been identified in this study, it has been of great importance for psychiatric nosology in terms of reliability requirements.
22 Susanna N. Visser et al., "Trends in the parent-report of health care provider-diagnosed and medicated attention-deficit/hyperactivity disorder: United States, 2003-2011", *Journal of the American Academy of Child & Adolescent Psychiatry,* vol. 53, nr. 1, 2014.
23 For methods in World Mental Health Surveys, see Kate M. Scott et al., *Mental Disorders Around the World: Facts and Figures from the WHO World Mental Health Surveys,* Cambridge: Cambridge University Press, 2018, chapter 3.
24 World Health Organization, "Depression and other common mental disorders", Global Health Estimates, 2017. See also Stephen Hayes, *A Liberated Mind: The Essential Guide to ACT,* London: Ebury Publishing, 2019, p. 4.

25 For summary, see Richard Wilkinson and Kate Pickett, *The Inner Level: How More Equal Societies Reduce Stress, Restore Sanity and Improve Everyone's Well-Being*, New York: Penguin Press, 2019, p. 35.
26 Ronald C. Kessler et al., The global burden of mental disorders: An update from the WHO World Mental Health (WMH) surveys", *Epidemiology and Psychiatric Sciences*, vol. 18, nr. 1, 2009.
27 Martin E.P. Seligman, "Why is there so much depression today? The waxing of the individual and the waning of the commons" in *Contemporary Psychological Approaches to Depression*, New York: Springer, 1990.
28 Jean M. Twenge, "The age of anxiety? The birth cohort change in anxiety and neuroticism, 1952–1993", *Journal of Personality and Social Psychology*, vol. 79, nr. 6, 2000.
29 Jean M. Twenge, *iGen: Why Today's Super-Connected Kids Are Growing Up Less Rebellious, More Tolerant, Less Happy*, New York: Simon and Schuster, 2017; Jonathan Haidt, *The Anxious Generation: How the Great Rewiring of Childhood Is Causing an Epidemic of Mental Illness,* New York: Penguin Press, 2024.
30 See e.g. Owen Dyer, "US life expectancy falls for third year in a row", *British Medical Journal*, vol. 363, 2018.
31 On children's Rights in Society: Anna Holmqvist, "*Skola. Vård. Omsorg. Och den psykiska ohälsan.*", Mölnlycke, 2018. On psychosomatic problems: The Public Health Agency of Sweden, "Skolbarns hälsovanor i Sverige 2017/2018," 2018.
32 On the general increase in high income countries: Thomas Potrebny, Nora Wiium and Margrethe Moss-Iversen Lundegård, "Temporal trends in adolescents' self-reported psychosomatic health complaints from 1980-2016: A systematic review and meta-analysis", *PLOS ONE*, vol. 12, nr. 11, 2017. On Statistics Sweden-data: Statistics Sweden, "Hälsotillstånd, fysiska och psykiska besvär efter indikator, ålder och kön. Andelar i procent och skattat antal i tusental. År 2008-2009 – 2018-2018", 2019.
33 Scott et al., *Mental Disorders Around the World: Facts and Figures from the WHO World Mental Health Surveys*.
34 One methodological problem of measuring prevalence, as seen in the WHO's surveys, is that the different diagnoses – not least anxiety and depression – can vary between making life difficult for a few months or for the rest of a person's life. In order to get at this distinction, there is another way of measuring prevalence. Instead of asking how many people have ever met the criteria for a particular diagnosis, researchers attempt to estimate the "burden of disease" measured in terms of "disability adjusted life years" – i.e. how long a person has met the criteria for a particular diagnosis. In the Global Burden of Disease Study, this data is compiled annually, from WHO surveys, as well as from epidemiological data, patient registers and summaries of research reports which, using statistical methods, process different types of data in order to achieve the most representative results possible. This study is more complex than the WHO's survey studies, and consequently it is less transparent, but it is seen by many as being more exact, assuming the life expectancy of various countries is taken into consideration through a so-called age adjustment. The pattern is also evident here. Measures of both "anxiety" and "depression" show the greatest burden of disease in Europe, Australia and North America. If we add these two diagnoses to eating disorders, bipolar disorder, substance abuse, alcohol abuse and schizophrenia, then divide the burden of illness in line with the World Bank's classification of high income, middle income and low income countries, we see that the high income countries sit way above the others. Among high income countries, the burden of disease in life adjusted years per 100,000 people (adjusted for age) is close to 2,500, whereas the figure for other countries is around 1,600. See

Global Burden of Disease Collaborative Network, "Global Burden of Disease Study 2017 (GBD 2016) Incidence, Prevalence and Years Lived with Disability 1990-2017," Seattle, 2018.

35 On the poorest people in a country feeling worst: Wilkinson and Pickett, *The Inner Level: How More Equal Societies Reduce Stress, Restore Sanity and Improve Everyone's Well-Being,* p. 40. On the striking fact that high income countries show the highest frequency: Scott et al., *Mental Disorders Around the World: Facts and Figures from the WHO World Mental Health Surveys,* p. 326.

36 Lynne Friedli and World Health Organization, "Mental health, resilience and inequalities," 2009, p. v.

37 Dainius Pūras, "Special rapporteur on the right of everyone to the enjoyment of the highest attainable standard of physical and mental health", UN Human Rights, 2017, https://www.ohchr.org/EN/NewsEvents/Pages/DisplayNews.aspx?NewsID=21480&LangID=E [2020-02-27].

38 For a summary of studies and a discussion of method, see Matthew Nock et al., *Suicide: Global Perspectives from the WHO World Mental Health Surveys,* Cambridge: Cambridge University Press, 2012, p. 8. See also Ping-I Lin et al., "What have we learned from the time trend of mass shootings in the U.S.?", *PLOS One,* vol. 13, nr. 10, 2018, and Francesco Berardi, *Heroes: Mass Murder and Suicide,* London: Verso, 2015.

39 Nock et al., *Suicide: Global Perspectives from the WHO World Mental Health Surveys*, p. 1.

40 On the number of suicide attempts per death: World Health Organization, *Preventing Suicide: A Global Imperative,* World Health Organization, 2014, p. 9. On the number who have considered suicide: John A. Chiles and Laura Weiss Roberts, *Clinical Manual for Assessment and Treatment of Suicidal Patients*, Washington: American Psychiatric Pub, 2018. For a Swedish study with similar results, see E. Salander Renberg, "Self-reported life-weariness, death-wishes, suicidal ideation, suicidal plans and suicide attempts in general population surveys in the north of Sweden, 1986 and 1996", *Social Psychiatry and Psychiatric Epidemiology,* vol. 36, nr. 9, 2001.

41 See Meyer et al., *Explaining Suicide: Patterns, Motivations, and What Notes Reveal,* pp. 25–26.

42 Meyer et al., *Explaining Suicide: Patterns, Motivations, and What Notes Reveal,* pp. 25–26.

43 Meyer et al., *Explaining Suicide: Patterns, Motivations, and What Notes Reveal,* p. 36.

44 Meyer et al., *Explaining Suicide: Patterns, Motivations, and What Notes Reveal,* p. 37.

45 Meyer et al., *Explaining Suicide: Patterns, Motivations, and What Notes Reveal,* p. 36

46 Meyer et al., *Explaining Suicide: Patterns, Motivations, and What Notes Reveal,* p. 38.

47 Meyer et al., *Explaining Suicide: Patterns, Motivations, and What Notes Reveal,* p. 41.

48 Meyer et al., *Explaining Suicide: Patterns, Motivations, and What Notes Reveal,* p. 48.

49 Meyer et al., *Explaining Suicide: Patterns, Motivations, and What Notes Reveal,* p. 30

50 Meyer et al., *Explaining Suicide: Patterns, Motivations, and What Notes Reveal,* p. 104.

51 Meyer et al., *Explaining Suicide: Patterns, Motivations, and What Notes Reveal,* p. 115.

52 Meyer et al., *Explaining Suicide: Patterns, Motivations, and What Notes Reveal*, p. 47.
53 For the global distribution of suicide methods, see Vladeta Ajdacic-Gross et al., "Methods of suicide: International suicide patterns derived from the WHO mortality database", *Bulletin of the World Health Organization*, vol. 86, 2008 and Airi Värnik et al., "Suicide methods in Europe: A gender-specific analysis of countries participating in the European alliance against depression", *Journal of Epidemiology & Community Health*, vol. 62, nr. 6, 2008. For a summary of statistics over the number who shoot themselves in the head, see Lisa B.E. Shields, Donna M. Hunsaker and John C. Hunsaker, "Suicide: A ten-year retrospective review of Kentucky medical examiner cases", *Journal of Forensic Science*, vol. 50, nr. 3, 2005.
54 Meyer et al., *Explaining Suicide: Patterns, Motivations, and What Notes Reveal*, p. 172.
55 Meyer et al., *Explaining Suicide: Patterns, Motivations, and What Notes Reveal*, p. 33.
56 Meyer et al., *Explaining Suicide: Patterns, Motivations, and What Notes Reveal*, p. 103.
57 Meyer et al., *Explaining Suicide: Patterns, Motivations, and What Notes Reveal*, p. 155.

3

THE NATURE OF WORRY

"Listen, I don't care, it doesn't matter. I know what I've done, so people can think whatever they want. I don't care!"

At the edge of the dog park, there is a bench. A woman sits there sometimes, talking to herself. I've seen her before. If I'm perfectly honest, I've eavesdropped on her. Standing within earshot, pretending to be doing something on my phone.

"I said, go to your owner then. And she went. It's so … I don't want to cry. Should I be crying? And he, he thinks he's so fucking dangerous, but he doesn't know what I've been through. They can point a gun at me, but I'm completely powerless. No use getting worked up if you're powerless."

This isn't the first time I've noticed that there is a "you" in her monologues. I initially assumed she must be hallucinating, that she really does think she is talking to someone. But listening to her now, I'm not so sure.

Is what I can hear simply an example of someone "speaking their mind"?

If I were to put my own stream of thoughts into words, it probably wouldn't sound so different. It would be incoherent, even to me. All those injustices, prejudices, things other people have said, fears, and losses, they would probably be interspersed with lecture-like digressions about how the world works. There might even be an unspecified *you* from time to time. A shifting *you,* even. A *you* that might be someone else at times, myself at others.

"Love's obviously the important thing. I don't know if she's coming back. You talk about love – I want love! *Physical* love!"

She wraps her arms around herself and leans forward.

On previous occasions, most of what I have heard was confused and angry – as though she was furious with us passers-by. She has the posture of

DOI: 10.4324/9781003514930-4

a labourer, the hair of a labourer, the hands of a labourer. She has a broken body, a body that needs crutches. It has been six months since I first walked past the woman on the bench, but I've never seen her sitting with anyone else.

"I didn't just come out and say it. What the fuck are you doing here? Imagine if I had? I should have done. What the *fuuuck* are you doing here? And what am I doing here?"

I have to shout a few times before she hears me.

"Excuse me! Excuse me!"

She stops talking. When she turns to me, the eyes that meet mine are alert.

"I have to ask you something," I say from the other side of the fence. "Why are you thinking aloud?"

"Huh? Is it bothering you?"

"No, no, I was just wondering. Did you realise you were doing it?"

"Of course I did," she says, now more concerned than anything. "What, do you think I'm a bit, you know, funny or something? A bit weird?"

"What you're saying doesn't sound strange. The strange thing is that you're saying it."

A plane roars overhead, drowning out the warm morning with its rumbling, a fading beeping sound. We both look up at the sky.

"I've got a friend who's always nagging me, he nags so fucking much. 'Can you speak up?' His hearing's not great. I have to shout every time I see him. I shout at him and he shouts back at me. It can go on all day."

I sit down beside her on the bench.

"Is that why you think aloud?"

"No. Err, I don't know why."

She smiles. Her gums reveal a society in which dental care isn't universal.

"Guess you can see I've been drinking, huh? Not much, though. A glass of wine. Do you think that's a lot? One glass is enough. Otherwise, I'm as quiet as a mouse. I go into town, buy what I need, head home again. I'm perfectly normal, you know? No, not normal. I drink. You're not normal, you don't act normal when you drink. I'm not looking to talk to anyone, really. I just want a bottle of red wine. Where are you from?"

I tell her that I'm writing a book about worry, and she shares her thoughts on the subject. She tells me that she has worked in psychiatric care for much of her life. That she was interested in sociology when she was younger. These days, she's retired.

As we talk, I have the sense that she is listening as attentively as anyone else. Sure, she might be fond of the kind of rant where one subject drifts into another, but what surprises me is the self-consciousness with which even she seems to live. She is self-conscious of her own thoughts. Of other people's thoughts about her.

"Do you want to feel how warm my hands are?"

I reach out and touch her hand.

"They are warm," I say.

"Hang on. There, there." She grips my hand. "In other countries, people can touch each other like this without thinking about sex. They don't think about anything. They're just human. But us Swedes, we can't do it. We're all, no! But look, I don't feel any sex appeal from your hands, or from your body. I'm not even looking at your body. You know, you've just got to trust that it, it... When you're sitting here, watching people ... some of them, they look so fucking tired. But they haven't asked for that. It's the loneliness that does for people. Loneliness. Do you agree?"

Thoughts About What Isn't There

One of the basic approaches of sociology is attempting to understand what is considered deviant through what is considered normal. The difference doesn't need to be especially big. A person who talks to themselves on a park bench or on the metro might sound angry, self-obsessed, or crazy, but how would it sound if we all broadcast our thoughts? What would we hear then?

Two things we can say with confidence are: 1. Life would rarely be quiet. 2. Much of what we heard would be worries.

When we talk about worry, the standard definition is as follows: "A set of anxieties about an unknown future usually predicated on '*what if ...?*' questions."[1]

This definition can be made more precise. If we look at our thought processes phenomenologically – as in, in the way they appear to us – then *thinking* is the thing we see. An ongoing process, in other words. When we say that we have "a thought," we are therefore simplifying things. We are cutting out a particular section of the larger thinking movement and isolating it as a single thought.

This abstraction – something I too am guilty of in this book – also occurs when we talk about things like "a fear," "a concern" or a "what if question." The only concrete thing is a thought process whose parts we name, at the risk of forgetting the larger movement.

Because as far as worry is concerned, the movement is important. Worrying is a process. It shifts, relentlessly at times, sluggishly at others, but always in a circular motion. It also has a specific aim: to find safety through the movement of thought. This highlights one of the key differences between worry and fear: *worry aims to nullify itself.*

The difference is also evident in the language we use. Being afraid is a *state*, whereas worrying is an *activity*. We don't *worry* about spiders, for example; we're *afraid* of them. And if we are afraid of something, we make sure to watch out for it. We don't necessarily question whether we are doing the right thing by being afraid – fear is a relatively thoughtless emotion. But when we worry about something, we always question whether we are doing the right thing by worrying, and in an attempt to gain clarity we try to imagine various chains of events.[2]

If my worries take the form of wondering, "what if I left the hob on?", the thought doesn't stop there. As I try to remember, my mind will also be busy with a number of other *what ifs* linking back to the question of the hob: what if the ring gets so hot it's glowing red? But I turned it off, didn't I? Or did I? Does it really matter? Yes, because what if it causes a fire? But just because the ring is on doesn't mean it'll burst into flames, does it? No, but what if it does? And what if it causes a fire and one of the neighbours dies?

All these *what ifs* form a type of thinking that has been closely studied within the field of cognitive psychology over the past forty years. A particularly unreal way of thinking. To some extent, all thinking is removed from reality – thinking about something concrete like an orange or a tree can never encapsulate everything that an orange or a tree is – but thoughts need not merely revolve around objects and qualities that actually *exist*. We can also think about things *that do not exist*, things that *could exist* but *do not yet exist*, and *might never exist*.

What if questions revolve around representations of things that do not exist – or, as it is known in cognitive terms, *counterfactual thinking*.[3]

Even if the hob is not on, we can imagine what might happen if it was, and even if the stove doesn't burst into flames, we can imagine what might happen if it did. What we are thinking about here are not *facts* about the world. They are *counterfactual* thoughts. Not what *is* (in the present) but *what could have been* (in the past) or *what could be* (in the future).

A more academic definition of worry is *counterfactual thinking arising from unease*.

Counterfactual thinking has been studied in a whole host of experiments over the past four decades, with researchers investigating whether there are any patterns in our thinking about "that which does not exist." The answer is yes.

As early as 1982, the cognitive researchers Daniel Kahneman and Amos Tversky argued that we have a tendency to imagine the likely over the unlikely. If we miss a plane by a few minutes, for example, we will probably fret more about not making it onboard than we would if we had missed the plane by half an hour.

Similarly, we tend to get more caught up on the exception than the rule. If we get a flat tyre on the way to the airport, we will be more upset than if we miss our flight because of rush hour traffic. In this sense, there is a certain longing for realism present when we think about things that have not happened.[4]

However surreal they may be, counterfactual thoughts also have a real impact on our lives. Many of our emotions would simply be impossible without the ability to think counterfactually.

To take an example, *regret* covers more than our usual definition of an "emotion" – i.e., a reactive feeling with a bodily aspect such as a heightened pulse, shallow breathing or tears. At the heart of regret is a thought of the world as it is and as it could be – asking ourselves, "what if I'd acted differently?" A sense of *coulda, woulda, shoulda*, in other words. None of this is actually real, it doesn't exist. And yet regret is a very real feeling.[5]

This comparison between the real world and other, counterfactual worlds is just as fundamental to emotions like guilt, longing and indignation, or to the lighter emotions of relief, hope and expectation. Each has a mental aspect and therefore exemplifies just how hard it can be to separate our thoughts from our feelings.

The ability to think counterfactually is key to being able to explain fundamental human processes. But the *extent* to which the counterfactual world affects us is not a constant. Over the course of history, we have become increasingly concerned with thinking about things that are not real. And the more we have done this, the worse we have become at noticing things as they are.[6]

The Counterfactual Shift

During the rapid industrialisation of the Soviet Union in the 1930s, a Russian psychologist by the name of Alexander Luria became interested in how people's thought processes were affected by the new era.

Like his mentor Lev Vygotsky, Luria was critical of the dominant idea that a stimulus provokes a response as mechanically as with Ivan Pavlov's famous dogs, who began salivating the moment he rang his bell. Luria argued that in humans, something else took place in between stimulus and response: thought.

But unlike the phenomenologists who were popular in Europe at the time, Luria was unsure whether patterns of thought were the same in everyone, regardless of socio-economic context. He believed that socio-historical factors, such as whether one lived in an industrial or agrarian society, for example, likely had an impact.

In order to investigate his theory, Luria and a group of Soviet researchers carried out a series of cognitive experiments in remote mountain villages in Uzbekistan and China, where living conditions were still pre-modern. The majority of these communities were typically feudal and patriarchal, ruled by rich lords. Many of the participants had neither gone to school nor learned to read.

Luria worked like an anthropologist, attempting to establish contact and forge friendships in the villages he visited, but he also carried out small thought experiments in his conversations with the farmers. These thought experiments involved the type of counterfactual thinking in which a person is presented with two statements and asked to draw a conclusion – a so-called syllogism.

For example: "In the far north, where there is snow, all bears are white. Novaya Zemlya is in the far north. What colour are the bears there?"

In one conversation with a man called Rustam, a forty-seven-year-old farmer, the discussion went as follows:

Rustam: If there was someone who had a great deal of experience and had been everywhere, he would do well to answer the question.
Luria: But can you answer the question on the basis of my words?
Rustam: A person who had travelled a lot and been in cold countries and seen everything could answer; he would know what colour the bears were.
Luria: Now, in the North, in Siberia, there is always snow. I told you that where there is snow the bears are white. What kind of bears are there in the North, in Siberia?
Rustam: I never travelled through Siberia. Tadzhibai-aka who died last year was there. He said that there were white bears there, but he didn't say what kind.[7]

Luria found it difficult to get the farmers to engage with his thought experiments. This can partly be explained, as critics have since pointed out, by the fact that the farmers had little interest in the educated city dweller's concerns. But there was also a pattern to their answers, as can be seen below with Abdurakhm, a thirty-seven-year-old man from a village in Kashgar, China:

Luria: Cotton can only grow where it is hot and dry. In England it is cold and damp. Can cotton grow there?
Abdurakhm: I don't know.
Luria: Think about it.
Abdurakhm: I've only been in the Kashgar country; I don't know beyond that …
Luria: But on the basis of what I said to you, can cotton grow there?
Abdurakhm: If the land is good, cotton will grow there, but if it is damp and poor, it won't grow. If it's like the Kashgar country, it will grow there too. If the soil is loose, it can grow there too, of course.

Luria:	Cotton can only grow where it is hot and dry. In England it is cold and damp. Can cotton grow there? What do my words suggest?
Abdurakhm:	If it's cold there, it won't grow; if the soil is loose and good, it will.[8]

In addition to the fact that the peasants were unfamiliar with the type of questioning that school children get used to from an early age, the pattern was as follows: Rather than engaging in a thought world of absolute truths whose foundations they had no idea about, the peasants tied their answers to their experiences.

Putting experience to one side in favour of counterfactual truths seems to have been particularly alien to them with respect to the syllogisms involving cotton and agriculture – a subject where they had a certain amount of knowledge. Roughly sixty percent of the peasants Luria spoke to could solve syllogisms that fell within their own areas of experience, but when they did so they rarely tied themselves to the premise. Like Khamrak, a forty-year-old farmer, they tried to base their answers on what they had learned for themselves:

Luria:	Cotton can only grow where it is hot and dry. In England it is cold and damp. Can cotton grow there?
Khamrak:	No, if the soil is damp and chilly it can't.
Luria:	Now, in England it is damp and chilly. Will cotton grow there?
Khamrak's wife:	It's chilly here too.
Luria:	But there it is always cold and damp. Will cotton grow?
Khamrak:	Me, I don't know ... I don't know what the weather is like there!
Luria:	Cotton can't grow where it is cold, and it's cold in England. Does cotton grow there?
Khamrak:	I don't know ... if it's cold, it won't grow, while if it's hot, it will. From your words, I would have to say that cotton shouldn't grow there. But I would have to know what spring is like there, what kind of nights they have.[9]

If the syllogism fell outside the farmers' field of experience, as with the bears, only fifteen percent answered correctly. These experiments have been replicated with similar results in other societies where both school attendance and literacy levels are low. Luria's results showed that those who had attended school for a short period of time and learned to read, could, without exception, solve his thought experiments.[10]

In Luria's view, the results were hopeful. With industrial society's demands for literacy and abstract thinking, people would become better at thinking counterfactually. Rather than being tied to sensory experiences as their primary source of information, children would learn logical inference from a young age. Their imagination and self-reflection would reach new heights, and people would become freer and less bound to their immediate surroundings.

To a certain extent, he was right. Studies of how people in industrialised societies think show that counterfactual thinking has taken over. We spend a surprising amount of time focused on things that are not real. But have we, as Luria hoped, become freer in our thinking? It may be philosophically interesting that we *can* think about everything from parallel universes to imaginary conversations and unicorns, but are these really the type of thoughts that go through our heads as we brush our teeth or hurry along the street?

Is it even possible to say anything concrete about what people think about?

This broad question has been widely explored, and has caused several decades' methodological battles. Our thoughts are, of course, invisible on the outside, meaning they cannot easily be measured. Another problem is that we all have differing degrees of awareness of our thoughts. If you were to conduct a survey asking people what they typically think about, the answers could easily become misleading. Most people are not sufficiently observant or distanced enough from their own thoughts to be able to give an accurate summary after the fact.

One way of circumventing this is to conduct so-called experience sampling. This involves randomly sending signals to a group of participants throughout the day. The signal is accompanied by instructions for the participants to write down what they are thinking at that very moment. Since the participants make notes immediately when prompted, the distance between what they *think* they normally think about and what they are *actually* thinking about is reduced.[11]

This method has been fine-tuned and streamlined using information technology, making it possible – at least for the Westerners on whom the studies are typically carried out – to answer the question about their daily thoughts with a certain richness of detail. And no, it is hardly Fermat's Last Theorem, the problem of evil or the infinite nature of the universe that occupy our daily thoughts.

We think primarily to the past and the future. The most striking observation is that very few of our thoughts – particularly in terms of daydreams and brooding – are taken up by the present. Our thinking is mostly counterfactual, in so far as we think about things that are not real and, most of all, about things that are *not yet* real – i.e. the future. Even when it comes to positive thoughts, the future dominates, with things like hope and expectation.

In one study, thoughts about the future were almost twice as common as thoughts about the past.[12]

We think about ourselves above all else. When thinking to the past or the future, the topics that preoccupy us aren't so much the Thirty Years' War or the melting ice caps. In all thinking, there is a mid-point, and we call this mid-point *me*. Even when we consider ourselves unselfish in our thinking, the mid-point is usually there: we think about *our* children, *our* friends, *our* pets, *our* parents. And in terms of worrying, it isn't global warming or the rise of right-wing nationalist governments that dominate our thoughts, despite the fact that such developments will likely affect us. Our worries are often much narrower than that, linked to individual responsibilities, our own choices.[13]

Precisely what we, as individuals, worry about varies, partly depending on age. While worries, according to a British study, largely revolve around finances and work at the outset of our adult lives, this tends to pass once we reach the age of forty. Looking at our lives as a whole, the anxiety that comes out on top revolves around something else: our relationships with other people. We worry about what might happen to them, what they think of us, what we think of them.

In this respect, very little changes with age. The old seem to worry about their relationships just as much as the young. If the woman talking to herself on the bench had followed the normal trend, she wouldn't be especially worried about her finances or her work by this stage of her life. But her thoughts about what other people think of her, her fears of being abandoned and longing for love, those will never leave her.[14]

We think counterfactually more often than is good for us. In a large study published in the journal Science, an experience sampling study involving 5,000 people across eighty-three countries produced 250,000 samples. The study asked participants to answer questions about what they were currently doing, how they felt, and whether they were engaged in so-called "mind wandering" – thinking about things that were not happening right there and then – at various points during the day. This type of "stimulus-independent thinking," as it is also known, occurred in almost half of all responses, and the activity the participants were engaged in seemed to make little difference. In fact, the only activity that effectively prevented mental absence was "making love."

The most thought-provoking results from the study revolved around how the respondents felt at each moment of recording. The nature of the activity they were engaged in, for example, had little impact on how happy the participants were. What seemed to impact most upon happiness levels was mind wandering. When the participant was present in what they were doing, they rated their happiness levels higher, and the large number of samples also enabled the researchers to see more than a correlation here, that mental presence really was responsible for higher happiness scores. Oddly enough, this applied regardless of the emotional charge of their thoughts. Even with pleasant thoughts swirling around their minds, the participants felt less happy than they did when they were present in the moment.

The researchers concluded that:

> a human mind is a wandering mind, and a wandering mind is an unhappy mind. The ability to think about what is not happening is a cognitive achievement that comes at an emotional cost.[15]

Smaller studies have also pointed in the same direction. It isn't surprising that worries around relationships, finances and work have a strong correlation with diagnosable mental health issues. Daydreamers – particularly those who get lost in vivid daydreams – generally experience lower levels of life satisfaction than others. There can be advantages to daydreaming, of course – children who daydream frequently are much more imaginative and self-possessed than others. But children who daydream frequently also, on the whole, feel worse than others.[16]

Not Thinking About a White Bear

Luria would probably point out that it is only natural to experience friction during a period of great societal change, but that with time, mankind would learn to thrive in industrial society. So far, however, that hasn't exactly proved to be the case – though perhaps our methods have simply been a touch too primitive, overly focused on counteracting any thoughts we consider difficult and replacing them with more "positive" thoughts.

As I write, there are 891 books featuring the phrase "stop worrying" in their titles, and 923 with "positive thinking." In Google Books' collection of English-language titles, the phrase "don't worry" has reached an all-time high, having barely existed as an expression for much of the nineteenth century. More than ever, the prevailing wisdom seems to be: if you're worried because you're worried, just stop worrying![17]

Even a child could understand why this type of advice isn't particularly helpful. An example of this can be seen in Leo Tolstoy's memoirs, where he describes his brother Nikolai working out the basic problem at a young age, namely that it is impossible to intentionally refrain from thinking a certain thought.

Nikolai had tricked his three brothers into believing that there was a secret which, if revealed, would drive evil out of the human heart, paving the way for goodness and creating a "brotherhood of ants." The brothers often returned to the idea of this secret in their games, and Tolstoy became utterly convinced of its existence. As they waited for the secret to be revealed, the brothers would sit beneath chairs draped with blankets in reverent silence. Tolstoy would later recall that as he huddled alongside his brothers, he was often moved to tears by thoughts of the Ant Brotherhood and all the goodness that would soon be unleashed. He desperately wanted to know what the magic secret was, but Nikolai simply said that it was written on a green stick that was buried by the edge of the ravine not far from their home.

When the brothers decided to go out on an expedition to find the stick, Nikolai came up with a test that the boys would have to pass before they could join him: to stand in a corner and not think about a white bear.

Tolstoy threw himself wholeheartedly into the task, but no matter how hard he tried, he couldn't *not* think about a white bear. No sooner did he get into position in the corner than the bear always popped into his head. That white bear would haunt him for the rest of his life, and the idea of the redeeming powers of the green stick played such a key role in his work as an author that shortly before his death, he arranged to be buried in the spot where Nikolai had claimed the stick was hidden.[18]

While Nikolai's green stick is still waiting to be unearthed, his white bears came to life when Tolstoy started writing about his childhood during the autumn of his years. In 1863, his contemporary Fyodor Dostoyevsky mused on how difficult it is to do a favour for someone without expecting a debt of gratitude in return. "It is just like trying not to think of a white bear," he wrote. "Try this experiment on yourself: try not to think of a white bear and you will see that the cursed animal keeps returning to your mind."[19]

For a time, the white bears really did become part of the history of ideas. Following the psychoanalytical revolution, there was a great deal of focus on the opposite: on how easy it was to push back thoughts. It is remarkable how influential early psychoanalysis managed to make this idea. Not only was it considered easy to repress thoughts, it was also assumed that the most unpleasant thoughts were also the easiest to get rid of. Despite our experience of just how difficult "the worst" thoughts typically are to banish – grief, embarrassment, fear, injustice – Sigmund Freud's ideas about subconscious repression mechanisms won a degree of support that would endure for some time.

But the white bears also survived this epoch in the history of psychology. In the 1970s, more than a century after Dostoyevsky wrote about "the cursed animal," his words were printed in an issue of *Playboy* magazine. One of the readers of that article was a psychology student by the name of Daniel Wegner. Wegner couldn't know it at the time, but by the time of his death he would be associated more with the white bears than anything else. The white bears would provide him with a dazzling career, taking him all the way to leading the Mental Control Lab at Harvard University – not because his research revealed anything new or particularly breathtaking, but because (as so often in the world of psychology) using experiments as his method, he managed to prove what a child had already known 150 years earlier.[20]

The first experiments were carried out during the 1980s. One group of participants was asked – just like Tolstoy had once been – not to think about white bears. Another was asked to actively think about the bears. The method used two measures of "thoughts of white bears": participants were asked to verbalise their thinking for the duration of the experiment, and they were also asked to ring a bell every time their mind turned to white bears. By using this dual approach, the researchers were able to measure both when participants said something about white bears, or were thinking about them "in the background."

To a certain extent, the results were predictable. Those who were asked to think about white bears did so more than those who were told not to. But "suppression was never complete," wrote the authors of the article. Regardless of the instructions they were given, the white bears drifted into the participants' thoughts. At least once every minute, they popped by to say hello. The Tolstoy brothers' observations had now found scientific support.

One detail that has gained real importance in clinical psychology is what happened when the two groups were given the opposite task at another stage of the experiment. Those who were initially told to think about white bears found it easier to complete the task when they were later told not to think about them. Those who had been "suppressing" the white bears, however, were completely overwhelmed by thoughts of them when asked to think about them.[21]

This experiment is now among the most repeated in the world, and the results remain consistent. Not only is it difficult to suppress undesired thoughts, it is impossible, and attempting to think something away inevitably leads to those thoughts growing stronger.[22]

With severe anxiety, this "revenge of the thoughts" is a problem that can make it difficult for people even to get out of bed.

The Head's Main Opposition

For Arthur Schopenhauer, the inner conflict between positive and negative thoughts was one of the foundations of his pessimistic philosophy. "Any incident, however trivial, that rouses disagreeable emotion, leaves an after-effect in our mind," he wrote in one of many passages anticipating psychoanalysis. Following an unpleasant incident, we prefer not to think about it, which, according to the white bear logic above, means that the event "tinges all our thoughts: just as a small object held close to the eye limits and distorts our field of vision."

Attempting to avoid negative thoughts was something Schopenhauer was all too familiar with – as was failing. The fear of regretting his decisions meant he always had an "opposition party" ready and waiting:

> In my head, there is a permanent opposition party; and whenever I take any step or come to any decision – though I may have given the matter mature consideration – it afterwards attacks what I have done, without, however, being each time necessarily in the right... it often reproaches me when I do not deserve it. The same thing, no doubt, happens to many others as well; for where is the man who can help thinking that, after all, it were better not to have done something that he did with great deliberation.[23]

What Schopenhauer formulated so early on here is the idea that worry needs not be purely future-oriented. It often stretches back to past actions we regret or wonder whether we should regret because their consequences are still unknown. Within existential philosophy, this inner conflict is welcomed – celebrated, almost. True to nature, Kierkegaard made this conflict into a rule:

> If you marry, you will regret it; if you do not marry, you will also regret it ... Laugh at the world's follies, you will regret it; weep over them, you will also regret it... Believe a girl, you will regret it; if you do not believe her, you will also regret it ... If you hang yourself, you will regret it; if you do not hang yourself, you will regret it... This, gentlemen, is the sum of all practical wisdom.[24]

While clinical psychology would, in later decades, accept this embrace of "negative thoughts," opinion is still divided over why we so often find ourselves in the kind of regret that much of Kierkegaard's work focuses upon.

Schopenhauer's Buddhist theory was that mankind is plagued by a "will" that is expressed in the desire for what we covet and the fear of losing it. With this will, certain thoughts will always be pursued over others.

The French existentialist Jean-Paul Sartre concluded that the worst discomfort – anxiety – had to remain a permanent part of our lives. In attempting to avoid those thoughts we associate with anxiety, anxiety is inevitable in the same way that thinking of white bears is inevitable when we try not to think about them.

"I flee in order not to know," Sartre wrote in his most famous work, *Being and Nothingness*, "but I cannot avoid knowing that I am fleeing; and the flight from anguish is only a mode of becoming conscious of anguish. This anguish, properly speaking, can be neither hidden nor avoided." Or, as he also put it: "It is certain that we cannot escape anguish, for we *are* anguish."[25]

That sounds heavy, but perhaps in both Kierkegaard and Sartre there is a puerile contest to view anxiety as the ultimate expression of humanity. In Sartre's last book, a series of interviews from the difficult period towards the end of his life, once he had become an alcoholic and lost his sight, he said that he had never really understood the whole anxiety thing.

"... that's bunk. I talked about it because other people were talking about it, because it was fashionable. Everyone was reading Kierkegaard then."[26]

The interview was so unlike anything Sartre had previously said that his partner Simone de Beauvoir cried when she read it, concerned that a young upstart had manipulated a confused old man. But Sartre seems to have had enough presence of mind to insist that the book of interviews was published.[27]

"I have never known anguish. That was a key philosophical notion from 1930 to 1940. It also came from Heidegger. It was one of the notions we made use of all the time, but to me it meant nothing."[28]

It is possible that the elderly Sartre's daily diet of four corydrane (amphetamines), half a bottle of whisky and a handful of sleeping pills contradicted this statement. But more important is that towards the end of his life he became increasingly uninterested in speaking of human problems as "existential" in the eternal sense. While he maintained that mankind is doomed to freedom, his attention shifted to how our biographical and social position limits and determines the way we perceive this freedom.[29]

Perhaps free will does not have to generate anxiety, whatever the context? If we are free to attempt to flee from something in our thoughts, shouldn't we also be free not to flee it? What happens then?

Perhaps life with the white bears would be bearable if we simply stopped wishing them away?

Why did we decide that we had to stop thinking about them in the first place?

Notes

1 Francis O'Gorman, *Worrying: A Literary and Cultural History*, New York: Bloomsbury Publishing USA, 2015, p. xi.

2 For a more detailed phenomenology of anxiety, see Graham Davey and Frank Tallis, *Worrying: Perspectives on Theory, Assessment and Treatment,* Chichester: Wiley, 1996.

3 For the first chapter in the subject, see Daniel Kahneman and Amos Tversky, "The simulation heuristic" in *Judgement Under Uncertainty: Heuristics and Biases*, ed. Daniel Kahneman, Paul Slovic and Amos Tversky, New York: Cambridge University Press, 1982. The concept of simulative thinking formed the basis of this, and can, in turn, be split into the prefactual and counterfactual kind. For the sake of simplicity, I will, like the majority of others in this field, stick to the concept of counterfactual thinking.

4 Ruth M. J. Byrne, *The Rational Imagination: How People Create Alternatives to Reality,* Cambridge, MA: MIT Press, 2005; Roland Paulsen, "The counterfactual imagination" in *Theorizing in Social Science*, ed. Richard Swedberg, Stanford, CA: Standford University Press, 2014.
5 Byrne, *The Rational Imagination: How People Create Alternatives to Reality*, p. 8.
6 See ed. David R. Mandel, Denis J. Hilton and Patrizia Catellani, *The Psychology of Counterfactual Thinking,* Routledge, 2005.
7 Aleksander Luria, *Cognitive Development: Its Cultural and Social Foundations,* Harvard: Harvard University Press, 1976, p. 110. Note that I have omitted Luria's remarks in the quotations, and that Luria conducted his interviews with his colleagues, meaning the interviewer could be someone other than Luria himself.
8 Luria, *Cognitive Development: Its Cultural and Social Foundations*, p. 108.
9 Luria, *Cognitive Development: Its Cultural and Social Foundations*, p. 111.
10 One difference in later replications is that researchers found a higher frequency of correct answers the more counterfactual – i.e. disconnected from experience – the syllogisms were. See Sylvia Scribner and Michael Cole, "Unpackaging literacy" in *Writing: The Nature, Development and Teaching of Written Communication,* vol. 1, 1981; Sylvia Scribner, "Modes of thinking and ways of speaking: Culture and logic reconsidered" in *Thinking: Readings in Cognitive Science*, ed. P. N. Johnson-Laird and P. C. Wason, Cambridge: Cambridge University Press, 1977.
11 See e.g. Russell T. Hurlburt, "Descriptive experience sampling" in *The Blackwell Companion to Consciousness*, ed. Susan Schneider and Max Velmans, New York: Wiley-Blakwell, 2017.
12 Leonard A. Jason et al., "Time orientation: Past, present and future perceptions", *Psychological Reports*, vol. 64, nr. 3, 1989. See also: Arnaud D'Argembeau, Olivier Renaud and Martial Van der Linden, "Frequency, characteristics and functions of future-oriented thoughts in daily life", *Applied Cognitive Psychology,* vol. 25, nr. 1, 2011.
13 See Raymond A. Mar, Malia F. Mason and Aubrey Litvack, "How daydreaming relates to life satisfaction, loneliness, and social support: The importance of gender and daydream content", *Consciousness and Cognition*, vol. 21, nr. 1, 2012.
14 James Lindesay, et al., "Worry content across the lifespan: An analysis of 16- to 74-year-old participants in the British National Survey of Psychiatric Morbidity 2000", *Psychological Medicine*, vol. 36, nr. 11, 2006.
15 Matthew A. Killingsworth and Daniel T. Gilbert, "A wandering mind is an unhappy mind", *Science,* vol. 330, nr. 6006, 2010.
16 Anxiety around relationships, finances and work is strongly related to mental health problems: Lindesay et al., "Worry content across the lifespan: An analysis of 16- to 74-year-old participants in the British National Survey of Psychiatric Morbidity 2000", p. 1631. On children who daydream: Mar et al., "How daydreaming relates to life satisfaction, loneliness, and social support: The importance of gender and daydream content", p. 403.
17 The number of titles comes from Worldcat.org, the world's biggest bibliographical database. More titles than are covered there may, however, exist. The results from Google Books comes from their Ngram Viewer, and amounts (in the 2012 corpus) to 0.000003 in every thousand of the total figure, having risen from a frequency of roughly half that for much of the twentieth century.
18 Henri Troyat, *Tolstoy*, London: Grove Press, 2001.
19 Fyodor Dostoyevsky, *Winter Notes on Summer Impressions,* Northwestern; Evanston, IL: Northwestern University Press, 1988, p. 49.

20 Daniel M. Wegner, "How to think, say, or do precisely the worst thing for any ccasion," *Science*, vol. 325, nr. 5936, 2009.
21 Daniel M. Wegner, "Paradoxical effects of thought suppression", *Journal of Personality and Social Psychology*, vol. 53, nr. 1, 1987.
22 Daniel M. Wegner, "Setting free the bears: Escape from thought suppression", *American Psychologist*, vol. 66, nr. 8, 2011.
23 Arthur Schopenhauer, *Studies in Pessimism, Volume Four*, Pennsylvania State University: Penn State Electronic Classics Series Publication, 2005, p. 34.
24 Søren Kierkegaard, *Either/Or: A Fragment of Life*, London: Penguin Classics, 2004, p. 54.
25 Jean-Paul Sartre, *Being and Nothingness: An Essay on Phenomenological Ontology,* Methuen & Company, 1976 [1943], p. 43.
26 Jean-Paul Sartre and Benny Lévy, *Hope Now: The 1980 Interviews,* Chicago: University of Chicago Press, 2007, p. 54.
27 Hazel Rowley, *Tête-à-tête: Simone de Beauvoir and Jean-Paul Sartre*, New York: HarperCollins, 2005, p. 344.
28 Sartre and Lévy, *Hope Now: The 1980 Interviews*, p. 55.
29 On Sartre's whisky drinking and sleeping pills, see Rowley: *Tête-à-tête: Simone de Beauvoir and Jean-Paul Sartre*, p. 205 and 324.

4

IN THOUGHT'S CLUTCHES

As part of a thought experiment, the renaissance writer Michel de Montaigne imagined suspending a philosopher in a wire cage from one of the towers of Notre Dame. The philosopher, Montaigne supposed, would likely reason that it was impossible for him to fall. Yet despite this intellectual understanding, he would also discover that he "cannot help but the sight of the excessive height will fright and astound him."[1]

As I talk to Patrik in the hallway, I find myself thinking that many of us are like Montaigne's caged philosopher. We worry about things even when we know we have no reason to worry. Like the philosopher, we can see that the cage is safely chained to the tower, but we still can't quite internalise that knowledge. We become transfixed by the possibility of falling, however miniscule the chances.

Patrik keeps chatting. I don't get the sense that he is any less present in the room than I am, and yet I know he is preoccupied with other things: a constant stream of thoughts about how he is perceived, how he should have expressed himself differently, things he regrets and things that might happen. This parallel flood of thoughts is with him every second of the day. Every once in a while, it comes to the fore, stealing his focus, and when that happens Patrik is no longer here.

I know this because he tells me so. If he hadn't mentioned it, I never would have guessed. His thoughts are his own, after all, and they aren't visible from the outside. Patrik has been diagnosed with Generalised Anxiety Disorder (GAD), but anxious thoughts about what might go wrong aren't the only thing weighing on him.

"The alternative scenarios never end," he says. "I constantly have the sense that I'm a victim and that I've been treated unfairly. That means I get

DOI: 10.4324/9781003514930-5

really hateful and I'm angry almost all the time. I'm in a dispute with my landlord right now, because it's so fucking cold in here, and that means that on one level, I'm angry all the time until eventually it explodes and the world gets a huge rant about how fucking wrong everything is. I think there's some hubris in it too, the idea that *my* problems are so much worse than anyone else's."

The hallway *is* quite cold. Behind him, I can see a number of children's Wellington boots lined up beneath brightly coloured overalls and coats. Patrik also happens to be a father. A well-functioning one, I should think. Self-reflective at the very least.

"I notice it most with the kids. My son is almost seven, and when I think about that I feel like I haven't been there for a single day of his life. I can often see it happening, and I think: I should be happy now. I can watch him learning to walk or whatever, but I never feel happy. I'm constantly lost in thought, in what's going to happen, everything that could go wrong."

Patrik feels responsibility. Plenty *could* go wrong. Things have gone wrong at various points in his life, like when his parents got divorced and ended up in a custody battle. Or when his father became depressed and Patrik felt like he needed to make him happy all the time. But no matter how much responsibility he takes for his and his family's future, it's as though there is no end to his guilt.

"The guilt is just huge. And it's so heavy. I'm never happy in the moment, but I have got better. Sometimes it might be several years before I manage to feel happy about something. So when my partner talks about an event I was apparently present at, I can feel happy. But it's really not good. There are always problems to be solved, emotions to be curbed, outbursts to deal with."

Patrik has tried mindfulness, attempting to become present in whatever is happening as it happens, but he says it doesn't help. Talking helps, saying exactly what he is doing while he is doing it. *Now I'm holding the scrubbing brush, I've put some washing up liquid onto it, I'm going to work it into a lather to clean the plate, I'm rinsing the plate and putting it down there*, he says.

"But it's never any more than an interval, then I go straight back into my thoughts. Even when I'm talking, I've become really good at being somewhere else in my mind."

I ask him whether he ever engages in any activities that help him to be more present than otherwise.

"Hurting myself helps. That gives me a feeling of being right there in it," he says. "And violence. I'd like to be able to turn around and say that intimacy and sex can take me there, but I can't. It's violence, or violent actions, that get me there."

"What do you feel when you cut yourself?"

"A temporary sense of peace. A way to bring myself to an emotional state I know how to deal with. I know how to feel bad, I know how to feel anxious, but I can't feel happy."

The Limits of Logos

Ever since sociology was established as an academic discipline in the late nineteenth century, the *irrational outcomes of modern rationality* have been the subject of analysis. In our attempts to solve problems, we often reinforce the rationality from which the problem arose.

Solving too much bureaucracy with yet another layer of bureaucracy is one example of this. Using technology to remedy the problems caused by technology is another.

Thinking one's way out of too much thinking is a third, much trickier example. After all, how can a person deal with too much thinking other than through their thoughts? Is it possible to criticise the thinking without adding even more thinking?

The tangle of *what ifs* we often grapple with demands another form of intelligence.

It is clear that such a form of intelligence exists, as we will see in this chapter. And yet in modern psychology, intelligence is defined exclusively in terms of cognitive ability – what we do with our thoughts. This is why history is full of intelligent men and women who have lived unintelligent lives.[2]

One of the more mysterious examples of this is the Austrian logician and mathematician, Kurt Gödel. Gödel's significance in the history of both mathematics and philosophy cannot be overstated. His first incompleteness theorem was published in 1931, revolutionising mathematical logic by proving that there are theorems that are true despite being unprovable. This meant that, contrary to prevailing belief, mathematics is "incomplete." It may sound trivial, but the incompleteness theorems belong to mathematical logic's most prominent contributions. In *The Proof and the Paradox of Kurt Gödel*, the philosopher Rebecca Goldstein likens them to an artwork that itself explains the principles of aesthetics.

Gödel was such a genius that the word feels like something of an understatement. Among his peers, perhaps only his friend Albert Einstein was able to match him intellectually. The two men became acquainted at Princeton University in the early 1930s, having fled Nazi Europe, and would often go on walks together, to exchange ideas. Later in life, Einstein would say that one of the main reasons he went into the office was to enjoy the "privilege" of talking to Gödel.

In addition to his incompleteness theorems, Gödel contributed to the theory of relativity, to phenomenology and to the development of Platonic rationalism. His philosophical interests seem to have known no limits, and he devoted his last few years to developing a new ontological proof, proving the non-existence of time and showing why time travel is theoretically possible.[3]

On the surface, Gödel was rationality and logic personified. According to one of his landlords, he came across as dour. Introverted and preoccupied. He spent most of the day in his room, only venturing out at sunset, when he went for a walk that often lasted until after midnight. Deep thinker that he was, he walked with his hands behind his back, eyes on the ground; a stereotypical "man lost in thought," as the landlord put it.[4]

At least some of the unsolved problems of mathematics likely accompanied him when he left his desk, but Gödel also had other things to think about. Because not only was he the man who revolutionised logic and made Einstein tip his hat, he was also out of his mind.

That isn't to say that some sort of Mr. Hyde character peeped out the moment he got a chance. No, even in his madness Gödel was a logician through and through. An empiricist too, to some extent.

One detail his bibliographers were able to dig out from his library records was that Gödel repeatedly borrowed an academic work that had no connection to his research – a book by the name of *Die Kohlenoxydgasvergiftung*, or Carbon Monoxide Poisoning – giving us a glimpse of one of the many *what ifs* that plagued Gödel: His fear of gas poisoning. This *what if* hadn't been plucked out of thin air. Back when he lived in Vienna, his apartment was heated using coal and coke, which meant that the risk of carbon monoxide poisoning was certainly present. But in Gödel's mind, the risks grew the more he tried to reduce them. After his move to the USA, his complaints about "the gases" were a recurring theme, and would even lead to him getting rid of his bed (because it smelled of wood and varnish) and removing the radiators and refrigerator (convinced that both gave off noxious gases) from his apartment, which left it cold and uncomfortable during winter.[5]

Other thoughts that tormented Gödel included the idea that his doctors wanted to harm him, that they were lying about the medication they prescribed him, that the medical reference books also lied about medicines and that shadowy intruders were injecting him in his sleep.

But his biggest problem was linked to food. What if someone had poisoned the things he ate? The risk was always there, however small, though the way Gödel dealt with these risks suggests that he knew his *what ifs* likely had nothing to do with reality.[6]

Gödel's wife Adele found herself drawn into his anxiety about being poisoned. Throughout their marriage, she acted as Gödel's taster – a human poison detector. Only once she had tried the food could Gödel be sure it was harmless. Prior to their escape from Europe, Adele had saved him from self-inflicted starvation by hand feeding him, spoonful by spoonful, until his weight increased from 48 to 64 kilos, and he had been reliant on her ever since. If she was not around, his fragile eating habits – and therefore also his life – were at risk.

On one occasion, when Adele was sick in bed and Gödel was struggling with a critique of Alan Turing, he isolated himself in his apartment. His paranoia took over, and his weight plummeted. With the help of his friend Oskar Morgenstern – the founder of game theory – and a cocktail of psychopharmaceuticals, Gödel managed to pull himself back from the brink. In 1977, however, when Adele was admitted to hospital and Morgenstern was no longer alive, there was no one there to save him.

One of the last people to visit him at home was the logician Hao Wang. Gödel reportedly told his friend that he had "lost the power for making positive decisions".[7]

When Adele was eventually discharged, she convinced him to be admitted to Princeton Hospital, where he died in the foetal position, weighing just 29.5 kilos. The cause of death was listed as "malnutrition and inanition" resulting from a "personality disturbance."[8]

Even a game theorist like Morgenstern was, in his interactions with Gödel, forced to acknowledge that there was a certain logic to his many *what ifs* and the measures he took to deal with them. But Gödel imagined "too many plots," as Morgenstern saw it. They were, he said, logically grounded; the issue was the underlying premise, which Gödel never managed to gain any perspective on. Morgenstern described an occasion when Gödel was admitted to Princeton Hospital, only to announce to the doctors that his health insurance did not cover the treatment they were offering him. It is hard to imagine the doctors' reactions when the mathematician read aloud from his insurance contract to explain why he could not accept their help. His conclusions were likely correct, but why was Gödel unwilling to accept any principles other than logic's?[9]

In his biography of Gödel, the mathematician John Dawson writes that he was "unable to escape from the inner logic of his paranoia – to adopt, as it were, a 'metatheoretical' perspective."[10]

It seems unlikely that Gödel was not able to theorise his own theories (which is what metatheory is about, after all). It was probably metatheory that got him to ask his wife to try his food before him – he knew that the risk of poisoning was vanishingly small. It wasn't that he lacked theoretical perspective, it was that theory was all he was capable of.

The Risk of Falling

Montaigne didn't choose to suspend just anyone from the top of Notre Dame; it had to be a philosopher. In another variant of the thought exercise,

Montaigne imagined walking between the two towers of the cathedral: "Let there be a beam thrown over betwixt these two towers, of breadth sufficient to walk upon; there is no philosophical wisdom so firm that can give us the courage to walk over it as we should do upon the ground."[11]

Yet again, Montaigne seems to have had his sights set on philosophy, on the intelligence of thought and its impotence. He admits that he is guilty of this form of limited intelligence himself, and confesses to shaking with fear while walking in the mountains, "though I stood above my length from the edge of the precipice, and could not have fallen unless I would."[12]

Centuries before Kierkegaard looked down into his bottomless precipice, and close to five hundred years before cognitive psychology would develop the idea of counterfactual thinking, Montaigne understood that what troubles us is not the dangers themselves, but our thoughts *about* them.

Compared to Gödel's fears, the risk of death is certainly higher when walking across a beam between two towers – it is only a step away – but a philosopher knows that the link between risk and fear is not quite so simple. For someone driving a car on a motorway, death is even closer to hand than on Montaigne's beam. Every time we pass another car, death is no more than a twitch of the wrist away, and yet the majority of us perceive driving as a perfectly undramatic activity.

Today, the world is full of people who walk across beams suspended in the air on a daily basis. Many do it at much greater heights than the towers of Notre Dame, and under far more challenging conditions than those envisioned by Montaigne.

These high-altitude walkers first began to appear in the United States around the turn of the twentieth century, making it possible to build bridges and skyscrapers hundreds of metres above the ground. In his book *High Steel*, Jim Rasenberger describes the workers' daily lives. Their initial reaction on taking the construction elevator up to the twenty-ninth floor for the first time was always shock, Rasenberger writes. This shock stemmed partly from the height, which seemed much greater when looking down than it did from street level, but also from the "slap of the wind." No matter how calm a morning it is on the ground, the wind is always whistling at the top of a skyscraper, with nothing to act as a brake on it. On top of that, all skyscrapers sway – around half a metre horizontally is normal for a building of 200 metres. At first, you keep your eyes down to focus on "the hole" and any discarded bolts, scraps of wire or chains just waiting to be tripped over. But then a girder swings overhead, and you quickly learn that the risk of falling is not the only risk.[13]

In an interview with Rasenberger, an ironworker explains that the majority of newbies stop dead before going out onto the beams. Sheer reflex makes them turn back – assuming they don't sit down first. As a result, rather than walking on the beams, it is common to see the men "cooning" them for the first few weeks: straddling the metal and using the bottom flange to shuffle out. So far, Montaigne seems to have been right: for the majority of people, walking a beam in the air is a very different prospect to walking one on the ground.[14]

But there is some variation here. Certain ironworkers start walking the beams from their very first day on the job, quickly learning to deal with rain, ice, and anything else that might complicate matters. So what separates these natural sky walkers from others?

This question – with a focus on New York ironworkers in particular – has been the subject of reporting and anthropological studies for almost seventy years. Part of the fascination stems from the fact that a large proportion of the workers, even today, are Mohawks. Roughly ten percent of New York's ironworkers belong to the Mohawk people – a statistically disproportionate number, considering there are only around 30,000 Mohawks in total, 24,000 of whom live in Canada.[15]

The recruitment of Mohawks dates back to the late nineteenth century, when an official from a bridge building company in Manhattan noted that they seemed to climb the spans for fun once the working day was over. This reputation was reinforced during the 1950s, with spectacular reports in *National Geographic* and the *New Yorker*. Even in *Industrial Bulletin*, published by New York's Department of Labor, the message was clear: "the Mohawks," claimed a report from 1961, "alone among all Indian tribal groups, have an instinctive lack of fear of height."[16]

It is amusing to think that the fear of heights, something that crops up in both Kierkegaard's and Montaigne's writing as a starting point in the investigation of anxiety, should not be existential. Admittedly, for someone who has to walk out on a beam suspended in the air, the fear of heights does not fulfil any survival function. If anything, it actually increases the risk, as dizziness is destabilising; ironworkers know not to look down. And yet: shouldn't the height make it impossible to escape the kind of catastrophic thinking in which a person counterfactually stumbles, falls into "the hole" and bounces between the supporting structures?

In contrast to someone standing well away from the edge of a cliff, the risk of falling from a construction site is high. Every major skyscraper has a human cost. The old World Trade Center, the Arthur Andersen building and the Empire State Building each claimed five lives, older buildings considerably more. During the first half of the twentieth century, when the Mohawk phenomenon first began to attract attention, it is estimated that around two percent of ironworkers died, and a further two percent were left disabled. Between 1910 and 1914, the Bureau of Labor Statistics calculated that out of every 1,000 ironworkers, twelve died and another 353 suffered workplace accidents. Even today, between twenty-five and fifty ironworkers die in the

United States every year. As professions go, only timber cutting and fishing have higher fatality rates.[17]

So how can any beam walker avoid being paralysed by *what ifs*?

In his book, Rasenberger describes his astonishing observations at the top of the Time Warner Center construction site by the corner of Central Park. He sees a worker stop mid-beam to cup his hands and light a cigarette. On another girder, a man is busy counting the money in his wallet. Rasenberger sees another couple of workers come face to face on a twenty-five centimetre wide steel. They stop, share a joke, laugh and then pass each other. Elsewhere, a young man clears a beam in three swift steps, jumping over the metre-wide gap to the deck to grab a tool before running back the same way he just came. "He would either make a great ironworker," Rasenberger remarks, "or a dead one." In interviews, the ironworkers talk about several people who have fallen asleep sitting on a steel a hundred metres above the ground.[18]

It certainly seems as though some people possess the ability to walk along a high beam as though it were on solid ground. Like a reply to Montaigne's thought experiment – albeit without making reference to Montaigne – the *New Yorker* journalist Joseph Mitchell wrote in the late 1940s that the Mohawks were particularly adept in this absence of fear. Mitchell quotes a representative from a bridge building company, who claimed that they were "agile as goats" and that they would gladly "walk a narrow beam high in the air with nothing below them but the river... and it wouldn't mean any more to them than walking on the ground."[19]

To the extent that this claim is true, the reason cannot be that the Mohawks are simply more surefooted, as Mitchell claims in his article – statistics show that death is evenly distributed across ethnicities in the industry. "You almost fall three or four times a day," one of the Mohawks said in an interview, adding: "You don't even think about it until someone reminds you later on. They'll say, 'I thought you were going in the hole today.'"[20]

Do the Mohawks simply demonstrate how a *non-philosopher* deals with the beam? Someone who understands the risk without getting into the kind of *what if* paralysis we saw with Gödel? Is it possible that there is some sort of cultural variation in the extent to which we listen to our thoughts?

The Sickness of Thought

One observation each of us can make is that our experience comprises much more than just our thinking. In every single moment, we are experiencing something we are not thinking about. William James, considered by many to be the pioneer of modern psychology, called this thought-free experience "pure experience."

Pure experience can be difficult to communicate or even notice. We are thrown into pure experience the minute we are born, and to a large extent, the same is true when we sleep. But the minute we turn our gaze onto our experience, we start analysing and labelling things and it becomes "shot through with adjectives and nouns and prepositions and conjunctions," as James puts it.[21]

And yet, pure experience can be found in even the most absorbing of thoughts. If, for example, we read a book, our thoughts will latch onto whatever the book is about and occasionally drift off to other things. At the edges of this shifting focus, there are visual impressions, bodily sensations, sounds, and smells that we experience without thinking about them. If we get up and go for a walk, our body will coordinate our movements without us having to think about them. We experience all this without having to think about it.

Consciousness, as James pointed out, is bigger than thinking. Meditative traditions, regardless of religious origin, seek to draw attention to this thoughtless consciousness. Expanding James' pure experience is one part of the aim with meditation techniques such as vipassana and zazen. In some Hindu teachings, thought is equated with *maya*, the veil of illusion. Someone who has woken up from the dream state of thought could, according to the theory, walk along a beam a hundred metres above the ground and be utterly present in every step, rather than getting lost in counterfactual thinking about what one misstep could mean.[22]

The way different cultures relate to thought absorption is, to some extent, apparent in the way they classify mental health problems. In the latest edition of the American *Diagnostic and Statistical Manual of Mental Disorders*, five out of 947 pages are given over to a summary of "cultural" – i.e. non-Western – "concepts of distress." Page 834 reads as follows:

"*Kufungisisa* ('thinking too much' in Shona) is an idiom of distress and a cultural explanation among the Shona of Zimbabwe."[23]

According to the manual, *kufungisisa* covers such varied diagnoses as depression, generalised anxiety disorder, obsessive-compulsive disorder, post-traumatic stress disorder and persistent complex bereavement disorder. *Kufungisisa* is not about certain types of thought, but *all* thought. The anthropological research into *kufungisisa* suggests that for many people, the condition is seen as much more relevant than Western diagnoses such as "anxiety" or "depression."

In a study of Zimbabweans who sought treatment for mental health problems, eighty percent stated that their problems were caused by *kufungisisa*. The condition was described as so severe that two thirds of those affected were unable to work.[24]

Kufungisisa resembles what is known in Western psychology as rumination. A recurring metaphor is that of a cassette tape playing over and over in one's head. The associated physical symptoms include weariness, trouble sleeping, headaches and a loss of appetite.

The diagnosis also appears in other countries, under other names. In a sociological study of Ghanaian women's health, for example, researchers found that "thinking too much" was the most-reported problem – more common than somatic illness. The women said that as a result of their thoughts, they were distracted and struggled to sleep. This excessive thinking was often described in physical terms.

"What worries me is my head, and then the inside of my ears will be sounding 'wuu wuu wuuuu'," one woman explained. Another said that her thinking caused headaches: "When I think like that deeply then my head will ache me terribly. Sometimes I have to tie my head to feel better."[25]

Compared to the hundreds of psychiatric diagnoses Western medicine has to offer, *kufungisisa* may seem like much too broad a concept, but there is plenty to suggest that the Western enthusiasm for categorisation has come back to bite us. These days, the issue of comorbidity – the idea that our thoughts and feelings qualify for a variety of diagnoses – is increasingly debated, as not even anxiety and depression seem to occur separately to any great extent. With the exception of a few phobias, we tend to experience *both* anxiety and depression. The flames of anxiety transition so easily into the darkness of depression, and the darkness scares us back to our anxiety. Finding someone who suffers only from anxiety, without depression – as is sometimes needed for clinical trials – is so rare that, as one pharmacologist put it, such people are "worth their weight in gold."[26]

All things considered, "wuu wuu wuuuu" isn't a bad description of what it entails to feel bad.

If we delve deeper into the anthropological research, the idea of "thinking too much" recurs as a central description of illness in many cultures around the world. In Nigeria, excessive thinking forms the core of what is known as "brain fag," a condition that typically arises from too much homework, which is believed to damage the brain and lead to a feeling of burning and headaches. In Uganda, what Western medicine would class as "depression" is considered a problem of thinking too much, a *sickness of thought*. In Cambodia, such varied complaints as tinnitus, forgetfulness, heart problems, and *khyâl attacks* (a panic-like condition) are also attributed to too much thinking. Among the Inuit and Bhutanese peoples, it is considered the cause of even worse conditions such as dementia and psychosis.

In a summary of 138 studies into how "thinking too much" appears as a health risk around the world, the diagnosis occurred in eighteen different languages.[27]

The risk groups observed vary between cultures. In one study of overthinkers in Ethiopia, for example, young men in cities are described as a particular risk group because their material living conditions and freedom from household chores grant them excessive time for brooding.[28] In a study from Thailand, on the other hand, it is women who come across as relatively vulnerable. This is partly because of gendered subordination, but also because women (unlike men) are not educated in the *khit pen* meditation techniques considered effective against thinking too much.[29]

In places where Buddhist principles have shaped society, most notably in south-east Asia, how much a person thinks is partly a moral issue. Thinking too much is described, in these regions, more as a character flaw than an affliction. Excessive thinking represents a barrier to a person's spiritual development, as well as too much seriousness. The idea that seriousness should be a problem may seem objectionable to the Kierkegaardian mind, but there is a concern for solidarity worth considering here: since everyone suffers, fixating on one's own problems represents a self-obsessed blindness to the world.[30]

This may sound like a strict requirement for thought control – in which case it is likely to backfire, given what we already know about the difficulty of thinking away a particular thought – but the key difference is in how thinking is valued. In the Buddhist tradition, what passes through our mind is subordinate to how we relate to it. Those who fail to let go of their thoughts are trapped in an unwillingness to accept the present, death and the impermanence of the world. In order to accept these incomprehensible concepts, we must move beyond our thoughts.

Even practical tasks require us to overstep the logic of thought from time to time. While those of us in the West might carelessly say that something is "mindless" or that someone should "use their brain," the expression "to understand through the head" is considered disparaging in Japan. This kind of understanding is seen as superficial, roughly equivalent to someone knowing what a series of dance steps should look like without actually knowing how to dance. In order to achieve real understanding, thinking has to be done away with.[31]

The Mechanics of Thought

There is cultural variation in the fear of heights, or "acrophobia" as it is known within psychiatry. From 0.9 percent in Iraq, the lifetime prevalence – i.e. how many people will, at some point in their lives, experience this type of problem – rises to 7.1 percent in Colombia, with typical over-representation in high-income countries.[32]

Although we do not have statistics for the Mohawk people, this suggests that the fear of heights can vary considerably between countries. Does that also mean that certain people can balance on beams suspended in the air with the same ease as they would walk on the ground?

If that is the case, the road to this point – the habituation process – is a long one. No one begins without fear. The fact that many Mohawks have taken themselves through this habituation process is because they have been forced to do so in order to earn a living. In this sense, the Mohawks' high representation among ironworkers is no more mysterious than the usual generational legacy of occupations and habits. To the extent that culture plays a role, it is largely in terms of the employers' perceptions of different ethnicities.

"A lot of people think Mohawks aren't afraid of heights," said one worker. "That's not true. We have as much fear as the next guy. The difference is that we deal with it better."[33]

The mental chatter, the calculations of risk, the trade-offs and warnings aren't necessarily what separates someone like Gödel, who didn't want to eat, from a steelworker who falls asleep on a steel girder. What separates them is how much they listen to their anxieties.

If we turn to other types of *what if* problems, we can, through various psychiatric diagnoses, see countless differences between societies when it comes to this point. The proportion of a population that will, during their lifetime, meet the criteria for generalised anxiety disorder varies, according to WHO data, from 0.1 percent in Nigeria to 8 percent in Australia. For panic disorders, the figures range from 2 percent in China to 27 percent in New Zealand. These vast variations also appear with diagnoses like social anxiety and claustrophobia.[34]

Regardless of the cause of these differences, they demonstrate that our preoccupation with *what ifs* differs not just on an individual level, but on a group level, too.

Counterfactual thinking separates us from the here and now because, by definition, it focuses on a reality that does not exist. All thinking is shrouded in unreality because it takes place on a symbolic level where the world can be represented but never really exist. Thinking can help us to understand the world, but it can also obscure it. To be anxiously absorbed by our thoughts is to confuse reality with symbols, signs, words and ideas.

During the 1950s and 1960s, when Zen Buddhism was exported to Europe and North America, it came hand in hand with a critique of modern society's thought absorption that was unusual for Buddhism. For once, the problem was described as less existential and more social.

"All so-called civilized peoples have increasingly become crazy and self-destructive, because, through excessive thinking, they have lost touch with reality," said the Anglican priest Alan Watts, who would play a key role in popularising Zen Buddhist ideas in the West.[35]

"Images made by thought destroy human relationship," wrote his mentor Jiddu Krishnamurti, who, in distancing himself from conceptual thinking did not even profess Buddhism. "I think the central problem of our existence is thought, the whole machinery of thinking, and I would like to go into that because our civilisation both in the East and in the West is based on thought."[36]

"We must realize that modern civilization is thoroughly oriented toward dehumanizing humanity in every possible way," said Daisetz Teitaro Suzuki, a pioneer in exporting the teachings of Zen Buddhism to the United States. "[T]hat is to say, we are fast turning into robots and statues with no human souls."[37]

Buddhist literature from this period contains several analyses of how this dehumanisation is felt on an individual level, but the Buddhist critics failed to go into any deeper analysis of precisely *what* it is about civilisation that has driven us to a thought-filled existence. They preferred to consider civilisation as a done deal, and therefore saw the possibility of emancipation as a primarily individual concern.

In the following chapters, I will trace our obsession with thoughts back in history, starting at the very beginning of time.

Notes

1 Clarification: the philosopher in Montaigne's example was a man. Michel de Montaigne, *Complete Essays,* Stanford: Stanford University Press, 1965, p. 44.
2 For an early critique of the concept of cognitive intelligence, see Stephen Jay Gould, *The Mismeasure of Man,* New York: Norton, 1981.
3 Rebecca Goldstein, *Incompleteness: The Proof and Paradox of Kurt Gödel (Great Discoveries)*, New York: W. W. Norton, 2006.
4 John Dawson, *Logical Dilemmas: The Life and Work of Kurt Gödel*, Wellesley: Taylor & Francis, 2005, p. 160.
5 Dawson, *Logical Dilemmas: The Life and Work of Kurt Gödel*, p. 112.
6 Dawson, *Logical Dilemmas: The Life and Work of Kurt Gödel*, pp. 233–234.
7 Dawson, *Logical Dilemmas: The Life and Work of Kurt Gödel*, p. 253.
8 Goldstein, *Incompleteness: The Proof and Paradox of Kurt Gödel (Great Discoveries)*, p. 250.
9 Dawson, *Logical Dilemmas: The Life and Work of Kurt Gödel*, p. 238.
10 Dawson, *Logical Dilemmas: The Life and Work of Kurt Gödel*, p. 255.
11 de Montaigne, *Complete Essays,* p. 449.
12 de Montaigne, *Complete Essays*, p. 450.
13 Jim Rasenberger, *High Steel: The Daring Men Who Built the World's Greatest Skyline, 1881 to the Present,* New York: HarperCollins e-books, 2009, p. 14.
14 David Weitzman, *Skywalkers: Mohawk Ironworkers Build the City*, New York: Roaring Brook Press, 2014, p. 100.
15 Stephen Nessen, "Sky walking: Raising steel, a Mohawk ironworker keeps tradition alive", *WNYC*, 19/3, 2012.
16 See Weitzman, *Skywalkers: Mohawk Ironworkers Build the City*, p, 93.

17 Ibid, p. 101; Rasenberger, *High Steel: The Daring Men Who Built the World's Greatest Skyline, 1881 to the Present*, p. 25.
18 Rasenberger, *High Steel: The Daring Men Who Built the World's Greatest Skyline, 1881 to the Present*, pp. 122–123.
19 Rasenberger, *High Steel: The Daring Men Who Built the World's Greatest Skyline, 1881 to the Present*, p. 160.
20 Weitzman, *Skywalkers: Mohawk Ironworkers Build the City*, p. 99.
21 William James, *Writings, 1902-1910,* New York: Literary Classics of the United States, 1987, p. 783.
22 Ramana Maharsi, *Self Realization*, V. S. Ramanan: Tamil Nadu, 2003, p. 417.
23 American Psychological Association, *Diagnostic and Statistical Manual of Mental Disorders (DSM-5)*, Washington: American Psychiatric Publishing, 2013, p. 834.
24 Vikram Patel, *Culture and Common Mental Disorders in Sub-Saharan Africa,* New York: Taylor & Francis, 2013, p. 85.
25 Joyce Yaa Avotri, *"Thinking too much" and" worrying too much": Ghanaian Women's Accounts of Their Health Problems*, Hamilton: McMaster University, 1999, p. 135.
26 Quoted in Edward Shorter, *How Everyone Became Depressed: The Rise and Fall of the Nervous Breakdown*, Oxford: Oxford University Press, 2013, p. 52. See Shorter's book for a more in-depth discussion of the comorbidity of depression and anxiety. For a clinical study of the comorbidity of severe forms of anxiety and depression, see e.g. Robert M. A. Hirschfeld, "The comorbidity of major depression and anxiety disorders: Recognition and management in primary care", *Primary Care Companion to the Journal of Clinical Psychiatry,* vol. 3, nr. 6, 2001.
27 For summary, see Bonnie N. Kaiser et al., "'Thinking too much': A systematic review of a common idiom of distress", *Social Science & Medicine*, vol. 147, 2015.
28 Kaiser et al., "'Thinking too much': A systematic review of a common idiom of distress", p. 178.
29 Marjory A. Muecke, "Worries and worriers in Thailand," *Health Care for Women International*, vol. 15, nr. 6, 1994.
30 Kaiser et al., "'Thinking too much': A systematic review of a common idiom of distress", p. 177.
31 Angeline Lillard, "Ethnopsychologies: Cultural variations in theories of mind", *Psychological Bulletin,* vol. 123, nr. 1, 1998, p. 22.
32 Klaas J. Wardenaar et al., "The cross-national epidemiology of specific phobia in the World Mental Health Surveys", *Psychological Medicine*, vol. 47, nr. 10, 2017.
33 Weitzman, *Skywalkers: Mohawk Ironworkers Build the City,* p. 91.
34 Ruscio et al., "Cross-sectional comparison of the epidemiology of DSM-5 generalized anxiety disorder across the globe", Peter De Jonge et al., "Cross-national epidemiology of panic disorder and panic attacks in the World Mental Health Surveys", *Depression and Anxiety*, vol. 33, nr. 12, 2016; Wardenaar et al., "The cross-national epidemiology of specific phobia in the World Mental Health Surveys". While the diagnoses mentioned build upon so-called "downward" counterfactual thinking, thoughts of how much worse life could be following a potential catastrophe, we see in depression how "upward" counterfactuals take up more space – how much better life could have been, in other words. To the extent that depression involves downward *what if* anxiety, it is primarily centred around the idea that the depression might never end. Also with regard to depression (and specifically "major depressive disorder"), we can see similar

patterns in lifetime prevalence: from 2.9 percent in Romania and 3.2 percent in Nigeria to 18.0 percent in the Netherlands and 20.4 percent in France. See Anne Gene Broomhall et al., "Upward counterfactual thinking and depression: A meta-analysis", *Clinical Psychology Review,* vol. 55, 2017; Ronald C. Kessler et al., "Anxious and non-anxious major depressive disorder in the World Health Organization World Mental Health Surveys", *Epidemiology and Psychiatric Sciences,* vol. 24, nr. 3, 2015.
35 Alan Watts, "Bits of various seminars", *Hermetic Academy,* 20/8, 2019.
36 Jiddu Krishnamurti, *Facing a World in Crisis: What Life Teaches us in Challenging Times,* Boston: Shambhala, 2005, p. 25.
37 D. T. Suzuki, *Selected Works of D. T. Suzuki, Volume II: Pure Land,* University of California Press, 2015, p. 239

PART 2

Trickles of History

5

TIME HORIZONS

Elise is convinced that the majority of one-car accidents are secret suicide attempts.

"What do you mean?" I ask.

"I know it sounds cynical," she says, her gaze steady. "But it's actually pretty logical. Dying in a crash is awful, but it's not as bad as killing yourself. For other people."

I am just about to ask whether she knows of any research into the subject when I realise that her words are less a sociological statement than a confession. She is speaking from experience.

Elise always had the future on her side. When she was a girl, she knew she was going to start school, and she was looking forward to it. When she started middle school, she knew she would be given grades, and she was looking forward to it. When she started high school, she knew she would be going to university, and she was looking forward to it. Life felt like a series of stages of promises and realisation. There was worry, but there was even more expectation.

And planning – every day, more planning.

Elise tells me that for as long as she can remember, her life has been highly structured. Her parents planned everything down to the very last detail, and she can't remember ever seeing either of them stressed. Her mother worried about *becoming* stressed on a few occasions, like when she couldn't find her keys and had to leave to catch the bus – despite being ten minutes early. There was indirect stress like that, but it wasn't the despairing kind. It was prolonged stress, involving lots of waiting.

If Elise's parents were going to visit someone, they made sure to get there at least twenty minutes before the agreed time, and then when they arrived

DOI: 10.4324/9781003514930-7

they simply sat in the car to wait. Sometimes they listened to the radio, sometimes they drove around the block a few times.

"If the weather was nice, we'd pop into the shops or go for a walk. You couldn't arrive too early either, so we often had half an hour to kill."

If they were going somewhere they had never been before, they would scope the place out a few days in advance. Before Elise's mother went on a trip to Gotland, for example, the family made the hour-long journey to Oskarshamn to check where the harbour was the day before. Then they drove back home.

"They planned absolutely everything. It didn't matter if we were on holiday or if it was just a normal working week. Every Friday they wrote a shopping list and decided what we were going to have for dinner over the next week. And every morning at the weekend or in the school holidays, Dad would ask: 'so, how is your day looking?' I hated that question. It was like he was killing the feeling of being free. Because even if I told him I didn't have any plans, I'd feel bad. Like I should be doing something."

Elise grew up. She looked forward to having a romantic relationship. She began a romantic relationship. She looked forward to moving to the countryside. She moved to the countryside.

But then something happened. Elise no longer had anything to look forward to. Her future disappeared.

She woke up one night with such powerful sense of anxiety that she was sick. It happened again the next night. She hadn't realised it was possible to feel so anxious, but this went on for months. She had felt anxious before, of course, but this was something else entirely. This anxiety felt more physical than mental.

It was more an impulse than a plan. Right in the middle of an upward bend, Elise stepped on the accelerator. When she reached the crown of the hill, she closed her eyes. The car left the ground, and her body was thrown around. At this stage, Elise still had plenty of goodness in her life.

"I felt love towards people. I liked them, liked being around them. It's not like I was lonely, either. It was more that I didn't have the energy to deal with the project of life. I couldn't do it."

Elise is sitting in front of me now. She survived. Her car overturned, rolled once and – miraculously – landed back on all four wheels without crashing into anyone else. When she opened her eyes, she saw that she had broken the fence on the edge of a field of sheep. The creatures were staring at her from a distance, chewing their grass.

Still, that wasn't the turning point. Shaken by what she had done, she took out her phone and called her partner, said that she had been in an accident.

That evening, she woke feeling anxious again.

"I just couldn't see what life would be like, going forward. I couldn't picture it."

In a study of psychiatric patients who had been admitted to hospital, those who had previously considered suicide were compared to those who hadn't. Both groups suffered significantly as a result of their respective diagnoses, which included depression, obsessive-compulsive disorder and schizophrenia, among others. But it wasn't the degree of suffering that separated them. What distinguished the suicidal patients from the others was something else: they couldn't see how they themselves could change while remaining the same person. They shared Elise's problem. When asked how they pictured themselves in ten years' time, they were unable to answer.[1]

As a result of studies such as this, some have come to the conclusion that people need something to look forward to in order to feel good. And in an era in which both young and old alike believe that today's children will be less well off than their parents, it is easy to imagine that this might be one of the key causes of today's worries.[2]

But the future has not always been as important to us as it is today. Our *time horizon* – how far into the future we look – has, for practical reasons, been limited to no more than a few days for much of the history of mankind. Nowadays, our time horizon lies way beyond anything to do with concrete experience. When we think about "our future," it covers such a long period of time that just a few centuries ago, no one would have even considered speculating that far ahead.

With no more than an ounce of imagination, we now always have something to worry about. A child can worry about having no friends in twenty years. A smoker can worry about dying of cancer at forty. A student can worry about becoming a poor pensioner in fifty years' time. Elise can worry that she will be unhappy for the rest of her life.

But these futures do not exist. They are imagined, calculated, fantasies. All that exists is the here and now, where our earlier hopes and fears either come to pass or are shown to be nonsense. So how can something that does not exist cast such a long shadow over something that does?

A Time Without Time

When describing the history of humanity, it is the rule rather than the exception that the timeless period of our existence – without any clocks, without any calendars – is ignored. And yet this accounts for around ninety-five percent of our past, roughly 200,000 years.

What makes it possible for us to discuss the impact that time and future horizons have had on us is that traces of our timeless existence can still be found in various cultures. In the mid-1900s, anthropologists began to notice how differently pre-industrial and pre-agricultural societies relate to time. It is, of course, difficult to grasp other types of consciousness relating to time, but the effort that many anthropologists have put into understanding these cultural differences is among the most impressive achievements of the social sciences.

Prior to the publication of a study of the San people in Namibia, for example, the anthropologist James Suzman spent twenty-five years in their company in an attempt to learn their language and understand their culture. Until relatively recently, the San peoples' lives resembled a last bastion of the hunter-gatherer society. They are often called the oldest people on earth, and their adaptation to modern, paid work is, as yet, an unfinished process. They now live somewhere between modernity and ancient history, with factory-made clothes, tools, homes and trade with the outside world.

Suzman's study did not focus on the San people's perception of time. In fact, he only became aware of the differences thanks to the white settlers who, in the backwaters of colonialism, continued to exploit the native peoples' labour. They often did so by paying in food rather than money. This went against Namibian law, but many landowners insisted on paying in kind, claiming that the San people were unable to handle money.

"Bushmen don't understand time like we do," explained one of the farmers.

This was a common view. Since the San people's concept of time was like that of "small children's," they couldn't manage their money. If they were paid a month's wage, the money would be gone within the week. If they were paid in food, however, it lasted much longer.

The argument was complicated by the fact that the farmers themselves benefited from the arrangement. The idea of the San people's perception of time being similar to a child's also had a worrying resonance, as it had previously been said that the San people were more animal than human. It wasn't until an older San man spontaneously volunteered that the white farmers had a different understanding of time that Suzman began to investigate what these differences were.

Reading about how little importance both the past and the future plays to the San people is dizzying. The man who mentioned the white farmers' differing approach to time was advanced in years, but like many of the other older men in San society, he neither knew nor cared when he was born. The only way to estimate his age was to ask about historical events he had lived through, but his lack of interest in discussing the past meant that wasn't easy – "the farmers and Herero stole all the land," was the version of history he kept returning to.[3]

On the whole, Suzman's study confirmed what another anthropologist had observed with the San people fifty years earlier. In this study, the researcher was struck by how little the San people seemed to remember – even less care – about the past. When a person died, they were simply buried in the sand and forgotten. Who a person's parents or forefathers were was irrelevant.

The interview subjects were even less concerned about the future, which rarely stretched more than a few days ahead. Instead, their focus circled around what we call the present.[4]

The same now-centric concept of time has been studied in multiple hunter-gatherer societies around the world, including the Mbuti people in the Democratic Republic of Congo, the Hadza people in Tanzania, the Batek people in Malaysia and the Pandaram in southern India.

What these studies have shown empirically can also be logically derived from what it means to live as a hunter-gatherer: in a society in which settlements change on a monthly, weekly, or even daily basis, where neither food nor capital is stockpiled, where everything that is picked or hunted is consumed right away; in this type of society, the past and the future will play a marginal role in the way we perceive ourselves and the world around us.[5]

This analysis is one of the least speculative as far as hunter-gatherer societies are concerned. With regards to many other issues concerning the earliest peoples, the debate continues to rage on much less solid ground. The idea of finding some kind of "primordial" human state among hunter-gatherer societies is largely hopeless, as pointed out by anthropologist David Graeber and archaeologist David Wengrow, because there were many differences between these various societies.[6]

One common characteristic of hunter-gatherers that may explain their now-centric concept of time is the obvious: that they fed themselves through hunting and gathering.

Anthropologists call this work characterised by *immediate returns*, as compared with agriculture's *delayed returns*. In order to understand the difference, we simply need to imagine a life of collecting mushrooms, roots, berries and enjoying the occasional hunting success. How does one go about organising this type of work?

The answer is that there is little need to. Since such foodstuffs cannot be stored for long periods of time, they must be consumed right away. Finding food therefore becomes a process that has to be repeated on a daily basis.[7]

This is what we know. Exactly what the work looked like, however, varies. Some societies seem to have lived primarily off whatever they could pick from the ground, whereas others were focused more on hunting, aquatic organisms, and eggs. What each had in common was the daily recurrence of production and consumption, a hand-to-mouth existence which, in terms of future horizons, had three major consequences.

First, planning for the future was not only unnecessary, it was also impossible. The future we worry about and try to control today is a product of technology and society. Planning your finances for the next week, the next year or the next decade is only possible if money and necessities can be amassed in some way. If money rotted, there would be no point in stashing it away every month. Nor would there be any point in exercising restraint in the present in order to enjoy greater returns in the future. Thrift wouldn't be a virtue at all.

Second, as a result of the way they ate, hunter-gatherer societies have typically had less to worry about. Of course, the nature of a group's diet will have varied between desert gatherers and Arctic hunters, but generally speaking, people have been able to rely on over a hundred foodstuffs. Farmers have typically been more vulnerable in that they sated their hunger with only a handful of crops, sometimes almost exclusively one, like rice or corn. In this type of monoculture, weather conditions, crop disease, and parasites can have devastating consequences. For a long period of time, the average lifespan of a hunter-gatherer was higher than someone living in a civilised, agrarian society. That isn't to say it was high, however. According to one estimate, it was somewhere between thirty and forty, though if we discount the high levels of infant mortality then it was higher. A child who reached their teens had a good chance of living to over sixty. Some might even make it to eighty. Generally speaking, the age curve among hunter-gatherers seems to have followed that which Sweden first reached in the mid-eighteenth century.[8]

A third consequence of living off hunting and gathering is that there is no division of labour to speak of. In a handful of societies, the hunt seems to have been reserved for certain individuals, but on the whole, everyone was expected to be able to do everything. The need for organisation, for people who only carry out certain tasks and who immerse themselves in specialisation, did not, therefore, exist. Some hunter-gatherer societies have shown higher levels of conformity, with strong norms, but economically each individual enjoyed a level of autonomy from the collective that no modern person even comes close to today. Collecting purely for one's own use was, in certain societies, a possibility, and with a working day of around four hours in length, it wasn't too onerous a task either. Those who wanted to could also shut themselves off in certain societies. Among the Hadza people in northern Tanzania, for example, hunter-gatherers have been observed living as hermits.[9]

This is one of social science's clearest examples of how an individual is shaped by society. Without an address, without a profession, without any organisation or family bonds to tie my identity to, who am I? Who should I be? What should I be? For a hunter-gatherer, the type of society required to give those questions meaning was largely absent.[10]

Even in societies in which work pays immediate returns, it is, of course, possible to prepare for whatever may lie ahead. Making a fishing rod, arrows or a stick for digging are all examples of doing something for the future. A child practising with a bow and arrow can imagine their first hunt in several years' time. But possessing that power of imagination is not the same as spending the majority of one's life devoted to mental time travel. While the everyday life of nomadic peoples involved a greater spatial dimension than ours, the temporal dimension weighed lightly in their consciousness.

The question is what this consciousness looked like. The future takes up so much space today – what could have existed in its place?

The Intensity of Life

Every now and again, we experience the difference for ourselves. It may happen in a moment of euphoria, terror, or in some nameless convergence of the two. The causes vary. But whatever the reason, time is compressed to a quivering now without any before or after. It may feel like a disaster.

After a few years as a young socialist, at the age of just twenty-eight, Fyodor Dostoyevsky was sentenced to death by Tsar Nicholas I. The group of utopian socialists to which he belonged had been uncovered by the Okhrana, the Tsar's secret police, and following eight months of interrogations, sleeplessness, haemorrhoids, and epileptic attacks, he and fifteen other prisoners were taken to Semyonov Square in Moscow to be executed. The death sentence was read to the prisoners, and, dressed in white execution shirts, they were made to kiss the cross. A sword was broken over their heads to emphasise that they had lost their titles. While the first few prisoners were bound to pillars and the platoon loaded their rifles, Dostoyevsky calculated that he had five minutes left to life. Since those five minutes felt endless, he used the church clock to divvy them up.

First, he set aside two minutes to say farewell to his friends. He then spent two minutes pondering his fate: where he was heading and how everything – life and death – was connected. He imagined that he might be able to solve the mystery in two minutes, but quickly found himself lost in thought as he studied the golden roof of the church and the way it glittered in the sunlight. He would soon merge with those rays of light, he thought; they were already his new nature.

His last thought was that, if he survived, he would live the rest of his life with the same intensity he felt in that moment.

> What should I do if I were not to die now? What if I were to return to life again? What an eternity of days, and all mine! How I should grudge and count up every minute of it, so as to waste not a single instant!

Dostoyevsky was not executed. At the last moment, the gunmen were stopped and a letter of pardon from the Tsar was read aloud. Nicholas I had arranged the mock execution in order to intimidate the prisoners, and their real punishment was now dealt out: four years' forced labour at a prison camp in Siberia.

Dostoyevsky lived for another thirty years, and though he did his best – not least through his frequent trips to the casino, where he gambled everything he had – he failed to live the rest of his life with the same intensity.[11]

When we encounter this kind of intensity, not only do we feel a shift in perspective, we also go through a kind of awakening, a sense that we are finally seeing the world as it really is. This experience is often tied to specific events and activities, and in our day and age that could be anything from mortal danger, violence, pain and exhaustion, to romantic love.[12]

The fact that it takes such extreme measures for us to feel present in the moment can be interpreted in several ways. It could be seen as evidence that we are, by nature, made for counterfactual escapades. As though it were some evolutionary asset – being able to imagine future dangers – that comes with a side helping of mental absence.

But among those who have studied the living conditions of hunter-gatherers, the position is often the polar opposite, and these timeless moments of intense living instead provide us with a glimpse of the future-free existence that humans once inhabited.

In his memoirs, the psychoanalyst Carl Gustav Jung wrote that the tragedy of mankind is that we have started to live "more in the future and its chimerical promises of a golden age than in the present, with which our whole evolutionary background has not yet caught up." We live, according to Jung, "on promises, no longer in the light of the present day, but in the darkness of the future, which, we expect, will at last bring the proper sunrise."[13]

One problem with investigating our "evolutionary background" is that it is easy to become speculative when trying to understand how people perceived the world thousands of years ago. This has enabled theorists to really go all in.

One theory, for example, is that our distant history was imbued with what the philosopher Jean Gebser called an "ever-present" now. Gebser is one of many who have romanticised this state. Mankind's short future horizon meant a "magic consciousness," in his view. And this type of consciousness was particularly magical because it lacked all notions of an isolated self.[14]

The argument is not without its merits. Without a state to register a person's existence, without a school system focused on getting you to survive the competition, without career plans or decisions about life partners or whether to have children, buy a cat, a home, and an abundance of consumer goods – without even a sense of fixed belonging to a particular group – it is reasonable to assume that people possessed a different kind of individuality. The only question is whether life itself was *entirely* egoless as a result.

As a concept, egoless boundlessness has been around for some time. Sigmund Freud's term for the state was "oceanic feeling," and he argued that it is something everyone experiences in infancy. Freud saw it as a primitive stage, meaning that our longing to return to it was regressive, an infantile desire to crawl back into our mother's womb. For Jung, however, the desire to do away with the ego was something progressive, a search for an original form of wisdom beyond the cold rationalism of modernity. Jung, together with Gebser, laid the basis for the idea that the earliest people lived in ecstasy, and that this transcendental state of mind is our true and natural state. This is sometimes known as animism, a term for the religious idea that nature is animated and alive. Yet what is meant here is the mystical form of animism, a dissolution of subject and object in which "the external" – other people, animals, plants, mountains, the sky and stars – merges with "the internal."[15]

Other historians and anthropologists have argued that hunter-gatherer societies were characterised by a less ego-transcendent animism. In this view, the notion of doing away with the self, of becoming part of the universe, stems from the civilisation in which Jung and Freud themselves lived while fantasising about the primordial state of mankind. Hunter-gatherers had a sense of self, of course, but it carried little weight in their consciousness. It wasn't until a later stage of history, once we began to settle and grow restless, that we discovered meditative techniques and began experimenting with psychedelic drugs to dissolve our sense of self. Only then did the idea that the self was something to liberate oneself from take root.[16]

According to this school of thought, what characterised the consciousness before the age of planning was a sharpened attention span. In order to survive as a hunter-gatherer, every individual had to keep watch over a large area. They had to learn the rhythm of the seasons and the healing properties of various plants, while also keeping an eye on how they grew. Craftsmanship may be fading in today's industrialised society, but hunter-gatherer mastered a number of skills: Simply breaking off razor-sharp pieces of hornstone and flint to use as tools exceeds what the majority of modern men and women could achieve with their own two hands. Add to that the individual ability to deal with sudden changes in weather, aggressive predators, insect bites, injuries and illness. Nowadays, we turn to technology and specialists whenever anything similar happens, but back then it was something every single person had to be aware of.[17]

This heightened state of attention is not mysterious in and of itself; it is shared with countless other animals that live as hunter gatherers. But in the case of humans, it is also combined with something else: self-awareness. Researchers have used different terms to describe this state of consciousness. The American historian Morris Berman calls it living in "paradox" – partly in the knowledge of the uncertainty that individual existence entails, and partly in confidence of one's own ability to act.[18]

The American anthropologist Walter Ong called it a world view, and the British anthropologist Hugh Brody described it as a "receptive stillness." Yet another anthropologist by the name of Paul Radin, best known for his in-depth field studies of the Winnebago tribe in Nebraska, argued that these people's perception was so sharp that their surroundings "glowed." Not in the biblical, burning bush sense of the word, nor in any supernatural sense – more like Dostoyevsky's experience of intensity as he waited to be executed. As with the Mbuti people in Congo, there was no worshipping of a higher authority, but they did sense that the forest, their world, was living.[19]

The Widening of Future Horizons

How the hunter-gatherers' sense of presence was reflected in their mental well-being is something we cannot know. Studies that have managed to follow societies as they make the transition to agriculture (the Ik people in Uganda and the indigenous peoples around the Arctic, for example) have reported an increase in suicide and depression. But these studies are few and far between, and it is also unclear how rapid the process is. Perhaps even early agricultural societies were relatively spared from mental health problems. In a study of the Kaluli people (a farming community in Papua New Guinea), an anthropologist spent almost a decade interviewing around 2,000 adults and children about their experiences of grief. He found only one person – a woman who had been married against her will – who met the diagnostic criteria of clinical depression.[20]

And yet, the shift to agriculture laid the material foundations for a sense of worry that simply had not existed before. The arrival of agriculture came hand in hand with the first technologies based on foresight. The farmer suddenly had to consider the most unlikely of catastrophes that might strike in the next year, in two years' time, or even further in the future. Storing beans and wheat was not just for the next winter; crop failure and famine taught mankind to be more longsighted than that. Their stocks would have to last through the poor harvests that, to this day, remain impossible to predict.

A farmer who squints up at the clouds or drives a finger into the earth is engaging in a different kind of attentiveness to the hunter-gatherer reading the shifting terrain. The hunter-gatherer lives off the land as it is, whereas the farmer creates his own landscape. Whether we are talking about the drainage systems on terraced land, irrigation systems via kilometres of channels or the use of slash-and-burn cultivation, the farmer must make decisions that may have life-changing implications.

Should we sow, reap, fertilise, harrow, and plough or does the river level, the rain, the drought or something else we aren't even aware of require us to wait? This sense of responsibility – something that could never have been asked of a hunter-gatherer – is one side effect of a society that is increasingly reliant on calculation and specialisation.[21]

However crucial these conditions may have been, it is easy to overstate the transition between hunter-gatherers and farmers. As we will see, the shift was far from abrupt, it did not happen overnight, and even today, we can see significant differences in the ways various resident cultures relate to time.

Some cultures lack a word for "time" as we understand it. In Kachin in northern Burma, for example, the word "ahkying" refers to clock time and "asak" to the time in a person's life. "Na" means a long time, while "tawng" means a short time. As a single concept, time simply does not exist.[22]

Such linguistic features suggest a varied relationship with time. In a number of North American cultures, time is only ever referenced indirectly. The Sioux people, for example, have long lived without a word for "time," and therefore also lack words for waiting or being late. Something that further affects our understanding of time are the movements we use to measure it. Linking time to the movement of the planets is different to linking it to the movement of a clock, for example. Certain Burmese monasteries use the dawn light to know when it is time to get up in the morning. More specifically, a monk knows it is time to get up when he can see the veins on his hand. In this approach to organising time, life becomes dependent on the movement of light. Those of us who set our alarm clocks at 06:30 follow a more disconnected sense of time that sometimes involves daylight and sometimes night.[23]

These seemingly insignificant differences in the perception of time also encourage different types of attentiveness. A person who is used to following clock time would, for example, struggle to keep up during the vigil over a dead body among the Mi'kmaq people in eastern Canada. Their vigils are organised into distinct time periods, beginning with a time for gathering, followed by a time for prayer, then further periods to sing, rest and eat – none of which are related to clock time. The mourners move from one period to another on the basis of mutual agreement. So when is the moment to wrap up one time and move on to the next? Whenever the time is right.[24]

Such mutual decisions around what replaces one time with another can also be seen among the Nuer people in Sudan, whose calendar follows the seasons. In the month known as "kur," for example, they pitch their cattle camps and build fish dams. When does kur take place? Kur takes place when they pitch their camps and build their fish dams. The same applies to the period known as "dwat," when they leave their camps and return to their villages.[25]

To the extent that these measures of time have endured, it isn't because of an absence of clocks. Among the farmers in Kelantan in north-west Malaysia, for example, an anthropologist noted that they would rather make use of a "coconut clock" than a mechanical timepiece. In competitive contexts, the shell of a coconut with a hole bored into it is placed into a bucket of water. An interval is measured by the amount of time it takes for the coconut to sink – typically between three and five minutes. The villagers know their coconut clock is not exact, but they still prefer it to their wristwatches.[26]

Even in those countries that were among the first to introduce clock time, there was lasting resistance to the clock.

The first sundial was likely built around 3,500 years ago, and served above all to help arrange meetings between the naturally occurring times of sunrise and sunset. The sundial allowed for generous definitions of punctuality. "Hunting the shadow," as the ancient Greeks called it, remained an inexact practice, and the sundial's ability to shape people's lives was also limited by clouds and by nightfall.

For much of history as we know it, the sundial was used during the day and the water clock at night. The idea behind the water clock was to measure the amount of water that flowed through an opening in a vessel. The problem was that this hole could become blocked, at which point time would stop. It could also become lager, therefore speeding up time. Despite this, the water clock proved enduring as an horological instrument, with its use stretching all the way from ancient Egypt to the eighteenth century, when the pendulum clock was first introduced.[27]

The chequered history of the mechanical clock is tinged with mystery. How did *this* particular instrument of time come to structure our lives more than any other? Remember that the very first clocks lacked hands. Instead, they chimed. Their function was to alert people when it was time to pray, and that was all. Yet today, clock time eclipses all other measurements.

In 2014, the National Institute of Standards and Technology in Colorado announced that they had built an atomic clock that will be accurate to one second for the next 300 million years. Four years later, they topped this by revealing that their new atomic clock would not lose a single second in the slightly abstract timeframe "the age of the universe" (estimated to be around 14 billion years). As the astrophysicist Stephen Hawking pointed out, we are now able to measure time more precisely than anything else, so precisely that even distances are most accurately given in time (a metre is defined as the distance travelled by light in a vacuum in 1/299792458 of a second).[28]

The fact that this technological revolution was even possible is extraordinary given the scepticism with which the mechanical clock was long viewed. Until the nineteenth century, the clock was considered a poor imitation of natural time, and important meetings, duels and battles were still scheduled in accordance with dawn. Clocks were nothing but elaborate ornaments – fascinating, but not particularly useful, though their limitations were less technical than they were social. The number of clocks in existence quickly grew, but there was no standardised time; every person followed their own clock.

It was only with the rise of industrial capitalism that synchronised time began to emerge. With increasingly complex transactions and new technology like the railways, coordination became necessary. In Sweden, "rail time" coexisted alongside "local time" for a number of years, with several hands on the station clocks. Stockholm and Gothenburg both tussled to be picked as the national time, but in 1879 it was Askersund – a small town mid-way between the two – that proved victorious.

In other countries, this standardisation process took longer. As late as the 1860s, there were around seventy different time zones in the United States. This had been reduced to fifty by 1880, but there was still a great deal of resistance to increased standardisation.

In 1884, just after standard time was introduced, the essayist Charles Dudley Warner wrote in *Harper's* that clock time risked gaining increased importance over people's lives: "the chopping up of time into rigid periods is an invasion of individual freedom and makes no allowances for differences in temperament and feeling."[29]

As the clock began to capture a growing portion of our attention – from existing as a single clockface in the town square to adorning our living room walls, becoming something we carried around in our pockets, and eventually laying claim to our wrists – its critics grew more vocal. In the early twentieth century, the German writer Sigismund von Radecki declared the wristwatch the "handcuff of our time." This came almost 200 years after Jonathan Swift's Lilliputians mused that Gulliver's clock seemed to function as some kind of god to him, because he always consulted it before doing anything.[30]

Much of the criticism was based on the fact that, by using clock time, we would be estranging ourselves from the organic sense of time inherent in nature's cycles of day and night, summer and winter, life and death. Today, we can see a number of differences on this very point. To be like the indigenous peoples of the Andaman Islands and construct a calendar around the dominant scents from various trees and flowers at different times of year demands more of our senses than checking our mobile phones.

Oddly enough, no matter how dominant clock time has become, it has remained disconnected from our experience. The majority of people are incapable of developing any real sense of how quickly time is passing. Exactly how far out they are varies from person to person. In those suffering from mania, psychopathy, and paranoid schizophrenia, for example, people's internal clocks seem to move much faster, while time moves more slowly for those with anxiety disorders, depression and non-paranoid forms of schizophrenia.[31]

One result that has been seen in countless experiments is that the majority of us are more like melancholics than manics: we think that time is passing more slowly than it really is, and our misjudgements are often significant. In an early experiment, the French geologist Michel Siffre made himself into a human guinea pig by spending two months in a cave 115 metres below the ground. At the end of the experiment, he wrote that he had lost all sense of time. By his estimates, he was on his thirty-fourth day underground when his colleagues revealed that two months had passed.[32]

This same sluggishness in experienced time has also been observed in other experiments. In one study, several participants were made to live in isolation cells without windows for between one week and one month, estimating at intervals how much time they thought had passed. The average length of what they believed to be an hour was, in fact, one hour and twenty-eight minutes.[33]

Our minds need external input in order to be able to relate to abstract clock time, but this input no longer comes from nature – it now comes from the first screen we laid eyes on: the clockface. Though the cyclical elements of time, such as circadian rhythms and seasons, still clash with clock time and calendar years, clock time represents our adjustment to abstraction. As political theorist Ajay Singh Chaudhary observes, this *Zeitkrankheit*, or "time-sickness", can lead to a pervasive sense of exhaustion.[34]

With an other-worldly, linear sense of time, the future unfolds in an expanse of potential and risk, constantly in motion – depending on the choices we make.

The Fight Against the Future

Elise found a way out. She left her partner and started a new life, with a new future. These days, she has things she cares about. Things she is looking forward to. But she has also noticed that she has begun to approach time in much the same way as her parents. Every day is planned out, "in quarter-hour blocks," she says. If she is late for anything, she feels anxious. It makes no difference whether it is her fault or whether the train is delayed.

"It's a physical sensation. I feel claustrophobic whenever I'm late for something. It's like I'm trapped in time and I've lost all control over my life."

Even when she is free, she plans her days. She says that this is partly down to the desire to get as much as she can out of life. Days that unfold at random, that aren't centred on projects and plans, often feel like wasted time when evening comes round. And yet she also derives a strange satisfaction from diverging from her plans.

"I love changing my plans. It gives me a soft, warm feeling all over. But it has to be me who makes the decision. If my plans change because I'm late, or because the bus is, I feel a wave of stress."

No matter how much power time has over our lives, this is always lurking in the background: A longing to break free.

Much of the evidence suggests that this conflict has been present since the very beginning. As the anthropologist James Scott points out, it wasn't with the discovery of planted crops that people began to settle in one place. Between the first trace of cultivated seeds and the global expansion of agriculture, around 4,000 years passed. During this lengthy time, many fought, fled and otherwise refused to become a part of settled life.[35]

This refusal proved enduring. The fact that some societies chose not to develop agriculture is not because it was unknown as a method of subsistence. In a study of the San people, one of the interviewees replied: "Why should we plant, when there are so many mongongo nuts in the world?"[36]

This kind of question was likely even more charged in pre-industrial societies. In 1753, Benjamin Franklin noted that white children who had been captured by the indigenous peoples of North America and subsequently grown up with them could be unhappy once they returned:

> in a short time they become disgusted with our manner of life, and the care and pains that are necessary to support it, and take the first good opportunity of escaping again into the woods, from whence there is no reclaiming them.[37]

Nowadays, most people lack both the physique and the knowledge to be able to escape – not to mention somewhere to escape to. We live with an enforced future and a whole host of urgent choices relating to everything from work, family and diet – choices that are made even when we attempt to refuse them.

The choices we have to make would probably weigh less heavily on us if they were presented as absurdities, as *impossible choices* whose outcomes depend on so much more than what we ourselves decide. But that is not the case. Our worries are reinforced by the perception that our choices should be *rational* and ideally also *anchored within us*, a fact that encourages us to dwell on questions of who we really are.

In certain societies, the culture has humbled the population on this point, creating a counterweight to future-building technologies. One example of this can be seen in Kabylia, a mountainous coastal region in northern Algeria where the French sociologist Pierre Bourdieu spent four years on a field study beginning in the late 1950s. Markedly settled, and with a widened future horizon and all the risks that come hand in hand with agriculture, this society maintained a scepticism – if not hostility – towards too much long-term planning. Rational demands for planning were largely disapproved of, and if someone became too engaged in the future and behaved as though it could be controlled, people would say that "he wishes to make himself the associate of God."[38]

A person who wanted to eliminate future uncertainty through calculation was seen as a weak, someone struck by "hubris." All calculation was suspect, not just that which sought to maximise production. The number of participants in a meeting was never counted, the weight of grain set aside for sowing never weighed, and people never counted the number of chickens or eggs they had.

So how could they farm the land and make crop-related decisions that would have consequences for years to come? According to Bourdieu, a certain "confidence" was motivated by tradition. Storing a set amount of food, for example, was more a question of following the rules than making rational, financial decisions. Possessing this type of confidence was a way of honouring the teachings passed down by previous generations, approved by the community. Using calculations to rise above tradition, on the other hand, did not show confidence. Any individuals who relied on efficiency measures not only lacked humility for the future, they were also deceiving the collective.[39]

Perhaps this kind of openness to the future was more illogical than anything. But we have also seen – not least with Gödel – the irrationality inherent in consistent rationality. Accepting the future as uncertain, following "tradition" in the form of established behaviours rather than calculations of risk, is a must in life – there simply isn't enough time to calculate everything we do.

The degree of uncertainty permitted by a culture varies, however. The Kabylian reluctance to manipulate the future is made much easier if society prescriptively recognises the dignity of doing so. But if dignity is seen in minimising risk and maximising opportunity instead, the future horizon that mankind has been stretching since the rise of agriculture is expanded even further.

A glimpse of the Kabylian people's embrace of uncertainty can also be seen in the history of the West. Among the first known wage labourers, for example, there was no sense of value in accruing an ever-growing pile of money. In fact, for hundreds of years, the principle of working enough to be able to afford life's necessities – and no more – was the dominant approach.

In the thirteenth century, as the Black Death swept across Europe, this philosophy had a noticeable impact when a labour shortage arose and the workers were permitted more freedoms. Later in history, temporary advances of this kind would see workers negotiate for higher wages, but at this particular moment it was free time they prioritised. A religious fervour blossomed among the workers, and an increasing number of the medieval calendar's saints' days were made into public holidays.[40]

Right up until the industrial revolution – and for some time after – the European working classes seemed to view the future with much the same sense of indifference as the Kabylian farmers. The German sociologist Max Weber describes in detail the traditional workers' resistance when faced with capitalism's hunger for more manpower. "The type of backward traditional form of labour is today very often exemplified by women workers, especially unmarried ones," he writes. By "backward," Weber does not mean anything entirely negative:

> An almost universal complaint of employers of girls, for instance German girls, is that they are almost entirely unable and unwilling to give up methods of work inherited or once learned... Explanations of the possibility of making work easier, above all more profitable to themselves, generally encounter a complete lack of understanding. Increases of piece-rates are without avail against the stone wall of habit.[41]

That the employers were unable to get them to work longer hours even by raising their wages is worth noting. Weber asserts that the traditional workers were less interested in how much they could earn than in how much free time they could have: "The opportunity of earning more was less attractive than that of working less."[42]

In concrete terms, this might mean that the factories were temporarily left empty when the workers decided they had earned all they needed for the time being.

This resistance has appeared in various forms throughout the expansion of capitalism, writes Weber: "A man does not 'by nature' wish to earn more and more money, but simply to live as he is accustomed to live and to earn as much is as necessary for that purpose. Wherever modern capitalism has begun its work of increasing the productivity of human labour by increasing its intensity, it has encountered the immensely stubborn resistance of this leading trait of pre-capitalistic labour."[43]

How could this "nature," as Weber calls it, be transformed to such a degree that today, it is difficult even to imagine anyone who is oblivious to the risk of becoming unemployed?

In the answer, we find the primary difference between Europe's traditional workers and the San people who continue to hunt and gather in Namibia to this day: no matter how stubborn the European workers' resistance may have been, it wasn't stubborn enough.

Notes

1 See Lorraine Ball and Michael Chandler, "Identity formation in suicidal and non-suicidal youth: The role of self-continuity", *Development and Psychopathology,* vol. 1, nr. 3, 1989.
2 Deloitte, "The 2017 Deloitte Millennial Survey: Apprensive Millennials: Seeking stability and opportunities in an uncertain world", p. 5; Stokes, "A decade after the financial crisis, economic confidence rebounds in many countries", 2018, p. 12.
3 James Suzman, *Affluence Without Abundance: What We Can Learn from the World's Most Successful Civilisation,* London: Bloomsbury Publishing, 2019, pp. 114–128.
4 George Silberbauer, *Hunter and Habitat in the Central Kalahari Desert,* Cambridge: Cambridge University Press, 1980.

5 James C. Scott, *Against the Grain: A Deep History of the Earliest States*, New Haven: Yale University Press, 2017; James Woodburn, "Egalitarian societies", *Man*, vol. 17, nr. 3, 1982.
6 David Graeber and David Wengrow, *The Dawn of Everything: A New History of Humanity*, New York, Penguin Books, 2022.
7 Woodburn, "Egalitarian societies".
8 Michael Gurven and Hillard Kaplan, "Longevity among hunter-gatherers: A cross-cultural examination", *Population and Development Review*, vol. 33, nr. 2, 2007.
9 For a summary of working hours, see Roland Paulsen, *Arbetssamhället: Hur arbetet överlevde teknologin*, Stockholm: Atlas, 2017. See also Richard Barry Lee and Irven DeVore, *Man the Hunter,* London: Transaction Publishers, 1968, pp. 30–49. Anthropologists have long debated what the Neolithic shift to fixed residences and farming meant in terms of the opportunity to build equal societies of the kind the San people once lived in. See for example David Graeber and David Wengrow: "How to change the course of human history", *Eurozine*, 2/3, 2018; Scott, *Against the Grain: A Deep History of the Earliest States*. For hunter-gatherers who lived as hermits, see Robert Layton, Sean O'Hara and Alan Bilsborough, "Antiquity and social functions of multilevel social organization among human hunter-gatherers", *International Journal of Primatology,* vol. 33, nr. 5, 2012.
10 For discussion, see Anthony Giddens, *Social Theory and Modern Sociology,* Stanford: Stanford University Press, 1987.
11 Quote from *The Idiot* in which Dostoyevsky, according to the majority of his biographers, was describing his own experiences of mock execution. See Joseph Frank, *Dostoyevsky, The Years of Ordeal: 1850-1859,* Princeton: Princeton University Press, 1990, pp. 55–58.
12 For discussion, see Geir Oygarden, *Den brukne neses estetikk: En bok om boksning*, Uppsala, Uppsala Universitet, 2002.
13 Carl Gustav Jung, *The Earth Has a Soul: The Nature Writings of C. G. Jung,* North Atlantic Books, 2002, p. 141.
14 Jean Gebser, *The Ever-Present Origin,* Athens, Ohio: Ohio University Press, 1985.
15 To some extent, anthropological research confirms the idea of mystical practices among hunter-gatherers. In an analysis of 488 small communities in which the relevant ethnographies had been made, the American anthropologist Erika Bourguignon found that ninety percent carried out some form of religious practice involving a heightened state of consciousness – see Erika Bourguignon, *Religion, Altered States of Consciousness, and Social Change,* The Ohio State University Press, 1973, pp. 9–17. That said, we know very little about religious experiences prior to the growth of civilisation. The many interpretations of Palaeolithic cave paintings and various anthropological field studies that have been carried out remain the subject of interdisciplinary feuds. The anthropologist Felicitas Goodman has described the mythological models researchers have developed as snippets "cut from all sorts of religions, which are then assembled into a collage of doubtful value." See Felicitas Goodman, *Ecstasy, Ritual, and Alternate Reality: Religion in a Pluralistic World*, Indiana University Press, 1988.
16 See e.g. Berman, *Wandering God: A Study in Nomadic Spirituality.*
17 For a more in-depth discussion of this, see in particular Scott, *Against the Grain: A Deep History of the Earliest States.*
18 Berman, *Wandering God: A Study in Nomadic Spirituality.*
19 Colin M. Turnbull, *The Mbuti Pygmies: Change and Adaptation,* New York: Holt Rinehart & Winston, 1983; Paul Radin, *The World of Primitive Man,* New York: H. Schuman, 1953; Hugh Brody, *Maps and Dreams: Indians and*

the British Columbia Frontier, Vancouver: Douglas and McIntyre, 1981, p. 43; Walter J. Ong, "World as view and world as event 1", *American Anthropologist,* vol. 71, nr. 4, 1969.

20 For a summary, see Brandon H. Hidaka, "Depression as a disease of modernity: Explanations for increasing prevalence", *Journal of Affective Disorders,* vol. 140, nr. 3, 2012. The study of Kaluli: Edward L. Schieffelin, "The cultural analysis of depressive affect: An example from New Guinea" in *Culture and Depression: Studies in the Anthropology and Cross-Cultural Psychiatry of Affect and Disorder,* ed. Arthur Kleinman and Byron Good, Los Angeles: University of California Press, 1985.

21 See Scott, *Against the Grain: A Deep History of the Earliest States.*

22 Edmund Ronald Leach, *Rethinking Anthropology,* London: Athlone Press, 1961.

23 Edward Hall, "The dance of life: The other dimension of time", Garden City, NY: Doubleday, 1983.

24 Philip K. Bock, "Social structure and language structure", *Journal of Anthropological Research*, vol. 42, nr. 3, 1986.

25 Robert H. Lauer, *Temporal Man: The Meaning and Uses of Social Time,* New York: Praeger, 1981, p. 22.

26 Douglas Raybeck, "The coconut-shell clock: Time and cultural identity", *Time & Society*, vol. 1, nr. 3, 1992.

27 G. J. Whitrow, *Time in History: Views of Time from Prehistory to the Present Day,* Oxford: Oxford University Press, 1989, p. i.

28 Belinda Smith, "These atomic clocks are so precise they can measure the distortion of space-time", *ABC News*, 28/11, 2018.

29 See Jeremy Rifkin, *Time Wars: The Primary Conflict in Human History*, New York: H. Holt, 1987, p. 145.

30 See Helmut Kahlert, Richard Mühe and Gisbert L. Brunner, *Wristwatches: History of a Century's Development*, Atglen: Schiffer Pub., 2005, p. 14.

31 Rifkin, *Time Wars: The Primary Conflict in Human History*, pp. 46–57. John Edward Orme, *Time, Experience And Behaviour*, London: Iliffe Books, 1969.

32 Michael Siffre, *Beyond Time*, New York: McGraw-Hill, 1964.

33 Jürgen Aschoff, "On the perception of time during prolonged temporal isolation", *Human Neurobiology*, vol. 4, nr. 1, 1985.

34 Ajay Singh Chaudhary, *The exhausted of the Earth: Politics in a Burning World*, London: Repeater Books, 2024.

35 Scott, *Against the Grain: A Deep History of the Earliest States*, pp. 58–61. See also Claude Lévi-Strauss, *The Savage Mind,* Chicago: University of Chicago Press, 1966, p. 258. For a discussion of Lévi-Strauss' distinction between hot and cold societies, see also Giddens, *Social Theory and Modern Sociology.*

36 Lee and DeVore, *Man the Hunter*, p. 33

37 Walter Isaacson, *A Benjamin Franklin Reader*, New York: Simon & Schuster, 2005, p. 157.

38 Pierre Bourdieu, "Time perspectives of the Kabyle" in *The Sociology of Time,* ed. John Hassard, New York: Palgrave Macmillan, 1990, p. 226.

39 Bourdieu, "Time perspectives of the Kabyle", p. 233.

40 Peter Englund, *Förflutenhetens landskap: Historiska essäer,* Stockholm: Atlantis, 1991, p. 189.

41 Max Weber, *The Protestant Ethic and the Spirit of Capitalism,* New York: Scribner, 1958, p. 62.

42 Weber, *The Protestant Ethic and the Spirit of Capitalism*, p. 60.

43 Weber, *The Protestant Ethic and the Spirit of Capitalism*, p. 60.

6

DISENCHANTMENTS

Thinking back to what might have been and forward to what could be opens up our ability to think about something else: cause and effect.

Cause and effect is the language of science, of technology; it has helped us understand everything from the most minute processes in the division of cells to continental drift and the movements of landmasses over millions of years. Cause and effect has also made it possible for us to calculate risk, and ever-present within worrying is an analysis of cause and effect.

There are times when it feels like life is nothing but a relentless set of dominoes made up of cause and effect, as though everything follows the laws of mechanics in an endless process that no one can control. What is our purpose if we are nothing but organic machines surrounded by an even greater machine known as nature? Viewed like this, many things lose their meaning.

Disheartened, we might remember how big and mysterious the world seemed to us as children. How can that same world have become so pale and soulless?

A little over 100 years ago, the sociologist Max Weber was grappling with these very questions, and his reflections helped him to formulate one of social science's most widely debated contemporary diagnoses. He called it disenchantment.

A Life of Enchantment

It is worth mentioning here that Weber himself was an anxious man who struggled until the very end to make sense of his private life. That isn't to say that his life was a miserable one. During his time as a young professor,

DOI: 10.4324/9781003514930-8

Weber and his wife Marianne rented an apartment above a family who followed their every movement. When Weber got home in the evening, he often whipped the cushions on the sofa while Marianne stood to one side and screamed. The couple, it seems, were amused by the rumours that Weber disciplined his wife which spread through ultra-Catholic Freiburg.[1]

Among the many scholars who have written about the Webers' lives, there has been a tendency to leave out such marital pleasures as these. Instead, since Weber was unable to maintain an erection to "consummate the marriage" during their twenty-seven years together, the focus has often been on why their marriage was an unhappy one.

It may seem unnecessary to delve into yet another neurotic academic's tangled thoughts, but the interesting thing about Weber is less his problems and more how he related to them. Because unlike Kurt Gödel, whose paranoia we have already read about, Weber was a master of self-reflection. No matter what he was going through, his own analysis seeped into his anxiety. Explanations flourished – long, anxious and for the most part tinged by the late nineteenth-century doctrine of psychological problems stemming from a person's nerves.

To a modern historian, the many references to nerves reveal the concerns and traits that people at the time wanted to do away with. When, for example, Marianne apologised for her reluctance to invite people over to their home in the evening, she did so by making reference to their nerves: "unfortunately our nerves, our lords and masters, rarely permit that."[2]

In Weber's letters, "nerves" occasionally give way to "demons." They fulfil much the same function, with the key difference that nerves appear to be more value-free. Unlike demons, nerves have no will and appear as small, natural catastrophes.

By referencing nerves, the Webers could deal with his impotence as though it were nothing more than an unfortunate reading on the family's private Richter scale. For example, they kept a joint record of Weber's nightly ejaculations, or "emissions," as they called them. They believed that these were connected both to his sleeping problems and the limpness of his member. The most detailed descriptions of Weber's problems appear in the frequent correspondence between his wife and mother. Over the course of several years, Marianne reported to her mother-in-law about Weber's issues. Their communication knew no bounds.[3]

For a time, the two discussed – in consultation with psychiatry – whether castration might be the only way to "cut the Gordian knot." This was a thought that Weber himself had entertained (at around this time, he began making reference to the Russian Skoptsy sect which, during the eighteenth century, practised self-castration as a means of salvation). After much deliberation, they abandoned the idea. As Marianne wrote in a letter to her mother-in-law, it would "probably replace the emissions with a different evil."[4]

Weber's problems eventually caught up with him in his work as a young professor. He found that he was struggling to speak and was struck by a number of fixations, among them that an ape's mask was pressed on his face while he gave a lecture. Shortly after the death of his father, Weber collapsed, just thirty-four years of age, and for the next five years, he was unable to work at all. He was forced to step down from his position at the university, and it would be twenty years before he was in any fit state to take it up again.

Weber's breakdown led him to re-evaluate the "asceticism" that would recur as a societal diagnosis in his later books. To renounce the pleasures of life in order to devote himself to science was something he had long considered his salvation, and in a letter to Marianne, he wrote:

> After years of dreadful torment, I feared a profound depression would set in. It did not happen, and I believe it was because I worked constantly and did not let my brain or nervous system get any rest. Quite apart from my natural need to work, this is one reason why I am so very reluctant to make a really perceptible pause in my work.[5]

Weber's fears were realised to such an extent that he was on holiday when he collapsed. Despite this, he came to re-evaluate just how healthy it was to work in order to keep his demons at bay. After his breakdown, he wrote that it was like it was like an icy hand had let him go, "for my sickly disposition expressed itself in past years in a desperate clinging to scholarly work as to a talisman... the *need* to feel submerged under a workload is extinguished."[6]

For Weber, his breakdown was a moment of awakening. He could see his omnipresent suffering, and particularly the suffering inherent in academic self-flagellation. Among Weber's contemporary academics (all of them men), nervous problems were commonplace. The philosopher Heinrich Rickert suffered from agoraphobia and had to be accompanied whenever he went outside. The psychiatrist Karl Jaspers had facial tics that he eventually learned to control, though the price was a permanent strained look on his face. The art historian Carl Neumann suffered from deep depressions, and was admitted to hospital following a series of attempted suicides. And on the other side of the Atlantic, William James revolutionised modern psychology while, like Weber, being diagnosed as an incurable "neurasthenic" (the diagnosis of the day, which covered both depression and anxiety).

In private, Weber transitioned to a stubborn criticism of work. In countless letters, he exhorted his friends to beware of intellectual overexertion, claiming that it inevitably leads to collapse. The typical outcome is that it ends in suicide, he wrote.

In a letter to the sociologist Robert Michels, Weber gives detailed instructions on how to proceed if he wants to survive:

> Give up for a year *all* lecture trips abroad and *all* hurried work, go to bed every (*every*) day at 9:30, spend two weeks *at a time* in the summer relaxing without books (without *any* books) in the isolated German *forest* (full board: 3-4 marks), and you will know after a year how much work capacity/capital you have left.[7]

Over time, this awakening would solidify into an even stricter need to be in control. He became particularly fixated on the idea that stimulation during the day would reappear as insomnia at night. This might apply to anything from getting a bit of fresh air to meeting friends, and Weber's calculations were detailed. A walk in the forest would cost him three-quarters of a night's sleep, giving a toast at his sister's wedding three whole nights (which was the reason he refrained). He excitedly wrote to his wife whenever someone visited him in Rome, where he often took refuge from the German winter, but also complained about "the bill" he inevitably had to pay at night.[8]

With the help of these calculations, large quantities of sleeping pills and the bromine that was often prescribed as a sedative at the time, Weber attempted to piece his life back together. As he would later lament, every part of his body – including his emotions – was alien to him. The only thing he could trust was his "icy brain": "For years I used this icebox as a last hope, as something that remained 'pure' against the devils who had their way with me when I was ill (and probably before)."[9]

Sadly, it would be some time before he realised that his brain had deceived him to a far greater extent than both his demons and nerves were capable of.

The insight would leave its mark on his sociological work. The idea of modern man as a cerebral robot, fanatically believing anything science holds to be true, is a recurring ideal type in Weber's analysis.

It is important to note here that Weber was not hostile to science. Until his dying day, he saw science – *value-neutral science* – as his calling. And yet he also considered it "meaningless." Despite its claims to explain the world, science is unable to provide answers to the questions that most concern people, namely: "What should we do? How should we live?"[10]

Towards the end of his life, Weber asked the following in a lecture: "Who – apart from a few overgrown children, who are indeed to be found in the natural sciences – still believes that the insights of astronomy or biology or physics or chemistry could teach us anything about the *meaning* of the world, or even anything about the way in which to trace such a meaning – if one exists?"

In this lecture, Weber advanced the theory that modern society involves a growing gulf between humans and the world around them. While the pre-modern farmer knew his place within a cycle in which life's purpose is given from birth, modern man is born into a never-ending accumulation of wealth, knowledge, risks and problems in which he can never truly find a foothold. He may become "weary of life," but he can never be "fulfilled by it," and since it is impossible for him to reach the end with any real sense of having done his part, he approaches a death that cannot be seen as anything but meaningless.[11]

This lack of meaning is felt not only in existential questions about what we should do and how we should live. On a deeper level, too, the world recedes to such an extent that we, as individuals, understand increasingly less of it. Weber demonstrates this with the example of someone driving along a road. Unless the driver happens to be an engineer, they will typically have very little idea of how the car actually works and nor do they need to know. They turn the wheel and trust that a specialist will be able to help them if anything goes wrong, in the same way that they could help others in whatever narrow field they have specialised in. Only in the slimmest of areas do we know something about anything.

"The savage," writes Weber, "knows incomparably more."[12]

This aspect of disenchantment seems to have passed many people by. Because disenchantment *does not* mean that a truth is revealed, allowing us with absolute certainty to dismiss the existence of God or declare that nature has a soul. It doesn't mean that we gain any insight into the conditions of life at all.

The fundamental meaning of disenchantment is "the knowledge or belief that *if we only wanted to* we *could* learn at any time that there are, in principle, no mysterious unpredictable forces in play, but that all things – in principle – can be *controlled* through *calculation*."[13]

In other words, disenchantment is about a belief that the world is calculable – i.e. governed by causality, by mechanical laws that determine everything from planetary gravitational fields to the social lives of termites and all human activity. This stands in contrast to the notion of the world as "ensouled", a term used by German sociologist Hartmut Rosa. Consequently, a sense of "resonance" is diminished – the experience that the world is alive, which presupposes unpredictability.[14]

That it is *in principle* possible to understand the world in this mechanist way cannot be emphasised enough. As any astrophysicist or neurobiologist would say, "more research" is needed before we can fully investigate how parallel universes work, or how the human brain produces different states of consciousness. Despite the empirical deficits, disenchantment sprouts from the idea that cause and effect, *in principle,* can explain everything – that nothing that is currently inexplicable, not even consciousness or the idea of free will, can exist beyond the laws of mechanics.

Yes, in the world of disenchantment, even our inner cogwheels turn in accordance with the causality of the universe. And yet mankind is a manipulator who, using technology, learns how to take advantage of causality. This complicates things slightly. At times, disenchantment can be felt in the way we try to manipulate ourselves as though we were machines. Weber's own life provides several examples of this, with the complex calculations he used in an attempt to control his anxiety. As the Webers' repeatedly mention in their letters, science seems to have no idea how to help people like Weber, and yet that didn't stop the couple from counting daily stimulants and sleeping pills on the one hand, and nightly emissions and sleeplessness on the other.

Unfortunately, many of Weber's critics seem to have missed that it is precisely in this mechanist view of the world – with cause and effect governing everything – that disenchantment can be found. There have been plenty of studies about the world's "disenchantment" that refer to the percentage of the global population that still professes any religion, but in the strict sense of the term, disenchantment has nothing to do with religion.

Weber may well have seen secularisation as one of many expressions of disenchantment, but in his analysis disenchantment began *within* religion – more specifically, in the deterministic currents of Protestantism. This particular analysis of history is, however, one of Weber's most criticised. In short, we can say that Weber's history of ideas did not go far back enough in time.

Like Clockwork

Just like the modern awareness of time, this mechanist worldview is intimately bound up with the clock – specifically, the astronomical clock. In an attempt to map the movements of the stars, the first astronomical clocks were built in China and the Arab world hundreds of years before they reached the West. Their function was to act as a metaphor for the movement of the planets, and when the Europeans finally started making their own astronomical clocks, they were so pleased with their creations that they began to think that the universe probably functioned in much the same way as the models they had built. Mechanically.

This shift came during the seventeenth century. In 1605, the German astronomer Johannes Kepler wrote that "the celestial machine is to be likened not to a divine organism, but rather to a clockwork." It is worth pausing for a moment here to consider this new worldview. Why did Kepler choose to distinguish between organisms and machines?[15]

To all extents and purposes, it comes down to differing views on nature as living or dead. Organisms are alive; they have goals and aspirations, and they are in control of themselves. Prior to the seventeenth century, it was seen as natural to view the universe as a living being. The stars were, as Aristotle put it, "partaking of life and initiative." As late as the sixteenth century, William Gilbert, one of the pioneers of magnetism, wrote: "We consider that the whole universe is animated, and that all the globes, all the stars, and also the noble earth have been governed since the beginning by their own appointed souls and have the motives of self-conservation."[16]

Copernicus, who revolutionised astronomy by replacing the earth with the sun at the centre of everything, also considered the universe to be a living thing. In justifying why he had placed the sun at the centre, he used both scientific and mystical theories, suggesting, for example, that the sun's central position explained why many had historically considered it a god. But even after the arrival of the mechanist epoch, philosophers like David Hume continued to question the causal machine model.

"There are other parts of the universe (besides the machines of human invention) which bear still a greater resemblance to the fabric of the world," wrote Hume. "These parts are animals and vegetables. The world plainly resembles more an animal or a vegetable, than it does a watch or a knitting-loom."[17]

That the machine, despite criticism, went from metaphor to model was more the result of technological developments than scientific ones. It was around this time that the first truly impressive machines began to emerge, after all. The machine became the triumph through which science could demonstrate its power. With the machine, the abstract calculations of mathematics could be performed with a precision that was impossible in nature. The machine was proof that the laws of science worked, that it was possible to calculate time, force and motion and build a technology that would previously have been considered a miracle.

This practical feat, which, through industrialisation, transformed society, made it so much easier to assume that everything in the universe functioned in the same way – particularly the solar system. But in terms of the plants and animals we continue to refer to as "organisms," it would be much more complex.

One man it is impossible to avoid in this context is the philosopher René "I think, therefore I am" Descartes. Shortly after Kepler proclaimed the mechanical movements of the planets, Descartes came up with a mechanist system for all life on earth. As the early scientist he was, Descartes worked empirically, taking a particular interest in the automatic movements of the heart, the digestive system and the respiratory system. Did these not prove the mechanical nature of the human body?

Keen to get to the bottom of the issue, he developed an impressive knack for cutting open live dogs to study the way their internal organs behaved. "If you slice off the pointed end of the heart in a live dog," he observed, "and insert a finger into one of the cavities, you will feel unmistakeably that every time the heart gets shorter it presses the finger, and every time it gets longer it stops pressing it."[18]

These vivisections may seem barbaric, but fortunately Descartes had determined that there was no moral dilemma there. One of his arguments was namely that if one could construct a machine with "the organs and outward shape of a monkey or of some other animal that lacks reason, we should have no means of knowing that they did not possess entirely the same nature as these animals." By the same logic, he concluded that the animal's ability to feel pain was equal to that of the machine's – non-existent, in other words.[19]

Since mechanist materialism has become virtually synonymous with natural sciences, it may be worth remembering that its origins were religious. Descartes remained a Christian, and he described how his mechanist worldview first came to him in the form of a revelation in the year 1619. In his theology, he was explicit in the devaluation of the body and flesh as mechanical and dead. Present alongside this material was, of course, the human soul. This "rational soul," as he called it, was unique to mankind, and the dualism between soul and matter enabled Descartes to maintain Christian notions of man's superiority over animals. He was unable to say exactly how this rational soul set the mechanical body in motion, but his hypothesis was that the meeting between the two took place in the pineal gland, a small pea-shaped gland in the brain.[20]

Today, the machine still functions as a model for the living, but it has, over the years, undergone a series of crises and modifications. After the astronomer Fred Hoyle presented his theory of the ever-expanding universe, the astronomical clock proved to be a problematic model for the universe. Descartes' mechanical organisms had, for similar reasons, difficulty surviving Charles Darwin's theory of evolution, according to which both plants and animals adapt to environmental changes.

Above all, the idea of a mechanical fauna designed by God simply could not be reconciled with the creative power Darwin saw in nature. While machines invariably have to be created by someone, organisms create themselves. A machine cannot heal itself if one part of it is destroyed. It cannot emerge as a single-cell organism, only to grow, develop new structures and propagate itself. Animals and plants do all of these things, and they also possess the ability to develop new characteristics in themselves – something that occasionally results in a new species.

Darwin was also explicit that consciousness was not a uniquely human phenomenon. "Nevertheless the difference in mind between man and the higher animals, great as it is, is certainly one of degree and not of kind," he wrote.[21]

Like other contemporary biologists, Darwin believed that behaviour could be passed down through generations. He gave several examples of environmental adaptations in parents being inherited by their offspring, which left the door open to concepts like habit, intent and aspiration – all parts of consciousness – also existing among plants and animals.

During the 1940s, this part of evolutionary theory was revised when it was established that organisms inherit their genes in unchanged form from their parents – assuming no random mutations have taken place. As a result of this theory (which would later be complicated by epigenetics), the notion of creative organisms vanished from evolution.

"Chance alone is at the source of every innovation, of all creation in the biosphere," wrote the Nobel Prize Laureate Jacques Monod in his book *Chance and Necessity*. The all-powerful engineer-God was replaced by Lady Luck, and organisms became machines subjected to another external power – a mysterious one.[22]

Over time, the mechanist worldview has been reproduced from both religious and atheist quarters. Not least has the question of human versus animal consciousness attracted speculation.

One example is Karl Marx, who insisted that free and conscious production was something uniquely human. Labour – with the exception of the most "primitive, instinctive forms" – is a process rooted in consciousness, argued Marx. Man gets the idea of what to do, and then shapes the world accordingly.

The labour of animals, on the other hand, is instinctive and inherited: "A spider conducts operations that resemble those of a weaver, and a bee puts to shame many an architect in the construction of her cells. But what distinguishes the worst architect from the best of bees is this, that the architect raises his structure in imagination before he erects it in reality."[23]

This is the reason why people, unlike animals, can become alienated from their nature. If human labour is no longer free, then it means that we have been stripped of the freedom that defines our species. Animals, in other words, are *unfree* in the sense that they exclusively follow their instincts, whereas humans are *free* in the sense that they can shape the world to their consciousness.[24]

Today, research in animal cognition – a field that has attracted an increasing number of researchers since WWII – has advanced to such a degree that we can say with reasonable certainty that Marx was wrong about animals' lack of freedom.

For example, jumping spiders appear to surpass Marx's criteria for creation (building something "in imagination") with aplomb, seemingly possessing the ability to mentalise – i.e. visualise the mental processes of others. This is clearest when they lure their fellow spiders into their webs in order to eat them. They do this by making their webs move and observing how the other spider reacts. Not all jumping spiders are equally skilled in this however; it is a skill they have to practise, and those who succeed become increasingly skilful the more prey they catch.[25]

If we turn to Marx's other example of the bee and her wax cells, we also know that bees and other members of the Hymenoptera order are able not only to come up with new ways to live, they can also learn from one another. Early on, Darwin speculated that the honey bee could learn from the bumblebee's behaviour, and he wasn't entirely wrong. If, for example, a bee learns a new method of extracting nectar, this skill often spreads to other bees – something that has been shown, on several occasions, to affect the behaviour of entire colonies and even future generations.[26]

In Australia, researchers have studied the ways in which mud wasps repair their funnel-like nests after inflicting artificial damage that would never occur naturally – by breaking them in two, piercing holes in them, or pushing a nest built by one colony of wasps into another. Time and time again, the researchers watched the wasps stop their work to repair or incorporate the new nest into their own.[27]

The primatologist Frans de Waal's research provides even more sensational examples of the ways in which animals, in a laboratory setting, solve problems and learn to master machines using actions that cannot possibly be inherited instincts. The German ethologist Karsten Brensing has also compiled evidence of different cultures arising within various species. In Japan, for example, crows have developed a system for cracking nuts that involves dropping them onto roads for cars to drive over, then flying down to collect them once the traffic lights change – a behaviour that has not been observed in crows anywhere else on earth. Certain species, such as the killer whale, have also developed certain norms which, in vulnerable moments, can sometimes be prioritised ahead of both survival and reproduction.[28]

I mention this not to refute the mechanist worldview but to emphasise that the disenchanted view of nature is something other than a logical consequence of scientific evidence. This is especially true of the mechanist understanding of mankind.

Homo Mechanicus

Our tendency to regard human activity as subordinate to mechanical laws differs from culture to culture. Westerners seem much more inclined to see human activity as an expression of cause and effect than the Chinese, Japanese, and Koreans, for example. They also show an interest in *fewer* causes in explaining a certain event. This has been demonstrated in a number of socio-psychological experiments and can even be seen in the way children are taught history. Japanese history teachers, for example, place more weight on the ways in which historical figures have acted in different situations, based on their context, whereas American teachers show much more interest in "causes" of the type, "The Ottoman Empire collapsed for three major reasons."[29]

These causes are easy to theorise in hindsight, but notoriously difficult to predict in advance. This explains why, despite our increasing awareness of what causes social and economic crises, we are always taken by surprise whenever they happen. Mechanical models have, as a result, become less common among historians and sociologists during the past century. But the more we narrow our focus to the individual and their consciousness, the more mechanist science becomes.

Explaining how matter can become consciousness is what the Australian philosopher David Chalmers calls the "hard problem" of consciousness. All we can say with certainty is that no one knows.

One of the difficulties in studying this problem is that we can only do so through our consciousness. I can, for example, perceive myself as something more than a robot, as someone who possesses the ability to act in a way that has not been predetermined by a neurological domino in my brain. If I then read a theory that this perception is nothing but an illusion, that it is, in fact, that very neurological domino that has made me believe I am something other than a robot, then I am faced with a dilemma. Should I trust my perceptions or the theory? Both perception and theory are transmitted through my consciousness, and the decision to trust the theory – as several philosophers have pointed out – represents an extreme trust in authority. Why should my conscious – and incredibly direct – experience of being something other than a robot be more illusory than a mechanist speculation that someone else has come up with using their own consciousness?[30]

If we consider the imagined models for the human machine throughout history, they have all been strikingly similar to the technology of the time. This is evident not least in the ways we have attempted to explain where the machine's "I" resides. While Descartes' dualistic vision of man was dominant, the body was a factory of whirring cogwheels. A miniature person, a *homunculus*, sat in the head, pulling on levers to guide the human factory in different directions. In the 1940s, this figure was often depicted as a telephone operator, and when air travel became more widespread, the figure also began to appear as a pilot. But the idea of a mini pilot in the brain does not work, of course, because the mini pilot himself must surely have a pilot in his brain, who has a pilot in his brain, and so on. And yet the *homunculus* metaphor persists, even to this day.

During the eighteenth century, when electricity began to dominate science, the nerves became central to explaining the human machine. The nerves were the feeling self's tentacles, responsible for determining a person's sensibility. Just as mistakes, lethargy or frustration can be attributed to "the brain," as though it were something other than us, a person's nerves – as we have seen with the Webers – filled the same externalising role. Nerves also varied from person to person. Among the upper classes, they were assumed to be incredibly delicate, finely-calibrated threads, which explained why they were better at art, science and business than the lower classes.[31]

These days, the PC is the obvious metaphor for explaining the man-machine. Few can have escaped the metaphors of the human brain's various memories and pre-programmed software in the form of genetic code. Like the mini pilots in the brain, we have a new group of actors who – not least in Richard Dawkins' theory of the "selfish gene" – possess a freedom of action that we, ourselves, are lacking. Our genes – or, more specifically, "molecules called DNA" – have, according to Dawkins, "built a vast range of machines to exploit. A monkey is a machine that preserves genes up trees, a fish is a machine that preserves genes in the water." Humans, too, are "lumbering robots" – albeit incredibly complex ones – notes Dawkins.[32]

The image of humans as mechanical and externally controlled now possesses a cultural power that far exceeds anything Weber ever experienced. And if we go over to the artificial intelligence enthusiasts, the speculation outstrips anything we have seen before.

In 2009, for example, the neuroscientist Henry Markram gave a TED talk in which he announced the following: "it is not impossible to build a human brain... we can do it within ten years." Markram envisioned being able to step inside his autistic son's brain and experience the world as he did.

His idea won a billion euros from the European Commission, in the kind of research venture rarely seen. Starting in 2013, the ten-year Human Brain Project planned to build a computer model of the human brain. After just two years, however, it became clear that the project was in disarray, and Markram was fired. And yet there is still a great deal of hope that we will one day be able to build a human brain – either that or a computer onto which a human consciousness can be uploaded and live on in virtual form.[33]

Viewing ourselves as biological robots requires a deep sense of disenchantment – one that not only involves the world around us but also ourselves.

Whether we really *are* biological robots is of secondary importance in this context. It could well be the case – "more research is needed," as the saying goes. And it could also be the case that we one day manage to build a human consciousness using aluminium, plastic, copper, tin, silicon and whatever else is needed for a computer. Whether these hopes are realistic remains to be seen.

One thing we can say with relative certainty is that the conviction that consciousness is a side effect of the brain's mechanical activity, colours the way we perceive ourselves and the world.

At around the same time that Weber was writing about modern man's disenchantment, Pierre Janet (the psychiatrist who developed a theory of "the subconscious" before Freud) noted that an increasing number of patients at La Salpêtrière psychiatric hospital had begun to see themselves as balls in a Newtonian billiards game.

"All our patients use the same language," he wrote. "The words 'machine,' 'robot' and 'mechanical' all reoccur constantly... 'I am just a machine,' says Lise... 'It is my body, it is not my will.'"[34]

The type of mechanics assumed to be controlling the game of billiards is of less importance. As the Austrian psychiatrist and Holocaust survivor Viktor Frankl pointed out, disenchantment can find nourishment in any discipline – even sociology:

> First of all, there is a danger inherent in the teaching of man's 'nothingbutness,' the theory that man is nothing but the result of biological, psychological and sociological conditions, or the product of heredity and environment. Such a view of man makes a neurotic believe what he is prone to believe anyway, namely, that he is the pawn and victim of outer influences or inner circumstances. This neurotic fatalism is fostered and strengthened by a psychotherapy which denies that man is free.[35]

Frankl's argument that a mechanist view of humans would encourage "fatalism" also presupposes a rock solid conviction that most of us lack. Looking to Weber, we can easily see that he occasionally felt that his own psyche solidified into something alien. But rather than fatalistically giving in to this, he tried everything he could to tame it. Nocturnal emissions, intellectual exchange, bromine and sleeping pills; he was willing to regulate everything in order to master his demons.

During his last few years, he admitted that he had failed in the simplest of tasks: partaking of what life had to offer without letting his calculations and theories get in the way. His judgement of Western men and women also applies to him: "specialists without spirit, sensualists without heart; this nullity imagines that it has attained a level of civilisation never before achieved."[36]

Notes

1 Joachim Radkau, *Max Weber: A Biography,* Cambridge: Polity, 2013, p. 46.
2 Radkau, *Max Weber: A Biography*, p. 88.
3 Radkau, *Max Weber: A Biography*, p. 156.
4 Radkau, *Max Weber: A Biography*, p. 166.
5 Radkau, *Max Weber: A Biography*, p. 124.
6 Karin Johannisson, *Melankoliska rum: Om ångest, leda och sårbarhet i förfluten tid och nutid,* Stockholm: Albert Bonniers Förlag, 2013, p. 160. English version of this quote found in Arthur Mitzman, *The Iron Cage: An Historical Interpretation of Max Weber,* New York: Grossett & Dunlap, 1971, p. 50.
7 Radkau, *Max Weber: A Biography*, p. 152.
8 Radkau, *Max Weber: A Biography*, p. 151.
9 Radkau, *Max Weber: A Biography*, p. 168.
10 Max Weber, *Max Weber's Complete Writings on Academic and Political Vocations,* New York: Algora Publishing, 2008, p. 39.
11 Weber, *Max Weber's Complete Writings on Academic and Political Vocations*, p. 36.
12 Weber, *Max Weber's Complete Writings on Academic and Political Vocations*, p. 35.

13 Weber, *Max Weber's Complete Writings on Academic and Political Vocations*, p. 35.
14 Hartmut Rosa, *The Uncontrollability of the World,* Cambridge: Polity Press, 2020, p. 28.
15 R. G. Newton, *From Clockwork to Crapshoot: A History of Physics*, Harvard: Harvard University Press, 2009, p. 74.
16 J. H. Brooke, *Science and Religion: Some Historical Perspectives*, Cambridge: Cambridge University Press, 1991, p. 119.
17 David Hume, *Dialogues Concerning Natural Religion*, Los Angeles: Enhanced Media, 2017, p. 46.
18 René Descartes, *The Philosophical Writings of Descartes. Vol. 2*, Cambridge: Cambridge University Press, 1984, p. 242.
19 René Descartes, *The Philosophical Writings of Descartes. Vol. 1*, Cambridge: Cambridge University Press, 1985, p. 139.
20 For examples of criticism of Cartesian and contemporary materialism, see Thomas Nagel, *Mind and Cosmos: Why the Materialist Neo-Darwinian Conception of Nature is Almost Certainly False,* New York: Oxford University Press, 2012 and Raymond Tallis, *The Explicit Animal,* London: Palgrave Macmillan UK, 1999
21 Charles Darwin, *The Descent of Man and Selection in Relation to Sex*, Princeton, NJ: Princeton University Press, 1981, p. 105.
22 Jacques Monod, *Chance and Necessity: An Essay on the National Philosophy of Modern Biology*, New York: Collins, 1974, p. 112.
23 Karl Marx, *Capital: Volume 1: A Critique of Political Economy*, London: Penguin Books 1992 [1867], p. 284
24 Karl Marx, *Economic And Philosophic Manuscripts of 1844*, Amherst: Prometheus Books, 1988 [1844], p. 74.
25 Frans De Waal, *Are We Smart Enough to Know How Smart Animals Are*? New York: WW Norton & Company, 2016, p. 252.
26 Sylvain Alem et al., "Associative mechanisms allow for social learning and cultural transmission of string pulling in an insect", *PLOS Biology*, vol. 14, nr. 10, 2016.
27 Andrew P. Smith, "An investigation of the mechanisms underlying nest construction in the mud wasp paralastor sp. (hymenoptera: Eumenidae)", *Animal Behaviour*, vol 26, 1978.
28 See Karsten Brensing, *What Do Animals Think and Feel?*, London: Head of Zeus, 2019; De Waal, *Are We Smart Enough to Know How Smart Animals Are?*
29 Richard E. Nisbett, *The Geography of Thought: How Asians and Westerners Think Differently - And Why*, London: Nicholas Brealey, 2011, pp. 127–129.
30 For discussion, see Thomas Pink, *The Psychology of Freedom,* Cambridge: Cambridge University Press, 1996.
31 See Karin Johannisson, *Melankoliska rum: Om ångest, leda och sårbarhet i förfluten tid och nutid,* Stockholm: Albert Bonniers Förlag, 2013.
32 Richard Dawkins, *The Selfish Gene*, Oxford: Oxford University Press, 2006, p. 21.
33 Stefan Theil, "Trouble in mind", *Scientific American,* vol. 313, nr. 4, 2015.
34 Pierre Janet, *Les obsessions et la psychasthénie, vol. 1*, Paris: Éditions Flammarion, 1903, p. 279.
35 Viktor E. Frankl, *Man's Search for Meaning: An Introduction to Logotherapy,* New York: Simon & Schuster, 1984 [1956] p. 279.
36 Weber, *The Protestant Ethic and the Spirit of Capitalism*, p. 182.

7

AN APPENDAGE OF THE MACHINE

I knew the answer to the unimaginably big question of what I wanted to do with my life from a young age. Before I even got to high school, I was sure that I wanted to be a psychologist. I had already caught glimpses of what anxiety and depression could do to a person, and I was looking forward to joining secular society's army of spiritual counsellors.

During my time in high school, I had visions of a minimal office in which my adult self would talk sense into people who had lost their way. I got the necessary grades and believed, upon graduating, that I had enough wisdom to provide guidance to addicts, newly divorced parents, and traumatised refugees of war. All that was left was to make it through a psychology degree.

Back in those days, there was an additional requirement of anyone wanting to study psychology in Sweden. Just getting the grades wasn't enough. In order to be accepted onto the course, you also needed at least one year's work experience. I explored the possibility of including my summer jobs, but it looked like I would have to work on the factory floor instead. Before long, however, I was forced to accept that no factory floor wanted me, and after consulting my network (Mum and Dad), I eventually found another job: as a waiter.

I spent a year mixing dry martinis and Irish coffees. I hurried between tables, taking orders, pouring beers, and balancing plates of pigs' feet stuffed with sweetbreads, and by the time I got to the other side of my civilian service, I no longer knew whether I wanted to become a psychologist. I didn't feel any anxiety – I was too tired for that.

After another year of setting tables, pouring drinks, polishing glasses, providing top-ups, wiping down surfaces, and clearing plates, any illusions I might have once had about the solution to people's problems being found

DOI: 10.4324/9781003514930-9

in a psychologist's office had vanished. I decided to train as a sociologist instead and have now spent a third of my life studying people at work.

Fortunately, the hundreds of employed and unemployed people I have spoken to over the years have been so diverse that I have had to revise several notions I had when I first began my research. I have interviewed people who love their work, others who hate it, people who are passionate about their jobs, and those who hate them, people who take their work home and others who try to avoid work. I have spent months in offices, watching other people as they work. Some have been so stressed that they barely had time to use the bathroom. Others struggled to find a single task to fill their working day with.

The varied nature of working life makes it difficult to say anything unequivocal about the impact that work has on our lives, and one factor that complicates matters further is that journalists, researchers, and politicians – professions that enjoy an unusually large degree of autonomy in their jobs – seem to be practically the only groups permitted to say anything about the role of work in our lives. As a consequence, we are used to being told just how important work is as a source of community and purpose.

Another common notion is that paid work contributes to both physical and somatic health. A person with a job is, on the whole, healthier than someone without. But does that really mean that work makes us healthy? Or is it rather that unemployment – as shaped by our politics and authorities – makes us ill?[1]

Consider the following:

- Epidemiological research shows that when we retire, we enjoy an improvement in health equivalent to a ten-year gain.[2]
- Despite increasingly tough conditions for the unemployed or those with ill health, mental illness is more prevalent among those in precarious employment than those who have been completely excluded from the job market.[3]
- Historians have long asserted that large-scale economic crises in which a significant proportion of the population is pushed into unemployment typically lead to rapid increases in average life expectancy and reduced deaths from cardiovascular disease.[4]
- According to the socio-medical studies that have been carried out on working hours and health, those who work for longer than average run a higher risk of heart attacks and mental health problems such as depression, anxiety and obsessive-compulsive disorder.[5]

The idea that paid work improves our health is, in other words, dubious. But exactly *what* it is about paid work that affects our health is hard to say. "Stress" and "exhaustion" are often given as explanations for people's strains at work, but these terms cover a multitude of wildly different problems.

Stress could, for example, be what a carer feels when they do not have time to attend to everyone in a care home. It could also be felt by an idle security guard who spends too little time with their family. Or by a middle manager on annual leave, realising, to their horror, that family life is unbearable.

One thing that all work has in common is that it liberates us from questions about *what* we are going to do and *why* we are going to do it. In this sense, work is an institution in which disenchantment is felt not only ideologically, but in how we actually get through the day. Above all, it is evident in the increasing rationalisation of work. But again, there is something elusive here. An atmosphere. A feeling without a name. Or, as Evelina might put it: a sense of panic.

When I meet Evelina, she has just been declared fit to work by the Swedish Social Insurance Agency. She may be unemployed, but she tells me that she feels better than she has in a long time. Her problems first began while she was working as an illustrator at an advertising agency. The job drew a line under a long period of financial worries. Since graduating, she had got by as a cultural worker with many strings to her bow, but now she had a permanent job that paid enough for a middle-class lifestyle. The fact that this job would alleviate one worry while triggering a years-long battle with panic attacks could, perhaps, be explained away through "stress," but when I ask Evelina whether the job was stressful, she tells me it was actually quite laid back.

The problem was the people. Not that she was bullied, and not that they were unkind. Even now, she can't tell me exactly what the issue was.

"You get a certain type of person working in a place like that," she says. "That was the main problem with the agency. There was a certain kind of energy there, in the office."

Compared to other types of anxiety disorder, panic disorder is palpably physical. Evelina experienced sensations she didn't recognise. The overwhelming feeling was that there was no longer room inside herself.

"But in different parts of my body, in my stomach, chest, and throat. For a while, I felt like my tongue didn't fit in my mouth, connected to the fact that I was afraid of swallowing it and choking. And now, whenever I drive, it's in my feet. I feel anxious before it even happens, because I've had it before. I mean, it's all inside me. It's not coming from anywhere else. And that's really hard to accept."

Her first panic attack took place at a multi-lane crossing in town. Evelina couldn't breathe, she felt hot and began to lose focus. Afraid for her life, she kept driving until she could pull over at a petrol station. Her anxiety then grew to a sense of panic so intense that she thought she was going to die.

After that incident, she neither drove nor took the bus for eight months straight. She was signed off sick from work and eventually resigned.

Evelina tells me that she prefers life as part of the precariat, flitting between unemployment and various short projects. The question "is this how life turned out?" no longer feels like such a heavy weight around her neck. Yet again, it is the dull ache of financial anxiety she has to live with, an anxiety she tries to manage through various mental and practical strategies that are not always enough.

Surplus

Evelina's story is not representative. For many people, anxiety only becomes an issue when they lose their job.

Take Anne, for example. Like everyone else with generalised anxiety disorder that I interviewed for this book, the worry that she might not have enough money is part of Anne's catastrophic thinking. In her case, her finances are the dominant anxiety. That isn't so strange given that she is now unemployed, but her anxiety was also there when she worked in a shop.

"The problem is that I've become so forgetful, to the extent that I didn't come in when I was supposed to, that I didn't add up the till properly, and then I was really ashamed. And my forgetfulness is because of my anxiety, a kind of mental battle, because I was so busy thinking about things."

Aware that this mental battle could cause her problems one day, her anxiety about her anxiety has been following her for a long time. Ten years' cognitive behavioural therapy hasn't helped. At almost sixty years of age, she now finds herself outside the job market, where she has found new things to worry about – such as what her friends really think of her.

"I get stuck in a loop. Like at the moment, I have a friend I enjoy spending time with, but sometimes I get caught up on something she has said or done, and I keep going over it afterwards. What did she really mean? Why did she say that? Or why did *I* say a certain thing? Did I make a mistake? Did I put my foot in it? Did I sound distant?"

After a long period of depression, she was signed off sick from work. That helped, but then the Social Insurance Agency got in touch and said that she would have to repay 10,000 dollars because she had been too creative in her free time, which was classified as "artistic activity."

"I appealed, ended up going to court and won. But my sense of trust is completely eroded. You become so cynical when something as big as this happens."

Now, as she undergoes the fitness to work assessments that will determine just how much sick leave she can claim, her mind has started wandering like a lost soul.

"I constantly have to tell myself not to start babbling. Just say thanks, have a good day. But then I think, oh, I probably stand out anyway. They probably think I'm wrong, that I'm trying to cheat them, that I'm crazy. I always feel like I'm being judged. Always."

Both Anne and Evelina enjoy a material wealth far greater than the majority of people throughout history. Not working may still be associated with risks, but what is at risk here is hardly their survival. Instead, the risk is about something else: a life of worry.

About being unable to live on the same terms as one's friends. Questions like will I be able to stay in my apartment? Is the state going to hit me with non-payment of debts? Will I have any free time over the summer?

And it is about seeing your dignity put on the line. How do other people see me? Do they look down on me? Do they think I'm lazy? Stupid? Sick? Useless?

Humans have probably always compared themselves to others and thought along similar lines, but what seems less likely is that they have always – and equally one-sidedly – tied these thoughts to questions of how to make a living.

How did we end up here?

As a result of the delayed returns of agriculture – and the necessity of storing produce – something relatively new began to emerge: surplus. It was only with the arrival of surpluses that we got our first glimpse of the kind of financial inequality that we live with today. And the more efficiently we learnt to farm the land, the more this inequality spread from the economy to other areas of society.

The archaeological evidence of inequality stretches back at least 8,000 years. It can be seen in the defensive structures of the military hierarchy, the assembly spaces belonging to centralised power and the grand children's graves of those with inherited wealth. In a survey of 258 indigenous societies in North America, status and power-related inequality was almost exclusively found among those societies that produced a surplus.[6]

Even before the age of capitalism, there could be a high degree of inequality during periods of growth. In the Piedmont region of northern Italy, for example, the richest five percent of the population owned around thirty percent of all assets in 1450. Three hundred years later, their share had risen to close to fifty percent. High, but nowhere near today's global inequalities, where the richest five percent control around seventy-five percent of all wealth.[7]

The impact this inequality has on a person's sense of self and psyche depends on a number of cultural factors. In the three-estate system of early modern Europe, there was no job market in which people could "succeed" or "fail." For a pre-modern farmer, not even famine had to be an individual failing. But with the employment crises of industrial capitalism, the individual's responsibility was re-evaluated.

The bigger the surplus grows, the more the natural demand decreases. The fact that the poor continued to starve had to be explained in some way, and a new sense of work ethic quickly developed. In this view, *what* a person did for work was less important than *the fact that* they did something. Keeping this view alive became one of the state's main tasks.[8]

Anne's experience of being judged is part of this reality. It isn't all in her mind; she shares it with millions of other people in her situation. It is no coincidence that men in the poorest fifth of society run three times the risk of mental health problems than those in the richest fifth. Nor that those who receive a regular income from their own property are ten times less likely to develop an anxiety disorder than those who do not.[9]

This is not simply because of the economic hardship of poverty. Equally important is whether or not we consider ourselves successful or failures in comparison with others. A civil servant climbing one rung higher up the career ladder considerably reduces his or her statistical risk of developing depression even if their wage remains roughly the same.[10]

Status – the value assigned to a person in the narrowest of contexts – may, on one level, be nothing but empty symbolism. And yet status seeps into the way we see ourselves. Like a fragile crutch for the self, it helps and hinders us in line with the whims of fate. No matter how high a person rises, few manage to free themselves from the fear of falling. As a result, even the richest worry in unequal societies. International comparisons have actually shown that the richest ten percent of people in the most unequal countries are more worried than the poorest ten percent in the most equal.[11]

This worry is – like an inferiority complex, delusions of grandeur, self-contempt and other status-related afflictions – not universal. It demands a systematic division between winners and losers, a shared conviction that the only kind of life worth living is one that others envy.

The Loss of Craft

With economic uncertainty on the rise – thanks to growing unemployment, ever more fixed-term contracts and gig jobs with no regulation – many have concluded that the increase in worry is down to our working lives. There are, of course, plenty of examples to back this up. But on the whole, we are facing something much more paradoxical: *on the one hand, an economy that keeps us in uncertainty, and on the other, a working life that lulls us into a false sense of security.*

Financially, the majority of us live in uncertainty. We could lose our jobs at any moment and be forced into a life of unemployment. When we go to work, however, there is – for most people – little uncertainty over what the day will hold. The workload might be high, occasionally so high that we can't cope, but we generally know from the outset what our day will involve. We do not need to – and should not – question the meaning of this what. As long as we follow the rules, someone else is responsible for the outcome. In this sense, work provides us with a feeling of security.

While insecurity *surrounds* our work, the work *itself* is about peeling back uncertainty. From a young age, society's message is loud and clear: *only by enduring the boredom of scheduled life can you alleviate any worries about your finances or status.*

There are several parallel developments here. On the one hand, work has historically taken up an increasing amount of our time, with the twentieth century's statutory reductions in working hours being one of few countertrends. From having worked around four hours a day, the burden on agricultural workers gradually increased, eventually reaching more than twice that today – particularly if you include the time spent on housework and consumption (which is reasonable, given that the anthropological studies that estimated working hours in prehistoric societies made no distinction between these things). Even the ancient Greeks and Romans had longer holidays than we have today, and though medieval society saw working days of around eight hours, the work was connected to the seasons, meaning there were fewer working days overall – somewhere between 120 and 150 a year.[12]

The increasingly protracted activity we call work has fragmented over time into a series of different moments, specialisms and professions, in a process known within sociology as *division of labour.* What this means is that, for the majority of people, our work requires fewer and fewer of our skills. The work is adapted to pre-established rules and patterns, and it is drummed into us through education, at the cost of our own creativity and exploration. It is also incorporated into technological systems that we learn to control but rarely understand.

If we compare this to the hunter-gatherer or to the Kabyle farmer, they may well have been limited by rudimentary technology and traditional ideas, but as individuals, they were relatively autonomous in the way they chose to organise their labour. They faced more uncertainty, but they could also be confident that they possessed the ability to survive in their own hands. Even among pre-modern craftsmen, we find an experienced-based precision art that stretches way beyond the challenges the majority of modern workers face today.

In industrial society, work is constantly being made more efficient through new technology, yet those who develop this technology are not the people who use it. The type of creativity given an outlet among a tiny group of engineers ultimately leads to work losing its creativity for the vast majority. In other words, the craftsman's head is severed and given over to technical expertise, and the body left behind belongs to the worker.

At first, so-called crafts remained relatively unaffected when tools such as saws, drills, clamps, and grindstones were given motor power. Rather than shrink the craftsman's autonomy, this type of technology actually increased their possibilities. But once we introduced a drill stand on which the depth is determined by the machine, a multi-operation lathe on which the machine's movements are predetermined, a centrifugal governor enabling the rhythm of work to be determined by the machine's rev count, a unit counter measuring the worker's precision – then we moved from a situation in which the worker was *using* the machine to one in which the worker was simply *tending* the machine.[13]

Frederick Winslow Taylor, the engineer behind the rapid dehumanisation of work that took place around the turn of the twentieth century, was keen to talk up the benefits of allowing engineers like him to organise work. Traditional craftsmanship could not compete with the economies of scale inherent in standardised industrial work, and this was proved on a daily basis by the rapid growth in volume of the manufacturing industry.

But Taylor was, unlike today's management consultants, also explicit in his political aim to eliminate the traditional craftsman's power over their work. This was crucial in order to prevent workers from "underworking" – in Taylor's view, "the greatest evil with which the working people of both England and America are now afflicted."[14]

Those pre-industrial workers who had not learned how to behave were, as we have already seen, a source of headaches for the early industrialists. Andrew Ure, a doctor and one of the first organisational researchers, wrote, for example, that it

> is found nearly impossible to convert persons past the age of puberty, whether drawn from rural or from handicraft occupations, into useful factory hands. After struggling for a while to conquer their listless or restive habits, they either renounce the employment spontaneously, or are dismissed by the overlookers on account of inattention.[15]

As early as the eighteenth century, Adam Smith saw that the division of labour he advocated required that this easy-going nature was transformed into something new – albeit not particularly attractive:

> The man whose life is spent in performing a few simple operations, of which the effects are perhaps always the same, or very nearly the same, has no occasion to exert his understanding or to exercise his invention in finding out expedients for removing difficulties which never occur. He naturally loses, therefore, the habit of such exertion and generally becomes as stupid and ignorant as it is possible for a human creature to become.[16]

Even Taylor seems to have understood that the cause to which he had devoted his life would involve a radical curtailment of what it meant to be human.

But unlike Smith, Taylor argued that there was a pre-existing feeble-minded section of society he could recruit from:

> [O]ne of the very first requirements for a man who is fit to handle pig iron as a regular occupation is that he shall be so stupid and so phlegmatic that he more nearly resembles in his make-up the ox than any other type. The man who is mentally alert and intelligent is for this very reason entirely unsuited to what would, for him, be the grinding monotony of work of this character.[17]

With these words, the most rapid restructuring of human work that history has ever seen was set in motion. Oddly enough, in these passages Smith and Taylor have something in common with the young Marx's lament that the worker had been reduced to nothing but "an appendage of the machine." What none of them – not even Marx – showed any interest in was actually visiting the factory floors and asking the workers how they themselves perceived their work.

The Warm Embrace of Work

One of the most detailed descriptions of life in industrial society comes from the American journalist Studs Terkel's compilation of hundreds of testimonies in which workers talk about their experiences. Terkel conducted his interviews in the early 1970s, when industrial work still formed the backbone of the American economy, and the most frequent response described feeling like a machine.

According to one steelworker, "[w]hen the arms start moving, the brain stops."[18] Adam Smith's theory about forced mental lethargy gets real support here. "You push a button and you go this way," says a warehouse worker. "You become a mechanical nut. You get a couple of beers and go to sleep at night. Maybe one, two in the morning, my wife is saying, 'Come on, come on, leave it.' I'm still workin' that line."[19]

A receptionist confesses that she doesn't see the point of her job. "You know you're not doing anything, not doing a hell of a lot for anyone. Your job doesn't mean anything. Because *you're* just a little machine."[20]

In fact, references to feeling like a machine proved so common that Terkel himself remarks on the phenomenon in his foreword:

> For the many, there is a hardly concealed discontent. The blue-collar blues is no more bitterly sung than the white-collar moan. "I'm a machine," says the spot-welder. "I'm caged," says the bank teller, and echoes the hotel clerk. "I'm a mule," says the steelworker. "A monkey can do what I do," says the receptionist. "I'm less than a farm implement," says the

> migrant worker. "I'm an object," says the high-fashion model. Blue collar and white call upon the identical phrase: "I'm a robot."[21]

In our work, the disenchanted notion that we are machines, subordinated to the laws of cause and effect, reaches a concrete form that is not limited to ideas. If we spend our days behaving like robots, we may, over time, lose all sense of what actually separates us from them.

But in the same way that even the unhappiest of marriages can function as a fixed point in life, the most meaningless of jobs can also offer the security of being trapped. In a biographical testimony about the everyday life of factory work, the French worker Charly Boyadjian talks about how, despite its brutality, monotony, and meaninglessness, his job has over the years become a source of comfort in his life. He seeks it out, more than is strictly necessary from a financial viewpoint, and his friends all do the same – extra shifts on Sundays quickly fill up.

"I'm sure if you asked if they wanted to work seven days a week for a year, they'd do it."[22]

In the flow of work, our worries become redundant. The rules are clear, and we can focus our attention on two simple concerns: working as much as possible, and finding things to buy.

"A friend once said to me, half-joking (though all jokes have a grain of truth in them): 'When I'm not working, I don't know what to do with myself; I can barely cope, it's better when I'm at work.' The factory becomes your life."[23]

Boyadjian even discusses the way that sexual activity emerges as a threat to work and the rest required to make it through the day. He calculates that sexual intercourse – including the demands for intimacy afterwards – needs at least one hour, an hour that otherwise could have been spent sleeping. Other people, including those close to him, are seen as sources of disruption, and though he is part of an anti-racist committee with his union, he has noticed that his own reactions are becoming increasingly racist.

The more hostile the world seems, the more comforting it becomes to go to work. What Boyadjian is testifying to here is the way that work blankets our existence with a sense of security where questions like "what should I do with my life?" are removed from the equation. While our family and friends pale in significance, all thoughts revolve around a job that we, ourselves, do not control. What could be more comforting than that?

"When you're at work, everything feels really safe; there's nothing else you should be doing, everything has already been decided for you, you don't need to show any initiative. You get your money and you buy all the gadgets you can ... *It's real security, you don't have any other responsibilities; it's almost like going back to childhood.*"[24]

If we compare this way of living to that of the hunter-gatherers we met a few chapters back, it is clear that we have gone on a long journey to reach this point. Living an attentive life in the moment does not necessarily mean a more "harmonious" life. But being confronted by uncertainty on a daily basis – an uncertainty that, unlike the financial system's, is dependent on individual actions – means learning to live with uncertainty. For the vast majority of people, modern work represents the very opposite. It involves breaking with uncertainty.

While wages were based on piecework well into the industrial era, work itself quickly became increasingly regulated. Following the rise of agriculture and the introduction of standard clock time, our consciousness of time deepened further. Benjamin Franklin's motto that "time is money" gives only a hint of the symbolic power that clock time gained as a measure of performance. On factory floors and in offices, Taylorism's time-motion study men made their entrance. The smallest movements were registered to the hundredth of a second, and punctuality was elevated to the greatest of virtues.

In a time chart from the American Systems and Procedures Association, for example, we find the following target times: "open and close file drawer, no selection = .04 seconds; desk, open center drawer = .026 seconds; close center drawer = .027 seconds; close side drawer = .015 seconds; get up from chair = .033 seconds; sit down in chair = .033 seconds; turn in swivel chair = .009 seconds."[25]

Many would argue that this type of working life belongs to a bygone era with little relevance to the present day, and there is justification for this view. The service sector is currently close to the fifty-percent mark, globally, meaning that roughly half of all employees are involved in the production of services. Globally, the requirement for education is also increasing, which could suggest that working lives are becoming increasingly "knowledge-intensive."[26]

Yet even the service sector has become more rationalised and structured. The fact that Taylor's time-study motion men are no longer visible on office floors, stopwatch in hand, does not mean that they have become superfluous. A telephone operator today is subject to far more surveillance than a factory worker ever was, and the recording of data takes place automatically: the number of calls made, the length of those calls, what is said and what the phone operator does on their computer screen.

There are, of course, jobs involving more advanced "knowledge work" than this, but in terms of working processes, the studies that have been carried out have not, on the whole, shown any increased requirements for creativity. With the exception of a highly educated elite that utilises a broad range of knowledge in its daily work, the reality is that for the majority of people, work requires less and less of our abilities. The fact that we are also seeing increased requirements for education is an effect of so-called credentialism – the growing demand for formal proof of training for jobs that could previously be performed by someone without a high school education. For the actual work itself, however, neither digitisation nor automation require any real knowledge. The fact that the working process is complicated by various semi-automatic systems is irrelevant to someone whose only task is to make sure the lights remain green.[27]

An example of this is given in sociologist Richard Sennett's study of a bakery in Boston. When Sennett first visited the bakery in the early 1970s, the profession required many years' training. It was a physically demanding job, carried out in the heat of the ovens, with hands working flour and water. The bakers may have complained, but there was also a certain pride in their work; making bread wasn't something just anyone could do.

When Sennett returned to the bakery twenty-five years later, everything had changed. The bakers barely saw the dough anymore. What they *did* do was click the right icons on the computer screens. They themselves had no idea how to knead dough or how high to set the ovens, how long to prove the bread, but the machine did, and their job was to switch it on and tend to whatever came out the other side. If anything didn't work as it should, they would call a technician who also had no idea how to bake bread.[28]

Increasingly system-dependent, decreasingly material, work tests the individual in different ways. Requirements for dexterity are replaced by demands for cerebral functionality. What matters now is that the brain does not go on strike, and yet that is precisely what it does.

Mentally holding it together, not hitting the wall, steering clear of a breakdown. The further towards the present day we look, the more these become a part of our work.

The Life We Don't Have Time For

Time pressure, inadequacy, and guilt are among the most devastating aspects of working life. But for the majority of people, that is not what work is like. For the majority of people, work does *not* involve relentless performance at the peak of their abilities.

For my PhD, I interviewed around forty employees who spent roughly half their working time on private activities – something I call empty labour. The record among those I spoke to was held by a bank clerk who spent around fifteen minutes a day actually doing their job. Working life covers everything from a stressed-out extreme to an idle extreme. The majority of people find themselves somewhere in between.[29]

Regardless of our workload, we know what to expect when we get to work each day. There are rules and guidelines we have to adhere to. But when we go home and meet our families or friends, we have none of this.

The reason why we describe *relationships*, and not jobs, as "complicated" can be found here.

To a child, almost the opposite is true. A problem that developmental psychologists and educators have long studied is the refusal of children, once they reach a certain age – typically in their teens – to go to school. This refusal can take a number of forms. Just the thought of spending years at a desk, doing as the teacher says, leaves many children feeling down. But at the same time, children are right in thinking that their fates lie in their teachers' hands. This sentence, being given over to a system so far removed from the relative freedom of childhood, can feel like too much.[30]

Social workers and psychologists working with pensioners frequently experience the opposite problem. Many pensioners experience a sense of emptiness. Their sentence is no longer knowing how to "kill time" in a life without any structure or framework. This phenomenon is particularly pronounced among men, who have historically dominated the labour market. And despite the fact that for many, retirement brings with it a number of health benefits, there is evidence to suggest that elderly men run a lower risk of becoming depressed the later in life they retire.[31]

In the period between childhood and old age, something that once seemed unbearable becomes a source of security. Habit reshapes us. The child's enthusiastic ability to entertain him or herself is tamed to such an extent that the very thought of filling a day wakes more dread than desire.

This psychological about-face reflects the historical transformation of the working collective. The pre-modern worker who voluntarily took a break from work after building up enough money has been replaced by a worker so worried that they might even be willing to take a pay cut to save the company. The fear of being let go, of being a loser, constantly hangs over us, no matter how successful we are. The safety and comfort of work is also the safety and comfort of duty. Work represents both a means of combatting financial uncertainty and a safe space in which we do not have to make any decisions.[32]

Whenever a societal institution becomes so central to our lives, it is not without consequences for the rest of society. Why, for example, do we find family life so difficult? Why are romantic relationships so complicated? Why is loneliness so common? How can something as simple as living together be so hard?

One answer to these questions is that we get better at the things we do and worse at things we don't. If we spend our lives practising how to work, we become good at working. But how good will we be at everything else that sits at the heart of being human?

During the brief periods of holiday when we are freed from the yoke of work, these shortcomings rise to the surface. Without the structure of working life, we are left naked. The question of what we really want from life becomes pressing – and we don't necessarily find any answers. Not for nothing have repeated studies shown that the frequency of divorces rises towards the end of holiday periods. Not for nothing do many people attempt to minimise the amount of holiday they take. In the United States, the world's most hostile country to time off, barely half of people take the vacation days they are entitled to in their employment contracts. What makes people come to this decision? What is it about the short periods of "breathing space" we are offered?[33]

Over a three-year period, the sociologist Arlie Hochschild grappled with this very subject by following a number of employees at an American company that went under the pseudonym of Amerco. Successful and established, the company was able to offer its employees a programme to reduce their hours, with increased opportunities for part-time working, parental leave, and paid holidays. Given that the employees often complained about their lack of time – they worked a forty-seven hour week, on average, many for ten or twelve hours at a time – this should have been a welcome initiative.

And yet very few chose to seize the opportunity. Only fifty-three of the company's 21,000 employees cut their working hours in order to spend more time with their children (none of them men). The majority lost unused vacation days, and only one percent chose to work from home, despite the company encouraging it.

In her interviews, Hochschild found that this self-imposed lack of time could not be justified on grounds of potential lost income or fear of being let go. The explanation was less to do with the transformation of working life, as family life. Work was simply "more fun" than life at home, as one employee put it.[34] "I always tell people here that I come to work to relax," said another.[35]

That men prioritised their work over their family was something earlier research had shown, but Hochschild saw that the pattern was also present among Amerco's female employees.

Her explanation is a simple one: while a person's social life in the workplace is regulated and, among the more privileged professions, polite, with inbuilt social support networks, family life is dominated by an atmosphere of stress, conflict, chaos and guilt.

Hochschild describes the growth of a rationalised family life in which it is the children's successes that define good parenting, rather than the amount of time spent with them. Ferried from one activity to the next, children are expected to have their emotional needs met during the hour or so left over in the evenings. Any failings or deviations from the schedule are outsourced to babysitters or therapists, but that is not enough. The more people avoid the home, the denser the minefield becomes. Alienated spouses, whiny children, even whinier step-children and vengeful exes do not make for a restful existence. Hochschild's sympathetic depictions make it hard to feel too upset when one of the managers interviewed announces that he finds it more rewarding to take care of his "office children" (his subordinates) than his actual children.[36]

From the refuge of work, the rest of the world appears chaotic and incomprehensible. Outside the air conditioned office, failure looms. Living with risk – accepting it as a historical condition of our existence – could have been a possibility. But living with risk is also what work has helped us do away with. Better, then, to fight risk wherever it rears its head.

Notes

1 For a discussion and summary of studies, see: Paulsen, *Arbetssamhället: Hur arbetet överlevde teknologin*, pp. 99-102.
2 Hugo Westerlund et al., "Self-rated health before and after retirement in France (GAZEL): A cohort study", *The Lancet*, vol. 374, nr. 9705, 2009, p. 1891. The figure varies depending on the individual's satisfaction with the job they did prior to retirement, with those with who felt the least satisfaction seeing the most rejuvenation.
3 Sarah A. Burgard, Jennie E. Brand and James S. House, "Perceived job insecurity and worker health in the United States", *Social Science & Medicine*, vol. 69, nr. 5, 2009.
4 José Tapia Granados and Ana V. Diez Roux, "Life and death during the great depression", *Proceedings of the National Academy of Sciences*, 2009.
5 Cecilie Schou Andreassen et al., "The relationships between workaholism and symptoms of psychiatric disorders: A large-scale cross-sectional study", *PLOS One*, vol. 11, nr. 5, 2016; Andreas Holtermann et al., "Long work hours and physical fitness: 30-year risk of ischaemic heart disease and all-cause mortality among middle-aged caucasian men", *Heart*, vol. 96, nr. 20, 2010; Mika Kivimäki et al., "Long working hours and risk of coronary heart disease and stroke: A systematic review and meta-analysis of published and unpublished data for 603 838 individuals", *The Lancet*, vol. 386, nr. 10005, 2015.
6 Ain Haas, "Social inequality in aboriginal North America: A test of Lenski's theory", *Social Forces*, vol. 72, nr. 2, 1993. The surplus may even have been a more contributory factor than the deferred dividends of work. In Haas' study, the size of the production surplus played a greater role than whether they were farmers or hunter-gatherers in terms of material inequality. Those who did not manage to store grain, collect livestock or build lavish residences were considerably more equal than materially richer societies.
7 Walter Scheidel, *The Great Leveler: Violence and The History of Inequality From the Stone Age to the Twenty-First Century*, Princeton: Princeton University Press, 2018, p. 307. Credit Suisse, "Global Wealth Report", 2017, p. 17 (the study is based on estimates for which the confidence intervals are likely quite large, given that the amount of data is vast).
8 See Herbert Applebaum, *The Concept of Work: Ancient, Medieval, and Modern*, Albany, NY: State University of New York Press, 1992; Jan Ch Karlsson, *Begreppet arbete: Definitioner, ideologier och sociala former*, Lund: Arkiv, 1986; Paulsen, *Arbetssamhället: Hur arbetet överlevde teknologin*.
9 The poorest fifth (in England, for example): Kate Pickett and Richard Wilkinson, "Inequality: An underacknowledged source of mental illness and distress", *British Journal of Psychiatry*, vol. 197, nr. 6, 2010. On people with income from

property (from the US, for example): Carl I. Cohen and Sami Timimi, *Liberatory Psychiatry: Philosophy, Politics, and Mental Health*, Cambridge: Cambridge University Press, 2008, p. 133.
10 Michael Marmot, *The Status Syndrome*, New York: Henry Holt and Co., 2004, p. 1.
11 Wilkinson and Pickett, *The Inner Level: How More Equal Societies Reduce Stress, Restore Sanity and Improve Everyone's Well-Being*, p. 35. Note that the countries compared are limited to OECD countries.
12 For a historical summary of the research into how much pre-industrial people worked, see Juliet B. Schor, *The Overworked American: The Unexpected Decline of Leisure*, New York: Basic Books, 1991 and Marshall Sahlins, *Stone Age Economics*, Chicago: Aldine-Atherton, 1972. For a summary of working hours in horticultural societies, see Raymond Hames, "Time, efficiency and fitness in the Amazonian protein quest", *Research in Economic Anthropology*, vol. 11, 1989. Yet another summary of anthropological research in the field is offered in Wanda Minge-Klevana et al., "Does labor time decrease with industrialization? A survey of time-allocation studies", *Current Anthropology*, vol. 21, nr. 3, 1980.
13 See Harry Braverman, *Labor and Monopoly Capital: The Degradation of Work in the Twentieth Century*, New York: Monthly Review, 1998 [1974], pp. 130–131.
14 Frederick Winslow Taylor, *The Principles of Scientific Management*, New York; London: Harper & Brothers, 1919, p. 14.
15 See André Gorz, *Kritik av det ekonomiska förnuftet*, Stockholm: Alfabeta, 1990, p. 31.
16 See John Cunningham Wood, *Adam Smith: Critical Assessments*, Beckenham, Kent: Croom Helm, 1984, p. 164.
17 Frederick Winslow Taylor, *The Principles of Scientific Management,* Gutenberg: Project Gutenberg, 2004 [1911], p. 20.
18 Studs Terkel, *Working: People Talk About What They Do All Day and How They Feel About What They Do*, New York: Ballantine Books, 1972, p. 5.
19 Terkel, *Working: People Talk About What They Do All Day and How They Feel About What They Do*, p. 241.
20 Terkel, *Working: People Talk About What They Do All Day and How They Feel About What They Do*, p. 59.
21 Terkel, *Working: People Talk About What They Do All Day and How They Feel About What They Do*, p. xiv.
22 Charly Boyadjian, "Le temps en '3x8'", from *Travailler 2 heures par jour*, ed. Collectif Adret, Paris: Seuil, 1977, p. 22.
23 Boyadjian, "Le temps en '3x8'", p. 22.
24 Boyadjian, "Le temps en '3x8'", p. 22. Italics my own.
25 See Robert Levine, *A Geography of Time*, Oxford: One World, 2006, p.71.
26 International Labour Organization, "Ilostat database", data downloaded in September 2019.
27 See Peter Fleming, Bill Harley and Graham Sewell, "A little knowledge is a dangerous thing: Getting below the surface of the growth of 'knowledge work' in Australia", *Work Employment Society*, vol. 18, nr. 4, 2004; Paul Thompson, Chris Warhurst and George Callaghan, "Ignorant theory and knowledgeable workers: Interrogating the connections between knowledge, skills and services", *Journal of Management Studies*, vol. 38, nr. 7, 2001.
28 Richard Sennett, *The Corrosion of Character: The Personal Consequences of Work in the New Capitalism*, New York: W. W. Norton, 2011, pp. 66-69.
29 See Roland Paulsen, *Empty Labor: Workplace Resistance and Idleness*, Cambridge: Cambridge University Press, 2014.

30 Jack H. Kahn, Jean P. Nursten and Howard C. M. Carroll, *Unwillingly to School: School Phobia or School Refusal: A Psychosocial Problem*, New York: Elsevier, 2014; Gerard McShane, Garry Walter and Joseph M. Rey, "Characteristics of adolescents with school refusal", *Australian and New Zealand Journal of Psychiatry*, vol. 35, nr. 6, 2001.
31 John L. Oliffe et al., "Masculinities, work, and retirement among older men who experience depression", *Qualitative Health Research*, vol. 23, nr. 12, 2013, p. 1628.
32 See André Gorz, *Farewell to the Working Class: An Essay on Post-Industrial Socialism*, London: Pluto Press, 1982. The phenomenon has been repeated, as during the 2008 financial crash when several Swedish unions introduced reduced wages for the duration of the crisis. See Paulsen, *Arbetssamhället: Hur arbetet överlevde teknologin*, pp. 54–75.
33 Megan Leonhardt, "Only 28% of Americans plan to max out their vacation days this year", *CNBC*, 27/4, 2019; Julie Brines and Brian Serafini, "Seasonal variation in divorce filings: The importance of family ritual in a postsentimental era", *111th Annual Meeting of American Sociological Association (ASA). Seattle: American Sociological Association*, 2016.
34 Arlie Russell Hochschild, *The Time Bind: When Work Becomes Home and Home Becomes Work*, New York: Metropolitan Books, 1997, p. 70.
35 Hochschild, *The Time Bind: When Work Becomes Home and Home Becomes Work*, p. 186.
36 Hochschild, *The Time Bind: When Work Becomes Home and Home Becomes Work*, p. 64.

8

THE WORLD AS RISK

Two doctors came into the room. This is it, Helena thought to herself. They always come in pairs when they're about to give a cancer diagnosis.

"I assume you've got bad news?" she said.

But they didn't. Her test results looked good, and the younger of the two doctors was simply shadowing the other. The older doctor asked whether Helena had brought anyone with her. She had been told to, just in case.

"No, I'm on my own, but it makes no difference because I'm a hypochondriac," Helena replied.

"Ah, I see," said the doctor.

He squeezed some gel onto her breast and pressed the ultrasound wand to her skin. As he moved the device back and forth, he talked about the anatomy of the female breast. Then he took a deep breath and smiled.

"He put his hand on my chest, like this," says Helena.

"There was a nurse there, so it wasn't creepy or anything. He put his hand right here and said: 'Feels good, doesn't it? You don't have cancer.' And I started crying. I just cried and cried. I was *completely* euphoric."

Helena didn't have cancer. She had been given the all clear yet again.

A few weeks passed before she noticed the next symptom. She was having some stomach issues. Could that be a sign of pancreatic cancer?

She asked her partner to google it for her. No, he said. If you have pancreatic cancer, your stools turn yellow. That same day, she called her adult son into the bathroom. Wasn't her poo yellow? Bright yellow, he replied.

Her partner googled yet another diagnostic criterion. The stools should be oily, and they should also float on the surface of the water. Her son made yet another trip to the bathroom and confirmed what she suspected: her poo was oily, and it was floating.

DOI: 10.4324/9781003514930-10

This marked the start of a new cycle of desperate telephone calls, hospital visits in different local authorities, tests, money for private clinics and, ultimately, being given the all clear.

"Once I've found one symptom, it's like I just go full steam ahead. The only thing that helps is a doctor telling me it's nothing. It's such a strange feeling, because it really does feel like a motor inside me. It's like suddenly being in a deep depression."

After pancreatic cancer, she had a lasting fever and cancer of the lymphatic glands.

Then she developed an ache in her jaw and throat cancer.

Next, stomach aches and cancer of the large intestine.

That autumn, she spent 2,000 dollars on private medical appointments. She talked her way to the front of various queues, allowed keyhole cameras to examine her insides, underwent a gastroscopy without anaesthetic, had moles sent off for analysis, found out which laboratory had received them and convinced them to give her the results over the phone – despite that being against the rules.

Then she developed bruises and blood cancer... Helena pauses.

"But that was how it all started! God, it's all just so much."

Once upon a time, Helena was eight. She didn't know much about illness, and she wasn't afraid of dying. She was still learning to read.

"I remember reading the word cancer in a headline, but I don't know if that was what set it all off, because I also remember that it was one night around the same time that I realised eternity was a real thing. And what happened then was that I panicked. I was inconsolable for days. And somehow it felt like it all fit together – the cancer and eternity."

She lay down on her bed and pressed her fingers to her face. Got up and went to the bathroom to study her reflection in the mirror. Did she have any bruises? You bruise easily if you have blood cancer. Perhaps she should have pressed harder?

These days, Helena has to be strict with herself. If she hears or reads anything about cancer, she memorises every single word.

"It's like my brain becomes this big sponge, sucking up all the information. Seriously, it's like my brain just opens up wide."

A year ago, she set herself limits for how much information she can take in. She says that she is too much of a hypochondriac to be able to google things, that she would never be out of hospital if she did.

"If anything comes up now, I get my boyfriend or my son to google it, because I can't."

Something that neither Helena nor I fully understand is why cancer in particular worries her so much when she simply shrugs off the symptoms of other diseases. During our conversation, she tells me about a doctor who noticed she had an irregular heartbeat and called her in for an examination.

She also tells me that for a couple of weeks, she kept fainting because of a problem with her vestibular system. She takes out her phone and shows me a recent picture of her upper body covered in angry red eczema.

None of these things frightened her.

"Why is it that cancer scares you so much?" I ask.

"There's just something about cancer that's so disgusting. I guess that's why I... It's like, it's a filthy disease."

Before we even met, Helena had told me that she suffered from hypochondria, or "health anxiety," as it is also known. But with every new symptom, she questions this diagnosis. She knows that hypochondria is a real thing, but she also knows that cancer is real. While she was undergoing therapy for her anxiety, her mother was diagnosed with lung cancer. Cancer exists. Whenever she decides that a mole is a malignant melanoma, there is a risk it is simply her hypochondria speaking. But there is also a risk that she really does have cancer. How is she supposed to know?

It's impossible to say.

Just as being paranoid has no effect on the likelihood of being watched, suffering from catastrophic thinking is no protection against catastrophe, and being a hypochondriac does not lower our risk of contracting a disease.

The Rationality of Risk

The sociology of risk has two focal points: on the one hand, how risks are created, and on the other, how they are perceived. Civilisation has played its part on both levels.

Pre-historic nomads suffered, for example, nowhere near the same levels of infectious disease as we do today. This was partly because they were scattered in small clusters and rarely came together in larger tribes – a kind of natural quarantine at group level – and partly because the only animals they lived alongside were dogs. The majority of pandemics, from the Black Death to tuberculosis and SARS, come from so-called zoonosis – infectious diseases that have arisen through close contact between humans and animals. On this point too, agriculture represents a health risk, with falling life expectancies the consequence.[1]

When Europe began to colonise the globe, it had devastating consequences. The fact that so many indigenous populations died is primarily because of infectious disease. In America alone, around twenty million people are estimated to have died, over ninety percent of the indigenous population.[2]

Civilisation creates new risks while also reducing others, but the biggest change hinges on the second focal point for the sociology of risk: how we perceive and approach risk. Microscopes, X-rays, and laparoscopes are all part of an apparatus that helps us to see what was previously invisible.

Scientific discoveries also inform us precisely what we should be vigilant about.

Helena is vigilant. She is a part of the disenchanted understanding of the world as cause and effect. To her, there is no sign of providence in things. Ruthless laws could force the lifeless junk into new and terrible constellations at any moment. There is no god taking responsibility for the outcome. It is up to her to make sure that the tangle of causal links are diagnosed, manipulated, curtailed and redirected.

The hard part for Helena is that she is so rational in her assessment of risk. She has the science on her side. Every time she notices a new symptom, she asks herself the two key questions of any risk analysis. One: how likely is it? And two: how harmful is it?

Being diagnosed with cancer at some point in one's life is a likely occurrence. In Sweden, roughly one in three people will suffer the disease at some stage. Cancer is also harmful – the number one killer in high-income countries.[3]

The statistics give weight to her fears. The question is why Helena is less rational when it comes to other risks. Why wasn't she worried when the doctor expressed concerns about her EKG? Cardiovascular disease has long been one of the leading causes of death in Sweden, and globally still claims the most lives.[4]

Helena is not ignorant of this inconsistency. In fact, she knows all about it. And she knows that she could just as easily worry about countless other things she almost never even thinks about.

Whenever Helena opens the newspaper, she sees it on every page: things that could and have gone wrong. Terrorism, assaults, epidemics, the housing crisis, obesity, the refugee crisis, the unemployment crisis, segregation, environmental disaster, murder, stock market crashes, currency crises, abuse, extremism, war.

Each of these risks is very real, the media hasn't made them up. And yet these are not the things Helena worries about. This is the inconsistency: among all the likely and damaging disasters she hears about on a daily basis, Helena has fixated on just one. In this sense, she diverges from the norm slightly, but when it comes to causes of death, the majority of us actually have a skewed image of how great the risks really are. In studies of risk perception, where participants are asked to guess how great a risk various causes of death pose, the results show that:

- Eighty percent of participants thought that accidents were a more common cause of death than strokes, despite the fact that strokes cause almost twice as many deaths as all accidents combined.

- Accidents were assumed to cause, on average, around as many deaths as illness, but in actual fact illness is eighteen times more common a cause of death.
- Blood clots were thought to cause more deaths than asthma. In truth, asthma kills twenty times more people.[5]

The fact that we are aware of the risks does not mean we have any real understanding of how great they are compared to other risks. This is partly – but not entirely – down to which risks our journalists and politicians choose to bring into the public eye.

An example: Terrorism *can* affect us, but in high-income countries the risk is incredibly low. Each year, on average, one person per million dies as a result of terrorism. In the United States, the country that ploughs the most resources into protecting itself from terror, the risk is even lower. Between 1970 and 2013, terrorism was responsible for an average of one death per four million inhabitants (a figure that also includes the victims of 9/11). To put this into perspective, the risk of drowning in your bathtub is more than twice as high. The available statistics also indicate that incidents involving cars crashing into deer are responsible for twice as many deaths.[6]

Why, then, have the majority of people never heard about these risks? Shouldn't the many victims of drowning in bathtubs be given twice as much media coverage as terrorism?

The answer, of course, is that there are differences.

Firstly, terrorism provides good *stories*. It features both an evil mastermind and an innocent victim. It involves secrets, and often comes with political overtones. Drowning in the bathtub, on the other hand, takes place suddenly and in a nigh-on absurd manner. There is no guilty party. Even cancer, with its overarching themes of treatment and farewells, allows for powerful stories. Though a public information campaign on safety while taking a bath could save more lives than channelling even greater resources into fighting terrorism, the risk of drowning in the bath is perceived as a more natural type of accident.

Terrorism is also bound up with mental *images*. Images of chaos, of blood, exploding buildings and mangled body parts, dead children. It is difficult to imagine the true fear of a terror attack, but thanks to movies and news reports, the majority of us have enough images in our minds to know where to start. Likewise, the dying cancer patient already exists as a strong, clear image.

Drowning accidents in the bathtub, on the other hand, remain relatively abstract. It would be possible to paint pictures in order to provide these solitary accidents with more colour, of course, but the question is why anyone would think it was worth the effort. What would they stand to gain?

Terrorism is a risk inherently bound up with societal *power*. It generates economic activity. Terror creates jobs and growth. There is an entire industry built around researching how to prevent terror, a military–industrial complex ready to neutralise the enemy, a surveillance industry to find them, the production of war materials to defend ourselves. Politicians have also turned the fight against terror into a key election-winning issue.

The victims of drowning in bathtubs lack both financiers and social movements.

No matter which popular risk we zoom in on, we inevitably find that it is interwoven with *stories*, *images,* and *power*. That isn't to say that our awareness of risk is a perfect mirror of society's power structures, more that the risks that capture our attention are the result of a fight in which even likelihood and evidence are taken into account.

It is not uncommon for risks to be positioned against one another with heightened narratives and increasingly crude images as weapons. Something we initially considered a banality can be blown out of all proportion and given decisive importance.

For the past fifty years, for example, a war has raged between educators over the best way to teach children to read. In one camp, we have those who advocate a phonics-based approach – i.e. teaching children to sound out words one letter at a time. The other camp is made up of those who recommend learning to decode the entire word from the outset, also known as orthographic processing. Both sides criticise the other because they believe that the opposite approach involves not only a risk to the child's reading ability, but to their very health.

An American neurologist wrote that the sounding-out method leaves children "emotionally damaged" and subjects them to "all sorts of emotional and psychological distress." Another educator on the same side of the argument describes the approach as "almost a form of abuse." In the other camp, researchers condemn the "whole-language" method as "destroying" the innocent child. They claim that rapid decoding risks "killing the hopes, and the potential, and the mental health of the children who are the victims of this reading disability epidemic."[7]

Battles of this type sometimes end when one side "wins," at which point the old risks fall into obscurity. The pace at which these shifts take place has accelerated in recent years, and as a result, certain activities have been invaded by risk. Take eating, for example: in a study of fifty ingredients chosen at random from a cook book, researchers found that forty of them had been examined in scientific papers reporting their cancer risk.[8]

This incredible practice of calculating risk did not occur by chance. It is a part of the disenchanted worldview which, four hundred years ago, made us see an increasingly large part of life as a chorus of cause and effect.

The Morality of Risk

When the chains of cause and effect point to an unwanted outcome, we are dealing with risk. But inherent in risk is an element of uncertainty. Unlike machines, we cannot calculate the risks in life with complete precision. Risk is typically defined as the *likelihood* of an unwanted event taking place; it includes an unknown amount of causes and effects and must therefore be based on statistics rather than mechanics.

Statistically speaking, there is – not accounting for miracles and undiscovered laws of nature – almost always a risk. But what do we do once we have established this?

There are two options. Either we live with the risk, or we try to minimise it.

The word "risk" comes from the Italian *risicare*, "to dare." Etymologically, then, "risk" is bound up with a verb. To dare means to take a risk, and for a long time, it was seen as a heroic thing to do. Dionysus I of Syracuse, for example, believed that his position as ruler hung by a single thread. When one of his courtiers, Damocles, wanted to see what it was like to live like a king, Dionysius hung a sword by a single horsehair over the throne. The power of incorporating this "sword of Damocles" into one's everyday life has been celebrated since antiquity, when the Roman politician and philosopher Cicero rewrote the legend.

To some extent, this heroic ideal endures to this day, but it has gained competition from other ideals in recent times.

As far as Magnus is concerned, *responsibility* holds a higher position than *courage*. Just by looking at him, that might be hard to believe. He seems cheerful enough, carefree and leisurely. And yet Magnus lives with a constant sense of guilt. A sense that maybe, just maybe, he might have killed someone.

"If I'm the last to leave the flat, I find myself thinking that I'm responsible for everything that happens there until someone else gets home. So I walk around the place until I feel like everything is OK. These days I check things like the TV, the phone chargers, any bulbs that aren't switched on. I used to have to pull out all the plugs and even unscrew the lightbulbs and that kind of thing."

What preoccupies Magnus is the idea that all electronics involve a risk of self-combustion. This kind of accident has happened to other people: mobile phone chargers overheating, TVs that suddenly burst into flames. He often sees it on the news.

The thought he cannot bear is that *his* TV will be the one that goes up in a ball of flames, putting the other people who live in the building in danger. How can he be sure there isn't a risk? What if he forgot to unplug that wire after all?

Often, when he leaves the house, he has to turn back to check – sometimes several times. It can take him up to an hour to make sure everything is OK, and yet he never really feels confident.

"For a while, I used to go around the flat taking pictures of everything, just to be sure. It was like heroin or something. I was constantly checking my phone, and when I took a picture, I started thinking about how even that had to feel right."

Magnus knows he needs to confront his anxiety somehow. But ignoring the risks of spontaneous combustion means putting others at risk of fire. Taking responsibility is something he holds close to his heart, and taking responsibility involves not exposing himself or others to the risk of a fire. By avoiding risk, however, he exposes himself to the risk of wasting his life on pointless obsessive rituals. His problem is the same as Helena's: which risk should he choose?

Anxiety rarely involves just one risk. There is also an ambivalence inherent in the anxiety: we set the risks against one another. At times, there may be so many conflicting risks that we are left feeling confused.

In a high profile case involving a two-year-old girl who escaped from a nursery in the United Kingdom, a bricklayer fell into this very confusion. He saw the young girl walking along the road, but rather than pull over to help her, he drove straight past. "She wasn't walking in a straight line," he said afterwards. "She was tottering, and I kept thinking, 'Should I go back?'"

Not long later, the girl was found drowned in a pool.

In subsequent police interviews, the man explained that he didn't stop to help her because he thought someone might think he was trying to kidnap her.[9]

It is easy to understand why he did what he did – many men today would hesitate before asking a young child they do not know to get into their van – but the incident illustrates the multiplication of risks that arise from *risk aversion*.

When an entire society creates risk by avoiding risk, we eventually end up being overwhelmed by it. The German sociologist Ulrich Beck calls this type of society a *risk society*. His British counterpart Frank Furedi calls it a *culture of fear*. They mean roughly the same thing.

According to Furedi, the awareness of risk has spread fear from a few focal points to every aspect of our lives. Secular fears extend further than religious ones: the fear of God has been replaced by imagined catastrophes, and moral scruples have given way to risk analysis. While there used to be a value in fearing for one's life – in being "Godfearing" – the culture of fear derives a paradoxical strength from the illusion that fear is something that, with enough effort, we can shake off.

How far we will go in our attempts to combat risk has, as we have already seen, no bounds. The "altruistic" fears Magnus is plagued by – the fear that others will suffer – are particularly elastic. One early study in the field shows, for example, that the most common fear in larger households is that children will suffer.

The fact that children are taught to be suspicious – not to talk to strangers, for example – obviously comes from a place of concern, but it also stems from a risk-laden view of other people. This fear can be measured in the mobility of children, in how far they are permitted to stray from home without supervision. In the space of just a few generations, this distance has shrunk from kilometres to the fence at the end of the garden. Growing up in a world considered so dangerous that you should stay away from it doesn't exactly stimulate bravery.[10]

Furedi notes that it is only marginally helpful to be aware of the problem of fear. Since his first book on the culture of fear was published, the "culture of fear" itself has been described as a societal risk. For the most part, this discussion tends to stop at the mass media's tendency to focus its news reports on risks and catastrophes. There is every justification for this criticism of the media. The fact that people between the ages of fifty-five and seventy-four are most afraid of becoming victims of crime while also being those least exposed to crime is, for example, difficult to explain without reference to the mass media.[11]

What media and communication researchers have found is that the mass media has been key in blowing the less rational part of risk, the part that has nothing to do with likelihood – the stories and images of risk – out of all proportion. The most radical impact of this is a warping of the way we perceive risk. As a rule, we have very little idea of how likely a catastrophe really is, but the *possibility* – the macabre images of the catastrophe – can completely dominate our attention.[12]

In an attempt to challenge this risk analysis, the Norwegian philosopher Lars Svendsen has argued that the likelihood of a child being murdered by a stranger is so small that it should simply be ignored: "Occasionally, a child is killed by a stranger, and when that happens it is without a doubt a terrible tragedy, but it is so rare an event that it is hardly a good idea to make that slim possibility the basis of children's relations to all strangers."[13]

The fact that so many continue to base their parenting on risk is down to the active sense of imagination we have developed when it comes to tragedies of this type.

There is often a self-reflexivity here, too. We already know that our risk assessment rationality leaves much to be desired. That our thought processes are not unconscious. Painfully aware of the irrationality of our fears, our images, and obsessive thoughts, we seek help. After a moment of searching, we find it, too – among the swelling ranks of experts.

The problem with this is that even experts can be wrong, which is evident in the many issues on which they cannot agree. During the Coronavirus pandemic, the less restrictive Swedish approach (which involved keeping schools open, for example) came in for fierce criticism from many experts in both Sweden and abroad. And yet the restrictions in Sweden were, historically speaking, strict. When "Asian flu" swept across the world in 1957, no measures of the kind we have seen in 2020 were taken – even though it was a brutal pandemic that killed many young people, with an estimated five million deaths globally.[14]

As Covid-19 began to spread, the question of whether the cure was worse than the disease reared its head yet again. The experts simply couldn't agree. Some pointed out that restrictions such as lockdowns and the forced closure of workplaces would lead to a financial crisis, and since unemployment and poverty are closely linked to alcohol abuse and increased suicide levels, there was a risk the drastic measures taken to prevent the further spread of the coronavirus would lead to an increased death rate in other areas.

On the other side, there were those who pointed out that the causality of crisis and mortality is not quite so clear cut. During severe crises, as I have already mentioned, it has been shown that the death rate often falls as stress levels go down and there are fewer accidents. According to some studies, it is actually prosperity that has a negative impact on health, because working hours increase and pollution worsens. These relationships do not seem to prevail in all crises and booms, however, so how can an expert know when the causality is there or not?[15]

No matter how much thought we put into weighing risks against one another, it is typically only with hindsight that the causal links become clear. After the 9/11 attacks, for example, security measures were introduced at airports around the world in an attempt to save lives. As a consequence, ticket prices went up and planes were often delayed. This meant that many of those who had previously flown short distances began driving instead. Since cars are a riskier mode of transport than planes, the number of fatal traffic accidents went up. Ten years after 9/11, it is estimated that a total of 2,300 Americans died on the roads as a direct consequence of increased security measures – almost the same number as died during the terror attacks.

Disasters of risk management can also be more direct, as seen in the 1991 cholera epidemic in Peru. Over 700,000 people fell ill and thousands died when the government decided to stop chlorinating the drinking water after it was discovered the process may cause cancer.[16]

Mistakes of this kind have not yet led to a reassessment of our approach to risk. Critical discussions of the talismanic power of risk can occasionally be heard in academic contexts, but within politics the demand for intensified risk monitoring continues to dominate. Rather than investigate different ways to relate to the world around us, we must instead become better at managing risk and the risks that come hand in hand with our aversion to risk. This "must" is based on neither calculation nor science; it is a cultural decree.

The Optics of Risk

Experiencing risk changes the way we perceive the world. To an overweight person, the fat around their stomach is more than just an accumulation of flesh. The fat points inwards, to who we really are. Fat has, to a certain extent, always carried symbolic weight, but the way it is now packed with meaning can only really be understood in relation to the risks associated with it.

Fat is enough of a reason for a close relative, a doctor or a complete stranger to feel compelled to pass judgement on the way we are living our lives. Fat affects the way others behave towards us, and the ways we think of ourselves. It creates the optics for perception.[17]

How likely or damaging a thing is does not really matter. Throughout history, people seem to have worried more about the kinds of things later generations will laugh at, while serious risks are given barely any attention at all.

In the late nineteenth century, for example, Sweden was a country with plenty of causes for concern. People were dying in poverty. The average life expectancy was barely fifty years, and epidemics ravaged the population. One in five children was dying before their fifth birthday, and the poor were dropping dead of "starvation fever." Only the richest members of society had the right to vote, and increasing numbers of people were becoming vagrants, only to be sentenced to forced labour. For the most serious of crimes, the punishment was beheading with an axe.[18]

Despite this, many were preoccupied by other problems. In the bestselling 1905 book *Mannens släktlif*, Swedish doctor and politician Wilhelm Wretlind reproduced many of the letters written to him by men seeking help. These men seem particularly unconcerned by all the death around them. Their thoughts are elsewhere. One man, for example, is tormented by something he did seventeen years earlier. He is afraid that his "burden" has ruined his health, and can see countless symptoms: "numerous nocturnal emissions," "weakness and weight loss," "sluggish defecation" and "nervous symptoms."

The man is almost thirty-five, but he has never been married or had intercourse with a woman, he writes. Like many other men at the time, he fears he is no longer capable of sexual relations because of his irresponsible behaviour. He wants to repair his body but does not know how. Water cures? Sodium bromide? Gymnastics? Surgery? He struggles to express the shame he has brought on himself. The best he can manage is "the vice of onanism."[19]

How could the risks associated with masturbation have troubled him more than the diseases claiming so many lives all around him? Was he not more anxious about dying as he travelled between villages? Having his cart break down in the forest in the middle of winter? Or catching himself on a nail and suffering the horrors of tetanus? Shouldn't the very real and tangible risks have inoculated him against the imaginary risks?

It is worth remembering that the writer of this particular letter has an ally on his side: science. And not just that. For more than 250 years, Christians and Enlightenment philosophers alike – including Voltaire, Rousseau and Kant – all condemned the act. Not so much as something ungodly, but as something damaging to one's health.

Compared to other medical risks, the risks of masturbation have proved tenacious since doctors first began to study them in the eighteenth century. And as medical risks go, they are by no means the most absurd. The idea that rotten food and damp air risked causing outbreaks of disease was, for example, a theory that influenced medicine in the nineteenth century. So-called "miscegenation" (or interbreeding) was studied under the umbrella of genetics well into the twentieth century and was thought to be responsible for everything from mental illness to criminality in offspring. In fact, as late as 2000, forty-one percent of Alabama's electorate voted in favour of retaining the last ban on "interracial marriage" in the United States.[20]

It is in the sphere of stories and images that the risks of masturbation really come into their own. In his book, Dr. Wretlind – who went on to gain international recognition as an expert on the subject – listed all the afflictions that a male "onanist" may suffer: a grey pallor, dull eyes, bluish bags under the eyes, poor posture, cold hands and feet, pimples, cold sweats, an irregular heartbeat and shrunken testicles. "Even the member itself may wither," he stresses. Strict empiricist that he was, however, he dismissed the eighteenth-century concerns about bone marrow deterioration.[21]

With statistics to back him up, he shows how up to 11.28 percent of "recently-admitted fools" in Swedish hospitals have gone mad as a result of masturbation. He writes about men who have gone under and about others who have, in desperation, cut off their testicles with a plane iron.

Will I ever be able to get married? asks one letter writer. No, it won't do, Wretlind replies. Not for "at least one year's time." During that year, the man must refrain from such things that may test his nerves – anything sexual, in other words, as well as staying up late, alcohol and gluttony. He must also adopt the usual routine: sitz baths, cold water cures, gymnastics and possibly even ice packs to ward off the nightly spilling of seed.[22]

Max Weber was clearly not alone in worrying about issues of this type around the turn of the century.

The most fascinating letters of all come from distressed parents who have discovered that their babies are onanists. According to one mother, her son began self-abusing at just five months old. With his cold scientist's eye, Wretlind explains how a newborn could manage something so motorically advanced:

> The minute the boy got onto his back, he swung his right leg over his left with such passion that he kneaded the member in between until it began to stiffen. His breath became more and more rapid, his cheeks reddening and his eyes taking on a peculiar glazed, fixed expression.[23]

Even among adults, suspicions flourished. One of the most famous complaints came from the composer Richard Wagner. When his friendship with Friedrich Nietzsche began to wane, he contacted his doctor to instruct him in the treatment of Nietzsche's migraines and worsening vision. Having seen others with the same symptoms, Wagner wrote that "I discovered, all too certainly, that these were the effects of masturbation."

In reply, the doctor confirmed that Nietzsche – despite his denials – likely was an onanist, but that it would be difficult to help him "given the well-known stubbornness of the sin."

There is evidence to suggest that Nietzsche found out about this well-meaning, if humiliating correspondence, and several researchers have since remarked that aesthetic differences of opinion were likely not the only reason the two men's friendship eventually transformed into hatred.[24]

From the profile of symptoms doctors like Wretlind painted, what emerges here is what, for a long time, must have been the most tangible risk of masturbating: the risk of anxiety. "A real *self-loathing* of the most intense kind is produced," Wretlind writes of his patients, continuing: "their melancholy often reaches such heights that they want nothing more than to escape the burden of life."[25]

Yesterday's sin, tomorrow's virtue. In 1968, masturbation as a pathological behaviour was removed from the American Diagnostic and Statistical Manual of Mental Disorders, and these days the medical consensus is that it is both a healthy and safe activity (not least as it protects the practitioner from all sorts of sexually transmitted diseases). Epidemiological studies also show that masturbation can have a strengthening effect on the immune system and that, in men, it can also reduce the risk of prostate cancer (a threshold effect, admittedly, that requires twenty-one ejaculations a month, according to the study in question).[26]

A risk's ability to disenchant the world towards suicidal territory does not necessarily need to be grounded in reality, in other words. Images and stories remain the active ingredients, even when we touch upon more likely risks, such as the fact that longstanding obesity can lead to death, or that a child being unwell may lead to the child dying.

But things could be different. Identifying a risk and what should be done about it does not have to mean being overwhelmed by it. Allowing the risk to "take over" is *kufungisisa*, the sickness of thought; it is getting caught up in the counterfactual world of thoughts at the expense of the real here and now.

Herein lies the liberating nature of risk.

Questions about what we want to do with our lives are replaced by *risk as a necessity*. Our own will is taken out of play, and we no longer have to think about it as much. This seems particularly welcome within politics.

The Politics of Risk

Shortly after the liberation of France in 1944, Jean-Paul Sartre summarised his thoughts about the Second World War in the American magazine *The Atlantic*: "Never were we freer than under German occupation."[27]

Sartre's point was that the occupation liberated the French from having to think about what they wanted to do with their lives. Suddenly resistance was the only right thing. For every thinking individual, goodness was a given. The occupation was the external necessity that allowed them to focus on the practicalities of doing – on the *how* rather than the *why*.

Life is rarely this simple, and knowing what is right and what is wrong seems anything but obvious. We might lack norms, or else they may be contradictory. Our own will keeps spinning like the needle of a compass at the geomagnetic north pole. We have no choice but to guess our way forward and find ourselves facing an uncertainty that sometimes endures for life.

Remaining in this uncertainty demands strength. It requires the ability to live with uncertainty. But what is a person supposed to do if they have never learnt to develop this skill?

For the same reasons the structured environment of the workplace can seem less demanding than the relative chaos of family life, we find ourselves in a situation where almost all politics involves searching for an external necessity – something forcing the decisions in a particular direction. It is striking how infrequently our notions of the ideal society take the focus in political debate. Instead, today's politics is more about how to best deal with the risk of something going wrong. As a result, the problems already plaguing the world rarely evoke as much enthusiasm as the possible catastrophes of the future.

But even here, things could be different. For one thing, the subject of this book – how we feel – could mobilise change. The fact that every sixth person is taking some kind of psychopharmaceutical drug in countries like the United States and Sweden – and that many more are struggling – could take centre stage in our politics. Yes, there are politicians who emphasise the importance of increasing access to mental health care, but that is also almost all they do. The question of *why* people feel so bad in the first place is strangely absent from contemporary public debate.

A few years ago, however, following a discovery linked to psychopharmaceuticals, political action was immediate. Since both sedatives and antidepressants pass through the body and ultimately enter the groundwater, a group of Swedish researchers decided to investigate the impact of the drugs now found in various watercourses on aquatic life. Their findings were striking. At even low concentrations of the anti-anxiety medication Oxazepam, perch become overconfident and greedy, and antidepressants such as Citalopram deprived both the three-spined stickleback and the zebrafish of their appetite and fertility.[28]

Around the world, large amounts of money are now being ploughed into tackling this problem – though not the other issue, the fact that people seem to be feeling so bad that they need chemical assistance in the first place. If animal populations are at risk of behavioural disruption, the problem is that the equilibrium of the ecosystem is under threat. Faced with this catastrophe, politicians are able to act on the basis of the necessity of the risk.

This gets to the very heart of the politics of risk: always seeing the worst in the future.

An imbalance in the ecosystem threatens the biological foundations of our very existence. No one can question the point of averting a future environmental disaster, but the fact that people are struggling is a catastrophe that has already taken place – and, apparently, one we can live with. The focus therefore falls on avoiding future catastrophe by expanding water treatment plants, meaning the medication can be removed from our drinking water.[29]

No matter the debate, and no matter which issue established politicians take up, the prevailing trend is for arguments be positioned against a risk. Politics has become "negative," as the German philosopher Jürgen Habermas puts it, a means of remedying the bugs that constantly seem to keep popping up in the system. Any counterfactual thinking, or questions about *what could be*, goes no further than that.

We can imagine countless ways in which society might collapse, but when faced with the question of what a more advanced democracy might look like, our imagination seems to desert us. This is the essence of what is sometimes referred to as "post-politics" – the bureaucratised administration of *things as they are*. Since risk management is all about preventing damage in the future, politics becomes fundamentally conservative as a result.[30]

What is new here is less the existence of this conservative politics than its all-encompassing extent. While risk-driven politics used to be challenged by a more risk-taking alternative, this tension has largely disappeared. Even right-wing populist governments are now in the business of risk aversion.

"Right" and "left" have largely become a question of how various risks are assessed and prioritised.

If we look back to some of the political reforms pushed through by radicals in the past, the types of arguments differ from those used by reformists today. The gradual expansion of voting rights to include women, the poor and the low-earning, recipients of state welfare and, as late as 1989 in Sweden, people with intellectual disabilities, is an example of reforms driven through *contrary to the calculated risks.* With each expansion of the franchise, workers' rights, welfare, or social security nets, conservative opponents have warned of the risks of political degeneration and misgovernment. And yet these reforms have been pushed through all the same. Not because another risk was cited as a counter argument, but because the reforms were considered to have their own ethical value – *whatever the cost.*[31]

Over time, even the longing for the unknown "no-place" from which the word *utopia* derives has become bound up in fear of ruin – so much so that utopia has become overshadowed by risk and reduced to a measure against future crises, often by the utopians themselves. This tendency is evident as early as Marx, who, particularly towards the end of his life, developed an obsession with capitalism's inherent self-destruction. Communism was not simply a utopia, in Marx's view, it was an "historic necessity" in the same way that capitalism had been in the past.[32]

In the years since, environmental toxins, the risk of atomic war and the self-obliteration of mankind have all given utopia a veil of necessity. As I write, the majority of utopian visions for society spring from the many – and very real – risks of global warming.

No one can question that it is right to take these risks seriously. Risks exist, and we would do best by tackling many of them. Even this book is based partly on risk analyses – for example, the risk of developing mental health problems. As some have suggested, there may also be situations in which it is more effective to appeal to people's fears than their longing to achieve change.[33]

And yet it is striking that the risks that are given real significance in the way we organise society are rarely those that truly threaten our existence. The fact that global warming is taking place and that very little is being done to stop it are facts that have been asserted and analysed in countless reports and scientific articles. These are not risks that have been hushed up. They have both narrative power and effective imagery (the icecaps melting at the North Pole, flooded coastlines, drought and starvation). The reason there has not yet been any significant popular mobilisation against this threat remains a mystery within social sciences and is itself a growing field of research. At least three risks can be discerned here, with a politics based on risk aversion.

Risk 1: Disaster becomes temptation. In the many warnings about disaster, there is an implicit assumption that disaster provokes terror, but this is worth discussing. I began this book by outlining the global statistics on depression and anxiety disorders, as well as the numbers of people who have seriously considered suicide. Appealing to fear and guilt implies that people are reasonably content with life as it is, but what if that isn't the case? The world's downfall is itself a narrative that sells – we see it frequently as entertainment, not least in family films. The end of the Earth is the subject of puppet shows, ballets, and operas. While criminality and terror strike nothing but fear into the hearts of people, there is a certain temptation inherent in destruction. It seems, as many sociologists and philosophers have speculated, that the Earth's destruction has, at least partly, become an end note to look forward to, an unpleasant plaster to tear off, enabling the longed-for change, whatever it may be, to finally come.[34]

Risk 2: Ethics gives way to calculation. The moment a risk is identified, the race to find a suitable counter-measure begins. This measure does not necessarily have to be political, and it doesn't have to involve any great societal reforms. In order to fight global warming, both renewable energy and nuclear power can act as solutions. Those who want to argue that the only solution is a different kind of society face a heavy burden of proof in terms of the technological advances capitalism will permit and how far state intervention can help us. The discussion immediately becomes technical, which leads us on to Risk 3.[35]

Risk 3: Risk is weighed against risk. In calculating how the risk of catastrophe should best be managed, every suggested measure is subject to yet more calculation of risk. For those who want something other than a conservative politics, it is difficult to pull off this arrangement of risk against risk, because any large structural changes will require a step into the unknown. In mathematical calculations of risk, more modest measures always fare better. One example of this is the American economist William Nordhaus' mathematical model for assessing how much global warming and the political attempts to fight it risk "retarding" the economy. This model, for which Nordhaus was awarded the 2018 Nobel Memorial Prize in Economic Sciences, essentially boils down to a numerical calculation of how much damage various temperature targets risk causing, based on the explicit premise that it may be better to allow coastlines to flood and species to die out than to harm economic growth. The ethical reflections are reduced to a bean-counting exercise in which the preservation of the status quo always wins.

Self-Fulfilling Risks

Helena is eating a cheese sandwich. She has managed to convince the kitchen at the rather fancy restaurant where we are sitting to make it for her. She is used to this type of negotiation, and knows to ask for things that aren't on the menu.

"One thing I've noticed is that there's something nice about my phases," she says. "When I get so depressed I don't have the energy to focus on anything else."

Centring her life around risk brings Helena a sense of respite. She simply has to complete the various stages and then the doctor will put a hand on her chest and tell her she is healthy. Like a cycle of despair and liberation. Like an adventure.

From time to time, however, Helena does worry about another type of illness – one where the sense of liberation is never quite as definitive.

"Twice during the past year, idiot men – both joking, and because they're sick in the head themselves – have called me a psychopath. And *that* hurt so much. So much. I can hardly even bear to talk about it."

Since, according to widely accepted symptom profiles, psychopaths are rarely aware of their own psychopathy, Helena has started asking around. Do you think I'm a cold person? Have I done things that were cruel without realising it?

Suspecting oneself of being a psychopath involves a more complex investigation than screening for lung cancer. If Helena went to a psychologist and told them all the terrible things she had done, the psychologist may well agree that she was a psychopath. But how could they possibly know for sure when there are no X-ray images or blood tests to back it up? When all they have is her word?

Helena has been here before. She remembers a similar episode taking place as a child, after she turned her guinea pig onto its back to look between its legs.

"I did it because I was curious to see what she looked like," she says. "Between her legs, I mean. But when I did it, I thought she looked offended."

She imitates her guinea pig's unhappy face.

"I mean, she looked at me like she was thinking: *what are you doing?*"

Helena felt like she had committed assault, and from that event and various associations, she spent a whole summer obsessing over the idea that, deep down, she was sexually perverted. It wasn't until she confided in a friend, dizzy with anxiety, that these fears seemed to run off her back.

That relief was more than her psychologist could give her when she sought help for her schizophrenia – if it was schizophrenia she had.

"Every session started with me telling her I thought I was schizophrenic. Then I asked her: do you think I am? And she said: 'No, Helena, you don't have schizophrenia. But you are confused.' That was how every session started."

Time passed, and Helena got nowhere. No matter how often her psychologist reassured her of the opposite, she couldn't escape the thought that she must be schizophrenic after all. Having a disease in her body wasn't something she could control, but having a disease in her mind widened the risk zone from matter to her thoughts and feelings.

After six months, Helena asked her usual question: "Am I schizophrenic?"

The psychologist gave her a resigned look.
"I don't know, Helena. I don't know."
It was like her fears of going crazy had driven her crazy.

Notes

1 Gurven and Kaplan, "Longevity among hunter-gatherers: A cross-cultural examination".
2 Jared Diamond, *Guns, Germs, and Steel*, New York: Norton, 1999, pp. 175–177.
3 Gilles R. Dagenais et al., "Variations in common diseases, hospital admissions, and deaths in middle-aged adults in 21 countries from five continents (PURE): A prospective cohort study", *The Lancet*, 2019.
4 Dagenais et al., "Variations in common diseases, hospital admissions, and deaths in middle-aged adults in 21 countries from five continents (PURE)".
5 For more examples and discussion, see Daniel Kahneman, *Thinking, Fast and Slow*, Farrar, Straus and Giroux: New York, 2015, p. 138.
6 John E. Mueller and Mark G. Stewart, *Chasing Ghosts: The Policing of Terrorism*, Oxford: Oxford University Press, 2016, pp. 137-139.
7 Frank Furedi, "The Phonics v Whole-Word battle has always been about politics, not pedagogy", *Times Educational Supplement*, 6/8, 2015.
8 Jonathan D. Schoenfeld and John PA Ioannidis, "Is everything we eat associated with cancer? A systematic cookbook review", *The American Journal of Clinical Nutrition*, vol. 97, nr. 1, 2012. For more on the multiplication and acceleration of risk, see Ulrich Beck, *Risk Society: Towards a New Modernity*, London; Newbury Park, CA: Sage Publications, 1992.
9 Frank Furedi, "It's time that we all 'interfered' more", *The Telegraph*, 4/6, 2006.
10 Mark Warr, "Altruistic fear of victimization in households", *Social Science Quarterly*, vol. 1, nr. 3, 1992; Ben Shaw et al, "Children's independent mobility: An international comparison and recommendations for action", London, 2015.
11 This result has been reproduced in a number of surveys, from an early study in the U.S. that showed that young black men were those who worried least, despite the fact that they were most often affected by crime, to the Swedish National Council for Crime Prevention's latest safety study, which shows that people between the ages of 55-74 are the most fearful in Sweden. See Eleanor Singer and Phyliss M. Endreny, *Reporting on Risk: How the Mass Media Portray Accidents, Diseases, Other Hazards,* Russell Sage Foundation, 1993; Swedish National Council for Crime Prevention, "Nationella trygghetsundersökningen 2019: Om utsatthet, otrygghet och förtroende", Stockholm, 2019.
12 Lars Svendsen, *Philosophy of Fear,* London: Reaktion Books, 2008.
13 Svendsen, *Philosophy of Fear*, p. 54.
14 Anders Bolling, *Dagens Nyheter,* 3/4, 2020.
15 Ralph Catalano et al, "The health effects of economic decline", *Annual Review of Public Health*, vol. 32, nr. 1, 2011; Ulf Gerdtham and Christopher J Ruhm, "Deaths rise in good economic times: Evidence from the OECD", *Economics & Human Biology*, vol. 4, nr. 3, 2006.
16 For fatal traffic accidents, see Garrick Blalock, Vrinda Kadiyali and Daniel H. Simon, "Driving fatalities after 9/11: A hidden cost of terrorism", *Applied Economics*, vol. 41, nr. 14, 2009. For Peru, see Henry I. Miller and Gregory Conko, "Precaution without principle", *Nature Biotechnology*, vol. 19, nr. 4, 2001; Anderson, "Cholera epidemic traced to risk miscalculation", *Nature*, vol. 354, nr. 6351, 1991. In retrospect, some have questioned whether the cholera epidemic was caused solely by the removal of chlorine, as there could have

been several interacting factors, see Joel Tickner and Tami Gouveia-Vigeant, "The 1991 cholera epidemic in Peru: Not a case of precaution gone awry", *Risk Analysis: An International Journal,* vol. 25, nr. 3, 2005.

17 See Susanne Brandheim, *A Systemic Stigmatization of Fat People*, Karlstad: Karlstads universitet, 2017.

18 Inga-Carin Enström, "Koleran slog till gång på gång", *Släkthistoria*, 30/6, 2017; Mats Karlsson, "Smittkopporna skonade ingen", " 9/3, 2018; Anna Larsdotter, "Livet för de fattigaste", *Släkthistoria*, 10/6, 2017.

19 Wilhelm Wretlind, *Mannens släktlif: I normalt och sjukligt tillstånd*, Stockholm: G.C. Gustafsons Boktryckeri, 1905, p. 91.

20 German Lopez, "Alabama used the States' right argument to ban marriages before – for interracial couples", *Vox*, 13/2, 2015.

21 Wretlind, *Mannens släktlif: I normalt och sjukligt tillstånd*, p. 85.

22 The case can be found here, in its entirety: ibid, pp. 124–127.

23 Ibid, pp. 69–70.

24 Martin Gregor-Dellin, *Richard Wagner: His Life, His Work, His Century*, New York: Collins, 1983, p. 452.

25 Wretlind, *Mannens släktlif: I normalt och sjukligt tillstånd*, p. 80.

26 Roy J. Levin, "Sexual activity, health and well-being – the beneficial roles of coitus and masturbation", *Sexual and Relationship Therapy*, vol. 22, nr. 1, 2007; Philip Haake et al., "Effects of sexual arousal on lymphocyte subset circulation and cytokine production in man", *Neuroimmunomodulation*, vol. 11, nr. 5, 2004; Jennifer R Rider et al., "Ejaculation frequency and risk of prostate cancer: Updated results with an additional decade of follow-up", *European Urology*, vol. 70, nr. 6, 2016.

27 Jean-Paul Sartre, "Paris alive: The republic of silence", *Atlantic Monthly,* vol. 174, December 1944.

28 Martin Kellner, *Selective serotonin re-uptake inhibitors in the environment: Effects of citalopram on fish behaviour*, Huddinge: Södertörns högskola, 2017; T. Brodin et al, "Dilute concentrations of a psychiatric drug alter behavior of fish from natural populations", *Science*, vol. 339, nr. 6121, 2013.

29 See Marie Granmar, "Ny teknik renar avloppsvatten från läkemedelsrester" *Sveriges Radio P1*, 25/4, 2019.

30 See Herbert Marcuse, *One-Dimensional Man: Studies in the Ideology of Advanced Industrial Society*, Boston: Beacon Press, 1991 [1964]; Jürgen Habermas, *Toward a Rational Society: Student Protest, Science, and Politics*, London: Heinemann, 1971.

31 See e.g. Linn Spross, *Ett välfärdsstatligt dilemma: Statens formuleringar av en arbetstidsfråga 1919-2002,* Uppsala: Uppsala universitet, 2016; Ulrika Holgersson and Lena Wängnerud, *Rösträttens århundrade: Kampen, utvecklingen och framtiden för demokratin i Sverige*, Göteborg: Makadam Förlag, 2018.

32 For an investigation, see Donald C. Lee "The concept of 'Necessity': Marx and Marcuse", *The Southwestern Journal of Philosophy*, vol. 6, nr. 1, 1975.

33 Hans Jonas, *The Imperative of Responsibility: In Search of an Ethics for the Technological Age*, Chicago, IL: The University of Chicago Press, 2000.

34 See particularly Pascal Bruckner, *The Fanaticism of the Apocalypse*, Cambridge: Polity, 2013, and Frank Furedi, *How Fear Works: Culture of Fear in the Twenty-First Century*, London: Bloomsbury Publishing, 2018.

35 For this reason, even radicals may feel that the only solution is systemic change. For an example of a radical who has, with great conviction, come round to the idea that renewable energy will never be able to replace fossil fuels, see Roy Scranton, *Learning to Die in the Anthropocene: Reflections on the End of a Civilization,* San Francisco, CA: City Lights Books, 2015.

9

THE SELF AS RISK

"Love doesn't exist, but the Oedipus complex does. Castration. Attraction. Impulse. Compulsion."

Annie's voice is full of sadness. She has been living with this truth for almost forty years.

"That was what struck me, that there is no love – and above all no selfless love. True love, without any intention to dominate, manipulate, hurt or just achieve sexual satisfaction, it doesn't exist."

Annie was a solitary child. So much so that rather than spending time with other children, she preferred to stay at home with her parents. She had her reasons for preferring solitude. No complex reasons, just reasons she would rather keep herself to herself. Yet when she was twelve, her parents sent her to a psychiatrist, having worried about her for some time. An understandable decision, she thinks in hindsight.

"They did what had to be done," she tells me, speaking slowly in French, keen for me to keep up. "They helped me speak to a therapist so I would start worrying less. It's just that at the time, psychoanalysis was the only real option."

This was Paris in the 1980s. During her first visit to the psychiatrist, there were three people in front of her. She noticed that they all spoke in a different way.

"It was like code. Everything they said, and everything I said, actually meant something different."

It was decided that Annie would begin psychoanalysis. Since she was only a child, two sessions a week would be enough.

Annie remembers the first few sessions being filled with embarrassed anguish. Her psychoanalyst was somewhere between thirty and forty. A

DOI: 10.4324/9781003514930-11

beautiful woman. Thin, with soft, straight hair. Annie waited in vain for her to start a conversation of some kind, or at least ask how she felt, but she didn't say a word.

The long silences made Annie clam up. Words caught in her throat. Her palms grew sweaty.

After a few hesitant months, Annie learned how to talk. She prepared ahead of every session. She gathered observations from school, spoke about things that had happened in the classroom, left openings for the psychoanalyst to make comments. With time, she even began to look forward to their meetings. Going to the psychoanalyst was like an intellectual workout. Annie enjoyed reflecting, questioning herself and learning to understand other people's behaviour. As she got older and began to read more adult literature, she found a great conversational partner in her analyst. She borrowed a few books by Sigmund Freud and thought that what she had read was convincing. She didn't understand everything, of course, but the fact that her psychoanalyst did was impressive.

"Back then, psychoanalysis felt like such a natural way to see the world, even outside of my sessions. We still use words and phrases that reveal its legacy today. We talk about the Oedipus complex, the castration complex, children being perverse. I remember learning that children are perverse and polymorphous at school, because we were taught there was an oral stage, an anal stage and so on."

Annie was now at the centre of things, where the mysteries could be revealed. But she didn't say a word about her solitude. Instead, she saw it deepen. She found new things to worry about and began to develop phobias, including what was known at the time as social phobia. She felt unable not only to play with her classmates but even to look them in the eye.

Still, none of this interested her psychoanalyst. She never asked how Annie was doing. The beautiful woman actually seemed increasingly uninterested in her patient in general. Her gaze was distant, and with each cigarette she smoked the haze in the room grew thicker.

It struck Annie that her parents had sent her to the analyst to get help. Shouldn't she make the most of the opportunity?

After three years in therapy, she finally summoned the courage to share one of her real problems: her fear of blood. Annie was so afraid of blood that she had avoided both sports and playing in the schoolyard. During her fourth year of secondary school, her biology teacher had shown an hour-long documentary about a heart transplant, and Annie's sense of panic lasted for several minutes – minutes that felt like hours – making her dizzy. After that, she was afraid ahead of every biology class.

But not even this seemed to interest the psychoanalyst. She seemed more annoyed than anything, but just as she was about to remark on Annie's confession, it was like she filled with an energy Annie had never seen in her before. Even now, Annie can still remember every single word the psychoanalyst said.

"You know very well why you're afraid of blood. Haven't you worked out what's bothering you? It's simple."

She asked Annie whether she had ever examined her genitals in a mirror. Annie replied that she hadn't, to which the psychoanalyst said that was abnormal at her age. Annie was afraid, said the analyst. But of what?

"What you are afraid of – as you well know – is the man's penis swelling and hardening to the extent that the veins and blood vessels become visible. It's the same with you: the labia fill with blood. Your phobia of blood is a repressed fear of sex."

At the time, Annie was fifteen years old, and had never come close to a penis in any state. She felt her cheeks grow hot. Embarrassed, she didn't dare look up, and spent the rest of the session in mute confusion. Her phobia of blood would just have to stay.

In reading Freud, Annie had come to realise that dreams were important, so she began sharing what the night had had in store for her. At first, this felt like relatively safe ground, but the psychoanalyst seemed to have her analysis of Annie ready, and she also found the most fantastical proof that it was right.

Take the time Annie told her about a dream that took place in a hospital, for example. In it, she was one of several people, only one of whom she recognised: The psychiatrist she saw a few times a year. He was strolling around with two buckets of milk in his hands, and he asked her if she would like any. That was the dream in its entirety.

It made a big impression on the psychoanalyst.

"You say there was milk in the buckets," she said. "But what if it was something else?"

Annie didn't know what she meant.

"What, other than milk, is white?" the analyst pressed her.

Since Annie didn't understand what the psychoanalyst was getting at, she was given yet another lesson in male sexuality. Semen was another white liquid, and with that in mind her dream could hardly have been clearer. What Annie wanted – subconsciously, of course – was the psychiatrist's semen. Ergo: she wanted to sleep with him.

"It's like a filter that makes everything negative," she tells me today. "Particularly romantic relationships."

Before long, it made very little difference what Annie said. All roads led to the phallus.

Her more obvious problems, dismissed by the psychoanalyst as "symptoms," increased to the point that she struggled even to leave the house. As a result, her first two years in high school went particularly badly. She stopped taking the bus or the metro, and began missing her therapy sessions, which led the psychoanalyst to suggest that she could always cycle.

Annie explained that the means of transport was irrelevant; she was afraid of leaving the house, of other people seeing that she was crazy, of having a panic attack and getting stuck in traffic. She would gladly cycle if she could, she had loved cycling as a child, but it just wasn't possible.

The psychoanalyst had another explanation for Annie's reluctance to cycle. A bicycle had a saddle, and beneath the saddle was a seat post. This post, so precisely positioned, wasn't there something about it that bothered Annie?

After seven years in psychoanalysis, Annie began to have trouble sleeping. She woke with palpitations and nightmarish thoughts. Was this really her youth? A time when her peers were living life to the full, making the most of the world? Her parents helped her visit the library, where she searched for books about different types of therapy, but when she told the psychoanalyst about this, the woman was unhappy. Psychoanalysis was the only thing that worked; everything else was nonsense.

Not long later, the psychoanalyst presented Annie with her explanation as to why she didn't want to go out.

"The fact that you find it so hard to be away from home is not just because you are afraid of your sexuality and being close to boys. Now that your mother has started working again, you are also trying to replace her by being close to your father."

Thus began the darkest period in Annie's life. She was gripped by a sense of disgust with herself and didn't dare look her father in the eye. She avoided touching pens, avoided looking at the poster of the space rocket in their hallway. No matter where she looked, she saw the male sexual organ, and that made her anxious.

It seemed as though her psychoanalyst had been right from the very beginning.[1]

Our Inner Self

During the Russian psychologist Alexander Luria's expeditions to the mountains of Uzbekistan in the 1930s, he not only investigated the impact of pre-modern ways of living on people's propensity to counterfactual thinking. In some fifty or so interviews, he also attempted to understand how the farmers saw themselves – how capable of "self-analysis" they were.

Among those who had some ability to read, the interviews went largely as expected. The farmers were able to discuss whether they were cheerful, honest, anxious or easily angered. But among those who had never learned to read, Luria found it difficult even to broach the subject: "As a rule, they either refused to name positive or negative qualities in themselves or dealt with the question by describing concrete and material aspects of their lives."[2]

With Nurmat, an eighteen-year-old peasant, the discussion went as follows:

Luria:	What shortcomings are you aware of in yourself, and what would you like to change about yourself?
Nurmat:	As for me, I have only one dress and two robes, and those are all my shortcomings.
Luria:	No, that's not what I'm asking you about. Tell me what kind of a person you are now and what you would like to be? Aren't there any differences?
Nurmat:	I would like to be good, but now I'm bad; I have few clothes, so I can't go to other villages like this.
Luria:	And what does "be good" mean?
Nurmat:	To have more clothes.[3]

When the interview subjects did not define themselves in terms of their financial situation, they described their character in terms of behaviour, as in the following conversation with Murza Shiral, a fifty-five-year-old peasant:

Luria:	Do you think that people are all the same or different?
Murza Shiral:	No, they're not the same. There are different ones [holds up fingers]: here's a landowner, here's a farmhand.
Luria:	Do you know what the differences are between individuals, say, between your acquaintances?
Murza Shiral:	Only they themselves know.
Luria:	Well, what are you like? Describe your character.
Murza Shiral:	My character is very good-natured. Even if it's a youngster who's before me, I use the polite form of address and speak courteously...
Luria:	Well, there are other people here in the village; are you the same as them or not?
Murza Shiral:	They have their own hearts and different conversations, and they speak different words.
Luria:	Well, compare yourself to them and describe your character.
Murza Shiral:	I'm a good-natured person, I talk to big people like a big person, to little people like a little person, and to middle-sized people like a middle-sized person ... That's all I can say, there's nothing else that remains.[4]

That Murza Shiral and Nurmat had thoughts about their "self" is clear, but when Luria asked them about their character, they seemed to think most about their situation and behaviour. The idea that they might be a certain way, intrinsically, seems to have been an alien concept to them. Even today, this difference is visible between cultures. Several socio-psychological experiments have, for example, shown that Americans gladly think categorically about what people *are*, while the Chinese, Japanese and Koreans tend to view both themselves and others in terms of situation and behaviour.[5]

This difference is key. A man in the nineteenth century might, as we have seen, worry about *having masturbated*, with all the risks that involved. But the worry of *being sexually perverse* is a later idea.

So where does this fear of *being* come from?

Almost 300 years ago, European doctors started warning about something that would soon be considered an epidemic. Today, we might call it an epidemic of anxiety, but it was around this time that medical terms for describing different types of anxiety began to replace one another. The Scottish doctor George Cheyne's concept of *nervousness* proved dominant for a long time, a diagnosis whose variants he presented in *The English Malady* in 1733.[6]

Like the majority of contemporary doctors, Cheyne was influenced by Descartes' mechanist view of the human body. Since Descartes' dualistic model saw the mind as divine in nature, it was not appropriate to speak of diseases of the mind. Cheyne's main contribution was to disseminate the idea of mental health problems as an issue of the nerves – an idea whose impact is still felt today, in the way we talk about "nervousness" and "neuroses."

Cheyne also provided the public with medical grounds to worry about anxiety.

"Of all the miseries that afflict human life, and relate principally to the body, in this valley of tears, I think nervous disorders, in their extreme and last degrees, are the most deplorable, and, beyond all comparison, the worst."[7]

His analysis covered more than simply an individual's nerves. Nervous problems were not caused by random wear and tear of the bodily machinery. Social conditions – in particular increased prosperity, extravagant lifestyles, increased consumerism, and an excess of brain work – had led to an explosion of nervous problems, particularly among the English upper classes.

The spread of nervousness was, in Cheyne's view, epidemic: "These nervous disorders being computed to make almost one third of the complaints of the people of condition in England," he wrote. This was likely the first estimate of an epidemiological nature as regards a psychiatric diagnosis.[8]

During the eighteenth century, attention was drawn to the nervousness epidemic by a number of doctors. In the Dutch city of Utrecht, an essay competition under the heading "the causes of the increasing nervous disease in our land" was organised.

"At the beginning of the nineteenth century," a doctor would later write, "we do not hesitate to affirm, that *nervous disorders* have now taken the place of fevers."[9]

With the epidemic growth in various types of anxiety disorders, there was a shift in the way people viewed mankind's spiritual life. Since madness affected functional citizens, and in particular the upper classes, whose sensitive nerves made them particularly vulnerable, it couldn't be the case that the *entire person* was mad. After all, the nervous, monomaniacal, phobic and neurotic person still functioned. They were fit to be around other people, typically managed to do their work, and occasionally went down in history for their performances. What doctors emphasised, therefore, was that madness affected only *a part* of the human machine.

With the breakthrough of psychoanalysis, this assertion became a theoretical foundation. Admittedly, psychoanalysis may have replaced Descartes' bodily focus with a more dynamic focus on "the subconscious" (a term that had long been in use within psychology before Freud popularised it with his unrivalled interpretative claims). But regardless of the starting point in the body or mind, a *dichotomous individual* was born. An individual suffering from "partial insanity", as the French doctor Philippe Pinel would put it. And, more importantly: *an individual whose healthy self could reflect on its sick self.*

This also marked the emergence of an approach in which a person's context was seen as irrelevant to understanding them. The fact that so many people could have developed the same kind of problem in such a short time certainly called for some kind of societal analysis among the doctors who first studied the issue of anxiety. But once psychology began to divide the individual into different levels of consciousness, anatomies of personality, cognitive schema, and neurotransmitters, the inner universe quickly became so big that there was no longer space for the society surrounding the individual in the analysis (other than as a "stressor"). Back in the wizard's hat of risk management, this time in a meandering terrain of reflexive spirals – thoughts about thoughts, emotions about emotions – the individual learned to be inwardly vigilant, while their context lost importance in terms of how he or she felt.

Alone Together

One thing Annie cannot understand is why her psychoanalyst never asked about her most obvious problem: her solitude.

"It wasn't exactly complicated. I was solitary. They knew that, but they never asked me why."

The explanation was simple. Annie liked her parents. She enjoyed being around them. They were the people she was closest to, and she was their only child. But their apartment was small, just forty square metres, and as a result, she avoided inviting friends over. She didn't want them to see where she lived, and she didn't want them to ask why her parents were unemployed.

Because that was the thing: Annie's parents weren't doing particularly well either. They were depressed and often suffered from such bad anxiety that they might not set foot outside the apartment for days on end. The pain of this was not unknown to Annie. She knew that sitting in the psychiatrist's waiting room when one of her parents was there made her sad. She was all too aware of the difficulty of giving an acceptable answer to the question of what her parents did all day.

When she was five, she made a promise to herself: she would protect her parents from a world that, as far as she could see, did not wish them well. She would protect them from shame. She would protect them from expense. She wouldn't ask to go to the cinema or the circus, to her classmates' birthday parties, because she knew that her family would be expected to repay the favour. Out of loyalty, she deepened her own sense of solitude.

Her years of psychoanalysis would help her cut the last few social ties she had left. When the analyst brought up the theory of the Electra complex – Freudian for daughters who are sexually fixated on their fathers – this even poisoned her relationship with her parents.

"It's the same process you might see in a sect. Isolate the individual, even from their own family – from their father, in my case. But the minute I started to feel doubts when I looked at my dad, I said stop. They drag you into something that's *their* fantasy, *their* perversion. And they want it to become yours."

Despite her solitude, Annie's experience fits into a larger pattern. Historically, the atomistic understanding of the individual as an isolated unit coincided with a growing loneliness in the way we live our lives. This development took place over a long period of time; layer by layer, the people in our immediate vicinity fell away. The clans of nomadic society, the village, the religious community, our relatives – today, much of the daily contact a person might once have enjoyed has been replaced by work and our immediate families, if that.

During the twentieth century, it became increasingly common for people to live entirely alone – a phenomenon that barely seems to have existed before pre-industrial society. This development accelerated during the second half of the century, and today almost half of all households in a country like Sweden are home to single residents – a limit that has already been passed in Paris, not to mention Stockholm, where over sixty percent of households are now single resident.[10]

Living alone does not, of course, mean that a person lacks a social context outside of the home, but as the American sociologist Robert Putnam has shown, the spread of single-resident households is preceded by a wider waning of local groups, social movements, political parties and other types of social gathering. This growth in solitude is also evident within a family context. "[V]irtually all forms of family togetherness became less common over the last quarter of the twentieth century," writes Putnam. It has become increasingly rare for us to spend dinners, vacations, and religious holidays together. Just sitting and talking or watching TV together is also becoming much less common.[11]

From the 1960s onward, between thirty and fifty percent of people in high-income countries have reported feeling lonely, and between ten and thirty percent that they felt intense loneliness. Often, this has to do with more than just a feeling. An American study examined how many close friends people had, for example. In 1985, the most common answer was three. Twenty years later, the most common answer was none.[12]

Few links between how we feel and how we live are as well documented as that between loneliness and mental health issues. And this is not just about correlation. In longitudinal studies stretching over a long period of time, the evidence shows that loneliness typically *precedes* mental health problems. Loneliness is followed by despair, which in turn is followed by anxiety and depression. The effects are huge. Those who lack friends or a supportive partner may even be more likely to suffer from depression than not.[13]

Compare this with internet addiction: Today, there is a common belief that social media is programmed so devilishly that people get caught up in its web and use it so much that they forget to see others face-to-face. But much of the evidence suggests more of an interplay. The typical pattern is that people who are already lonely go online looking for distractions and a sense of context. Once they become hooked, they make less of an effort to see other people, which simply makes them even more lonely.[14]

Not everything about this development is negative. Throughout history, there have been plenty of repressive communities that modernity has gradually wiped out. But the rise in loneliness does present us with new problems. Aside from the fact that loneliness makes us less happy, it also makes us vulnerable. Convinced that the solution to mental suffering is processing it internally – if only with the right psychopharmaceuticals – loneliness not only makes us more receptive but also more eager for someone to tell us what the problem is. What is *really* going on in there. As many social bonds fall away, a new one arises: with the psychological expert.

Interpreting our Interior

The notion that some part of us is broken would likely be much easier to grapple with if it weren't for the idea that this broken part is hidden away. Since what is broken is subconscious, we have no way of knowing how bad the damage is. There is only one person who can tell us what is lurking within: the expert.

Just how strange this faith in experts is only really becomes apparent when someone lacks it. An illuminating example can be seen in the aftermath of the 2004 tsunami in Sri Lanka. With so many lives lost following the devastation on the shores of the island nation, aid organisations around the world sent a battalion of psychotherapists, in what has been described as the greatest psychological intervention in history. The aid organisations' aims were clear: People should be treated for post-traumatic stress disorder (PTSD), and they should be treated through "debriefing" – the retelling of traumatic experiences with a focus on the thoughts they provoke in the individual.

One of the few people who questioned this intervention was the Sri Lankan-American psychologist Gaithri Fernando. Prior to the tsunami, she had studied the ways in which Sri Lankan children dealt with violence and loss caused by the country's long civil war, and she therefore knew that the diagnosis of PTSD was not entirely applicable, despite Western psychiatry's claims of universality.

Fernando continued to interview Sri Lankans about their experiences following the tsunami, and she found that those who had been injured or lost close relatives gave less weight to "interior" processes in the form of painful memories or brooding. Instead, they emphasised that the disaster had left its mark on people's moods and conflicts in their immediate communities. What they worried about most was the social imbalance and the prospect that they might fail in their commitments to their family and community. Like Luria's illiterate peasants, they seemed more concerned with matters outside the self than within.

Given that this reaction was difficult to shoehorn into the Western model of treating trauma, the humanitarian effort quickly became a confused affair.

"Two weeks after the tsunami there were hundreds of counselors doing nothing or getting in the way," said a doctor from the World Health Organization. Many of the trauma therapists were convinced that the catastrophe had been so severe that the inhabitants of the island were still in shock. In a BBC interview, one expressed concern that the local children seemed more interested in going back to school than talking about their painful experiences. According to the therapist, they were "clearly in denial." Only later would they realise "the full emotional horror of what has happened to them."[15]

This type of analysis is now so common that few react to it. Repressing a painful experience, closing one's eyes to injustice or denying an inappropriate reaction – none of these are unfamiliar concepts. We use them often, and willingly, both with regards to ourselves and to others. In this model is an assumption of *actual knowledge*. Deep down, we *know* something that we do not want to admit to ourselves. It is more than just a mistake, more than a lack of attention. There is something within us, but we don't want to know what.

Let's pause and take a closer look at this idea. It is possible that the therapist was right. If someone is "in denial," that means the person is unaware of it. Denial suggests something devious, evasive. If denial is present, we don't know about it. But if a person is not aware of what he or she is denying, then how can anyone else know about it?

Consider the following episode (a true story): Freud takes a train with his most promising disciple, Carl Gustav Jung. During the journey, Jung talks enthusiastically about some prehistoric remains that were recently discovered in northern Germany. He seems captivated by the findings. Freud, who knows that Jung sees himself as a possible contender for the throne of psychoanalysis, interprets this as an expression of Jung's oedipal desire to murder him. Freud faints.

According to Freud, Jung's excitement at the discovery of the prehistoric remains stems from his subconscious fantasies about Freud's death. Jung, in turn, interprets Freud's collapse as an expression of Freud's inverted form of oedipal obsession. In Jung's view, Freud is fixated on the notion that all men want to murder their father figure, and he is projecting this idea onto Jung, despite the fact that Jung simply thought the archaeological finds were fascinating.[16]

Who is right?

They can't both be right. Either Freud is right, and Jung was interested in the remains because of a subconscious desire for Freud to die, or Jung is right, and Freud was projecting an imagined threat onto him. Each implies that the other is wrong.

The problem illustrates a key difference between what the American sociologist John Levi Martin calls *first-person* and *third-person* explanations of human behaviour.[17]

Jung's own answer to why he wanted to talk about the prehistoric remains – that he found them interesting – is a first-person explanation. It is based on Jung's own experience. To Jung, experience is the most direct form of knowledge he can gain. He could, of course, focus his attention, reflect on why he found the remains so interesting, but no one has better access to Jung's subconscious than Jung himself.

A third-person explanation places the individual's experience in parentheses, in order to explain their behaviour on the basis of factors of which he or she is unaware. Jung may *think* it was the remains that interested him, but it was *actually* his subconscious desire for Freud to be transformed into prehistoric remains that led him to mention them. If Jung does not realise this, then he is "in denial."

Third-person explanations can be based on trauma or impulse, but also on social factors. Many sociologists, for example, are keen to explain how advertising and business culture affects us in ways we are unaware of. Other sociologists – and I count myself among this group – instead use first-person explanations to explore how these types of influences are recognised or reflected in our thoughts.[18]

Biological factors, such Cheyne's theory of nervous thoughts stemming from partial brain damage, can also be included as third-person explanations. In this instance, behaviour can be explained as a bodily *actually* that the individual themselves is not aware of.

People are often grateful when an expert presents an *actually* as an explanation to why they behave in a certain way. Regardless of what this *actually* is, it can bring comfort. But when a third-person explanation is based entirely in authority, when there is nothing we can do to refute it or even question it, this creates a power imbalance between the person doing the explaining and the person being explained. More often than not, we are *not* dealing with two equal parties who, like Freud and Jung, can parry a third-person explanation with another.

Latent Homosexual

Now that psychoanalysis has lost much of its scientific and therapeutic influence, we may question why its third-person explanation still deserve attention.

One reason is that although psychoanalysis has largely disappeared from science, it is still very much present in our society and language – as when someone, ironically or not, points out a "repression," a "projection," a "sublimation" or a "Freudian slip." Another, more crucial, reason is that psychoanalysis is responsible for some of history's most hilarious third-person explanation.

Freud's third-person explanations will likely endure as breathtaking curiosities – from the rat man's subconscious desire to engage in anal intercourse with his father, to Dora, whose cough revealed a subconscious desire to perform oral sex on a family friend. Countless words have been written about these "cases," yet very little has been established about the long-term effects of Freud's analysis on his patients.

One little-known exception is an American by the name of Horace Frink. Frink didn't come to Freud as a patient in the strict sense of the world. He was a psychoanalyst himself, and a successful one at that. As a co-founder of the prestigious New York Psychoanalytic Society, he was twice named president of the organisation. In his younger years, he had written a book about phobias and compulsion, and made such an impression on Freud during their meetings that the Austrian thought he could see an American Jung in him.

In February 1921, Frink travelled to Vienna for five months' teaching and analysis with Freud. Frink was thirty-eight at the time, a father of two, and had been married for ten years. He was widely seen as the most promising psychoanalyst in the United States.

But when he came home, he was a different man.

One thing that came up during his analysis with Freud was that Frink was a "latent homosexual." Frink himself felt no homosexual urges, but Freud had nevertheless seen an inherent homosexuality within him. In fact, the problem Frink had experienced on a conscious level was that he – like Jung and many other psychoanalysts of his day – had fallen for one of his patients.

Freud took pains to remind his disciples that, as psychologists, they could not act as advisors to their patients, but there is little doubt that this is precisely what he did in Frink's case: he instructed a confused Frink to divorce his wife and marry his patient.

Freud played such an active role in this decision that he actually summoned Frink's patient across the Atlantic to Paris, where he explained the situation to her. Angelika Bijur would later recall that Freud had been unequivocal during the meeting: the best course of action would be for her to get divorced and then immediately remarried, if not for her own sake then for Frink's, because he would "never again come back to normality and probably develop into a homosexual, though in a highly disguised way."[19]

Freud's words carried a lot of weight. Both Frink and Bijur divorced their respective partners, and they began a relationship.

Though Freud wrote in a letter that he had taken the side of Frink's "repressed desire," and therefore acted morally, Frink does not seem to have found happiness in his new marriage. He had to undergo more therapy with Freud, to whom he complained that Angelika had lost her charm. From being dazzlingly beautiful, he complained that she now looked "queer, like a man, like a pig."[20]

Still, more than anything, Frink was racked with guilt. He remained unsure whether he had done the right thing by leaving his first wife and their two children, and began to doubt the reasons for his divorce. Frink wasn't reassured when Freud asked whether Angelika, who happened to be incredibly wealthy, might like to make a donation to "the psychoanalytical fund."[21]

When Frink's ex-wife died, he fell into a deep depression. After a series of attempted suicides, he was admitted to the psychiatric ward at Johns Hopkins, and when it was revealed that he had mistreated Angelika, he was forced to resign as president of the New York Psychoanalytic Society. The two eventually divorced, and Frink was admitted to hospital again, for a longer period this time. He lived for another decade, during which he went through a handful of depressions, and died of a heart attack following a psychotic episode, aged just fifty-three.

Since Frink is the only one of Freud's subjects whose life we know about in any reliable detail, we can more easily assess his analysis with the facts in hand. Without even going into the idea of "latent homosexuality" that Freud applied to a number of people around him, it is clear that Frink regretted his first divorce for the rest of his life. Others could see that the plan was a bad idea at the time. Another of Freud's American patient/students who knew Frink and his patients told Freud that their marriage would never last because Frink and Bijur were too different. Freud replied that their marriage would be wonderful, thanks to their sexual attraction to each other.[22]

This is the most striking thing about Freud's accounts of his patients: His own cocksureness. This cocksureness reinforced the accuracy of his analysis. The patient's lack of certainty, on the other hand, was an indication of resistance, an attempt to defend themself against a repressed truth.

The ideas of "resistance" and "repression" represent psychoanalysis's biggest contribution to modern anxiety. With this pair of terms, all uncertainty and ambivalence can be reduced to symptoms. The slightest *what if* becomes a rabbit warren, and letting go of the thought – or accepting uncertainty as a part of life – is so easily reduced to a manifestation of resistance. Viewed like this, the psychoanalytical method is in stark contrast to the distanced observation of thoughts and feeling seen in meditation. A thought is never just a thought; each one comes fully loaded with clues as to what is going on in the repressed part of one's self.[23]

Angelika would later remark on her years spent in psychoanalytical circles by saying that she had "never met an analyst who didn't come across as an obvious neurotic, lost in theory and incapable of managing life." Her observation may partly explain why there was such a high frequency of suicide among the pioneers of the discipline. Of the 149 members of Vienna's psychoanalytical union, nine took their own lives between 1902 and 1938 – one in seventeen, in other words (today, the global suicide rate is one in 10,000). One of them, Viktor Tausk, addressed his suicide note to Freud, having been kicked out of the inner circle in Vienna. And when one of Jung's assistants committed suicide, Freud remarked on the issue in a letter: "Do you know, I think we wear out quite a few men."[24]

What if I've Killed?

In the book *A Father*, Sibylle Lacan describes how her father, the famous psychoanalyst Jacques Lacan, left the family shortly after her birth and then completely neglected her until his death. She describes herself as being "the fruit of despair," because her father had set his mind on divorce before she was even born.

A few years after the publication of her book, she took her own life. The back cover of the American edition features the following quote from the French historian and psychoanalyst Élisabeth Roudinesco:

> This book is the most beautiful testimony ever written about Lacan. Being the daughter of despair never prevented Sibylle from loving life so much that she could only leave it through a voluntary act.[25]

This quote is one of many examples of how psychoanalysis continues to give its practitioners wide scope for interpretation. Just as the saddle of a bike represents a phallus, suicide becomes an act of love towards life.

At this point, I need to emphasise that there are also plenty of fantastical third-person explanations outside of psychoanalysis, and that some psychoanalysts, such as Harry Stack Sullivan, gave more weight to the "manifest" – i.e. what their patients actually communicated to them – than to the "latent."

In the neurobiological paradigm, we can see how the subconscious finds a counterpart in neurological injuries that have not yet been empirically mapped, and therefore, in individual cases, simply represent an assumption. When a patient is being diagnosed, their behaviour is psychiatry's only measure, but the notion of a hidden deviation in the brain can occasionally give the interpreter as wide a scope as psychoanalysis.[26]

For example, in making a diagnosis such as psychopathy (which is explained, among other things, by underactivity in the amygdala and ventromedial cortex) the patient can easily find themselves in a catch-22 situation of *damned if you do, damned if you don't*. If they behave aggressively, that is an expression of psychopathy. But if they are friendly and helpful, this is also an expression of psychopathy, because they are manipulating their environment.[27]

The American sociologist Erving Goffman called this "looping" – a diagnostic situation in which the person making the diagnosis is unable to disregard their suspicions. Since looping largely takes place behind the closed doors of shame, it usually manages to escape the notice of any third parties. In rare cases, however, it becomes a public concern. And every once in a while, it can take the whole world by surprise.

One case that has already gone down in history is that of Sture Bergwall, also known as Thomas Quick – "Sweden's first serial killer." Through therapy, Bergwall was able to gain access to a large number of repressed memories. Some were about the supposed abuses his parents had subjected him to, but the spectacular aspect of the case was that he was also helped to recall repressed memories of a string of murders. With the aid of his therapist, he confessed to over thirty murders and was later convicted of eight.

A decade after his conviction, however, Bergwall was acquitted of every single charge. He had come to realise that he had neither murdered anyone nor been abused during childhood. His memories were not memories at all, they were suggested fantasies, shaped by strong psychopharmaceuticals and a tangle of third-person explanations in which his uncertainty was consistently interpreted as "resistance."

Despite countless analyses, books, and a national commission, researchers will likely continue to return to the Quick case in an attempt to make sense of the power and dynamics of third-person explanations. Most surprising is that there were no witnesses or forensic evidence to support any of Bergwall's morbid claims. The police certainly did their best to find the bodies. In the investigation into the disappearance of one young girl, Bergwall was taken back to the supposed scene of the crime in a Norwegian forest, with the Norwegian police turning the area into a no-go zone and enforcing a no-fly zone overhead. During the visit, Bergwall is said to have recalled an image of him cutting up the girl's body on the edge of a forest tarn, then swimming naked into the middle and letting her body parts sink to the bottom. This led to the largest crime scene investigation seen in Norway since World War II. The forest tarn was drained, with the Norwegians pumping out a total of 35 million litres of water. They even dug up the sediment at the bottom, going so deep that they reached 10,000-year-old material. The water was filtered twice, but no sign of the girl was ever found. And yet, in 1998, Bergwall was convicted of her murder.[28]

Given how often Bergwall changed his story, his hesitations, mistakes and vacillating, the convictions are a mystery. The convenient explanation is that they were the result of status-seeking on the part of the team of therapists, investigators, prosecutors, lawyers and memory experts, all thrilled by the prospect of going down in history for discovering Sweden's first serial killer – an example of "group think" in which there was no time for critical questioning.[29]

But the historically interesting question is how the justice system and the general public could accept the idea that Bergwall had recalled memories of murders that he was previously unaware of.[30]

While much of the debate around Bergwall/Quick revolved around the idea of repressed memories, the theory of "resistance" also permeated the case. The memory expert who gave Bergwall's retrieved memories scientific legitimacy was a professor of psychology by the name of Sven Å Christianson. Christianson wasn't a psychoanalyst, and instead borrowed from several schools of thought. In his book on serial killers, for example, he writes about a possible "issue of brain injury" in "some serial killers," without going into any detail. But what made the crime scene visits and interrogations of Bergwall possible was Christianson's prize theory of "psychological resistance."

Christianson argued that difficult memories of events such as murder can be "separated from other memories," becoming hard to access, and therefore recommended that suspected killers be interviewed repeatedly and at length. He also acted as a memory consultant in the "Kevin Case," in which two children were claimed to have confessed to the murder of another child (thirty-one interviews in total), and in the investigation into the so-called "scissor murder" in Hovsjö, in which a twelve-year-old was found guilty of the murder of an eleven-year-old (eighteen interrogations). In both cases, the children were later cleared of all suspicion.[31]

In his autobiography, Bergwall introduces another explanation as to how he could have confessed to so many murders, an explanation that seems to have passed the majority of people by.

Bergwall may have behaved like a pathological liar, but equally key is the fact that he doubted his own experiences. The idea of murder first came to him as a *what if* when he was a patient on a psychiatry ward, talking to another patient about their therapy sessions and all the terrible things a person can discover about themselves:

"What if I've killed?" Bergwall mused, reflecting further: "I was surprised by my question, then afraid, because Lars-Inge replied: Just the fact that you're asking makes me think you have."[32]

Even before he began therapy, Bergwall was alert to the nature of his thoughts. He was "crazy about psychoanalysis," he confessed in an interview, and began reading the Swiss psychoanalyst Alice Miller shortly after he was admitted to hospital. From day one, Bergwall and his therapists followed a template with fixed narratives and explanatory models. The horrible details he recounted proved the veracity of his confessions, in line with the guiding principle that "no normal person could come up with something so awful."

But the fact is that no one's imagination exists in a vacuum. Two works that inspired Bergwall in his – admittedly – impressive richness of detail were Bret Easton Ellis' *American Psycho* and Jonathan Demme's film *The Silence of the Lambs*. Bergwall first watched the film after Christianson recommended it during an investigation.[33]

"I couldn't separate fact from fiction," is a recurring observation in Bergwall's autobiography. Doubt, anxiety, all sorts of negative emotional reactions – these were all part of his resistance, and therefore confirmed the worst.[34]

"I dried my tears and thought that what I'd said must be true. All the crying and anxiety proved that my repressed memories had risen to the surface," he recalled in connection with a visit to a crime scene.[35]

Bergwall himself was surprised by the macabre details of his confessions, but the notion that his thoughts and fantasies indicated hidden horrors within disqualified any objections.

"Word by word, I went through the story; word by word, I painted pictures as I thought they would look, and which I thought were true but which I couldn't remember, because they were repressed."[36]

Bergwall was a product of analysis and expertise, someone whose experience was invaded by third-person explanations. Somewhere along the way, the idea that the individual – whether psychotic or not – is always the person with the best access to their consciousness was forgotten. The title of his autobiography neatly encapsulates the costly lesson he learned: *Only I Know Who I Am*.

The Eradication of Experience

Today, false confessions have evolved into a specific area of research within forensic psychology. So-called Lindbergh confessions are much more common than you might think, and often complicate policework. The term stems from the kidnap of Charles Augustus Lindbergh Jr., son of famous aviator Charles Lindbergh, for which over 200 innocent people came forward to confess. The same phenomenon hampered the investigation into the murder of Swedish Prime Minister Olof Palme – a crime to which, to date, over 130 people have confessed.[37]

Among those who suspect themselves, there is always an idea that the crime must have been carried out in some sort of subconscious state that their conscious self is preventing them from remembering. When fourteen-year-old Michael Crowe was interviewed at length following the murder of his sister, he became convinced he was suffering from a split personality. "Bad Michael" must have stabbed his sister to death in an attack of violent jealousy, while "good Michael" had blocked the event from his memory.

"I'm not sure how I did it," he said. "All I know is I did it."[38]

It wasn't until his sister's blood was found on clothing belonging to another suspect that the police dropped all charges against Crowe.

The idea that we might house an evil Mr. Hyde within us was so strong that Crowe, like many others who have only been cleared once forensic evidence proved their stories to be false, was on the verge of being incarcerated. It may seem like an accident, but the idea that someone would so fundamentally question their own experience is not, historically speaking, a coincidence. It stems from an idea about the hidden self that first began to gain cultural traction in the nineteenth century.

The modern calculation of risk not only covers what we *do*, it is just as concerned with who we *are*. These two analyses can weave together into various patterns. As seen in the case of Freud's protege Horace Fink, we can, for example, worry that we should get divorced, only to blow this anxiety into a symptom of something that is wrong with us. Once in a frenzy of interpretation, anxiety cannot be accepted as simple anxiety. The very existence of anxiety indicates that something is wrong – if not in the world then inside me. Like the super-ego Freud wanted to lift from his patients' shoulders, this suspicion of oneself – the constant brooding about what we really want, what we really feel – can seem like a compulsion.

Annie tells me that she eventually reached the stage where her psychoanalysis had taken on the form of a fixation.

"Towards the end of my therapy, I was even struggling to touch door handles," she tells me. "I pictured genitals."

It was as though she had put on her analyst's phallus-detecting goggles, and was unable to take them off.

Looking back now, after twenty-five years of processing and alternative therapy, she can see that a cigar is nothing but a cigar. As the founder of a patient group in Paris for those suffering anxiety disorders, she has come into contact with others with similar experiences. Annie has also written about her psychoanalysis and taken part in public debates with practitioners. While it is relatively common to see French intellectuals grappling over the validity of psychoanalysis, it is rare to see a psychoanalyst actually lock horns with a patient. And though they have, to some extent, accepted her criticisms – including the allegation that she was manipulated and misled – it confuses both the analysts and the public in general when patients have the nerve to complain about their treatment.

"It's not part of their worldview that the patient might be able to give as good as she gets, that we're able to deliver a factual critique of what they have done. The patient doesn't have that right. The patient can only project. The patient is ill. The analyst is healthy."

Notes

1 From interview 13/8, 2019 and Annie Gruyer, "Sept ans de psychanalyse" in *Le livre noir de la psychanalyse: Vivre, penser et aller mieux sans Freud*, ed. Catherine Meyer, Paris: Les Arènes, 2005.
2 Luria, *Cognitive Development: Its Cultural and Social Foundations*, p. 147.
3 Luria, *Cognitive Development: Its Cultural and Social Foundations*, p. 148.
4 Luria, *Cognitive Development: Its Cultural and Social Foundations*, pp. 148–149.
5 Nisbett, *The Geography of Thought: How Asians and Westerners Think Differently - And Why.*
6 For an ideo-historical summary, see Allan V. Horwitz, *Anxiety: A Short History*, Baltimore: Johns Hopkins University Press, 2013.
7 George Cheyne and Roy Porter, *George Cheyne: The English Malady*, New York: Taylor & Francis, 2013, p. 2.
8 Cheyne and Porter, *George Cheyne: The English Malady*, p. ii.

9 See Horwitz, *Anxiety: A Short History*, pp. 53–54.

10 K. D. M. Snell, “The rise of living alone and loneliness in history”, *Social History*, vol. 42, nr. 1, 2017.

11 Robert D. Putnam, *Bowling Alone: The Collapse and Revival of American Community*, New York: Simon & Schuster, 2007, p. 107.

12 Snell, “The rise of living alone and loneliness in history”; John T. Cacioppo and William Patrick, *Loneliness: Human Nature and the Need for Social Connection*, New York: Norton, 2009. On the number of close friends: Miller McPherson, Lynn Smith-Lovin and Matthew E. Brashears, “Social isolation in America: Changes in core discussion networks over two decades”, *American Sociological Review*, vol. 71, nr. 3, 2006.

13 See George W. Brown and Tirril Harris, *Social Origins of Depression: A Study of Psychiatric Disorder in Women*, London: Routledge, 2012, p. 180. See also John T. Cacioppo, Louise C Hawkley and Ronald A Thisted, “Perceived social isolation makes me sad: 5-year cross-lagged analyses of loneliness and depressive symptomatology in the Chicago Health, Aging, and Social Relations Study”, *Psychology and Aging*, vol. 25, nr. 2, 2010.

14 See e.g. Junghyun Kim, Robert La Rose and Wei Peng, “Loneliness as the cause and the effect of problematic internet use: The relationship between internet use and psychological well-being”, *Cyber Psychology & Behavior*, vol. 12, nr. 4, 2009; Yasin Demir and Mustafa Kutlu, “The relationship between loneliness and depression: Mediation role of internet addiction”, *Educational Process: International Journal*, vol. 5, nr. 2, 2016.

15 For an ethnographic analysis of the diagnosis of PTSD, see Allan Young, *The Harmony of Illusions: Inventing Post-Traumatic Stress Disorder*, Princeton, NJ: Princeton University Press, 1997. For a summary of Fernando’s research, see Gaithri A. Fernando, “Assessing mental health and psychosocial status in communities exposed to traumatic events: Sri Lanka as an example”, *American Journal of Orthopsychiatry*, vol. 78, nr. 2, 2008. For the therapeutic effort in Sri Lanka, see Ethan Watters, *Crazy Like Us: The Globalization of the American Psyche*, New York: Free Press, 2011.

16 Peter Gay, *Freud:A Life of Our Time*, London: Dent,1988.

17 John Levi Martin, *The Explanation of Social Action*, Oxford; NewYork: Oxford University Press, 2011

18 See e.g. Roland Paulsen, “In the mood for obedience: Despair, cynicism, and seduction among employment service employees”, *Culture and Organization*, vol. 24, nr. 5, 2018; Roland Paulsen, “Slipping into functional stupidity – the bifocality of organizational compliance”, *Human Relations*, vol. 70, nr. 2, 2017.

19 See Lavinia Edmunds, “His master’s choice”, *Johns Hopkins Magazine,* vol. 40, nr. 2, 1988.

20 Edmunds, “His master’s choice”.

21 See Silas L. Warner, “Freud’s analysis of Horace Frink, MD: A previously unexplained therapeutic disaster”, *Journal of the American Academy of Psychoanalysis*, vol. 22, nr. 1, 1994, p. 142.

22 See Warner, “Freud’s analysis of Horace Frink, MD”, p. 144.

23 See Matthieu Ricard and Wolf Singer, “Neuroscience has a lot to learn from Buddhism”, *The Atlantic*, 17/12, 2017. For those who have nevertheless tried to create a synthesis of psychoanalysis and Buddhism, see Daisetz Teitaro Suzuki, Erich Fromm and Richard De Martino, *Zen Buddhism and Psychoanalysis*, London: Souvenir Press, 1993.

24 Elke Mühlleitner and Johannes Reichmayr, *Biographisches Lexikon der Psychoanalyse: Die Mitglieder der Psychologischen Mittwoch-Gesellschaft und der Wiener Psychoanalytischen Vereinigung*, 1902-1938, Edition diskord,

1992. English version of this quote found in William McGuire, *The Freud / Jung Letters: The Correspondence between Sigmund Freud and C. G. Jung*. Princeton: Princeton University Press, 1974, p. 485.

25 Sibylle Lacan, *A Father: Puzzle*, Cambridge: MIT Press, 2019.

26 For a discussion, see Allen Frances, *Saving Normal: An Insider's Revolt Against Out-of-Control Psychiatric Diagnosis, DSM-5, Big Pharma, and the Medicalization of Ordinary Life*, New York: William Morrow, 2013.

27 See Roland Paulsen, "Mediated psychopathy -- A critical discourse analysis of newspaper representations of aggression", *Kritike*, vol. 4, nr. 2, 2010; Jon Ronson, *The Psychopath Test: A Journey Through the Madness Industry*, New York: Riverhead Books, 2011.

28 Hannes Råstam, *Thomas Quick*, Stockholm: Ordfront, 2014, p. 89.

29 See Dan Josefsson, *Mannen som slutade ljuga berättelsen om Sture Bergwall och kvinnan som skapade Thomas Quick,* Stockholm: Lind & Co, 2013.

30 For a discussion of the psychoanalytical legacy in general, and its importance in the Quick case, see Frederick C. Crews, *Freud: The Making of an Illusion*, 2017, p. 509. See also Josefsson, *Mannen som slutade ljuga berättelsen om Sture Bergwall och kvinnan som skapade Thomas Quick*.

31 Sven-Åke Christianson, *I huvudet på en seriemördare,* Stockholm: Norstedts, 2010, p. 365, 434–435; Dan Josefsson, "Fallet Kevin. Avsnitt 1: Hemligheten, Avsnitt 2: Huvudvittnet, Avsnitt 3: Minnen", *Dokument inifrån, SVT*, 2017; Juan Flores, "Saxmordet i Hovsjö: 'går inte att bevisa vem som gjort det", *Dagens Nyheter,* 14/3, 2019.

32 Sture Bergwall, *Bara jag vet vem jag är*, Stockholm: Forum, 2016, p. 32

33 Råstam, *Thomas Quick*.

34 Bergwall, *Bara jag vet vem jag är*, p. 122.

35 Bergwall, *Bara jag vet vem jag är*, p. 120.

36 Bergwall, *Bara jag vet vem jag är*, p. 375.

37 Saul M. Kassin and Gisli H. Gudjonsson, "True crimes, false confessions", *Scientific American Mind*, vol. 16, nr. 2, 2005; Ulf Kristiansson, "Palmemordet - det hopplösa uppdraget", *Helsingborgs Dagblad*, 14/2, 2010.

38 Kassin and Gudjonsson, "True crimes, false confessions", p. 249.

10

SELF-SUSPICIONS

In the growing body of autofiction in which writers share their most personal experiences, self-reinforcing worrying takes many forms. In *Dancing in the Dark,* one of Karl-Ove Knausgård's many worries sees him plagued by fears that someone – his girlfriend, for example – might decide that he is gay. Knausgård is not attracted to men, and he is afraid of this misreading of him, of someone thinking something about him that, while not true, is difficult to rebut.

This worry becomes a worry in and of itself. Whenever homosexuality is mentioned, even if it is just on TV, he worries that he might react strangely – which he sometimes does:

> [O]ne of the characters in the British series we were following was a homosexual, and when this was mentioned or referred to I blushed. Not because I was homosexual and unable to tell her, but because she might have thought I was. And that was ironic because if I blushed whenever the word "homosexual" was mentioned she would definitely have thought I was, and the idea of that made me blush even more.

Since self-reinforcing worrying is a relatively overlooked phenomenon in Western culture, Knausgård becomes increasingly afraid that the Freudian stereotype is true the more he blushes: "In my absolutely worst hours I used to imagine that I really was homosexual."[1]

In Rachel Cusk's *A Life's Work: On Becoming a Mother*, we find a similar dynamic, this time in relation to her daughter, whose birth Cusk occasionally regrets. On coming home from hospital with her new baby, she feels "bludgeoned by tragedy." The furniture and rooms in her house remind her of a life

DOI: 10.4324/9781003514930-12

lost, and her thoughts terrify her. She experiences a "panic of confinement," an "adulterous desire" for the childfree existence she feels she has betrayed.[2]

Cusk's fears of having made a mistake simply make her worry even more. But unlike Knausgård, she directs these anxieties outwards. She worries that her baby can sense something is wrong, that the child does not like her, and therefore seeks out her father "like a plant towards a new source of light." When her daughter develops colic, she decides this must be because she lacks a mothering instinct.[3]

All sorts of *what ifs* about the way her defective inner self is affecting her daughter begin to pop up: "Is my milk polluted by its passage through my unclean self? Is it carrying messages? Is the dark turmoil of what I feel being broadcast by my daughter's cries?" She views the slightest of failings, like when she loses her patience and screams over the crib, as proof that her ambivalent mind makes her a bad mother.[4]

When *what ifs* take over in this way, the worry becomes self-fulfilling. "What if I'm gay?" and "what if I'm a bad mother?" are thoughts which, simply through being thought, are awarded a degree of truth in the individual who has learned to suspect their own self.

Thinking about what we think about is also thinking about the self. Thoughts about thoughts involve a transition from what Jean-Paul Sartre calls "the pre-reflective to the reflective," or from "cognition to metacognition," as others would put it. Thinking "I'm so sick of her crying" and then, as the next step, thinking "what if what I just thought makes me a bad mother?" charges the first thought with new meaning. Thoughts about thoughts inevitably transform the thoughts we had first.

But thoughts about thoughts do not necessarily need to take root as self-suspicions. It is possible to think "what if I'm a bad mother?" without digging any deeper into the question. What takes root as self-suspicion is determined by the culture in which we live. Thoughts around whether one's cynical thoughts reveal bad parenting can hardly be understood without the idea of parenthood as a re-birth in which the child becomes the centre of one's universe, the very pinnacle of life (something which, historically, is a recent idea).[5]

The *way* we worry is just as dependent on context as *what* we worry about. For example, the fear of being bewitched or accused of being a witch in the seventeenth century is no more a coincidence than psychiatrists seeing patients who were worried that everyone around them was part of some kind of conspiracy in the early 2000s. This fear, which in some tipped over into delusion, first began to spread after the premiere of *The Truman Show* in 1998, a film in which the main character is the subject of this exact type of conspiracy.[6]

The way that pathological worry latches onto cultural fears and stories is easy to see in some cases, but often the worry is so strange and removed from reality that it seems more like proof of individual sovereignty arising from a sick soul. The link between culture and worry in the most widespread form of *what if* – the obsessive-compulsive thought – is particularly obscure. Since obsessive-compulsive thoughts are often absurd to the point of being grotesque, it is easy to assume that they must stem from a mix of genes and chemical imbalances – that the thoughts are not social, but antisocial.

A mother who can't stop thinking about suffocating her baby? A man who avoids going into the kitchen because he is afraid he might stab his wife to death? Are these minds in disarray or souls in touch with the spirit of the age?

Territories of Risk

Those who find themselves getting caught up in anxiety may show a greater sense of discomfort than others when it comes to certain risks, but the types of risk they focus on are no different to what other people worry about. Nor is the way they try to "neutralise" – i.e. alleviate – their worry. The risks of anxiety disorder always reflect a historical worry, and this is particularly evident in relation to obsessive-compulsive thoughts.

Today, one common type of obsession is worrying about being infected by bacteria and viruses, which leads, amongst other things, to repeated handwashing as a neutralisation strategy. This obsession would have been impossible before the mid-nineteenth century, when the Hungarian doctor Ignaz Semmelweis discovered that puerperal fever was dramatically reduced when caregivers washed their hands. It likely also requires Louis Pasteur to have theorised about the possibility of something like bacteria even existing.[7]

In line with new medical discoveries, asbestos became the subject of many obsessive-compulsive thoughts in the 1970s, and during the 1980s and 90s, there were many cases of HIV-related compulsions. In *The Boy Who Couldn't Stop Washing*, the American psychiatrist Judith Rapoport writes that a third of her obsessive-compulsive patients in 1989 were preoccupied with HIV and aids. These obsessive-compulsive thoughts were part of a wider worry – a worry which, in their obsessive-compulsive thoughts, took on a more concrete form.[8]

From time to time, obsessions will take root in incredibly local risk profiles. An example of this, *koro*, stems from the risk that a person's sex organs might shrivel away or recede into the body. This obsession, which is more common among men and has periodically been widespread on the island of Hainan Dao in the South China Sea, can lead to repeated measurement of penis length as a neutralisation strategy. As many have remarked, *koro* reflects the belief that various parts of the body (including the breasts, nose, and tongue) can retract, something considered to be life-threatening. These beliefs, which have survived in certain parts of southern China, also reflect a general reluctance to talk about sexuality.[9]

In every society, there are what I like to call *territories of risk* in which worry thrives. Over the following pages, I will analyse four contemporary territories of risk in which the culturally conditioned anxiety towards "the inner self" is particularly tangible: *religion, sexuality, aggression,* and *relationships.* As the attentive reader will no doubt have noticed, I have already discussed several religious and sexual sources of concern. This is not because religion and sexuality necessarily involve danger but because these are areas which, for a variety of historical reasons, attract worry in the same way we perceive terrorism to be a greater danger to us than drowning in the bathtub. Studying the why means not just understanding individual concerns in their societal context. It also means understanding society through the individual's concerns.

Territory of Risk 1: Religion

One of the first people to devote a medical study to obsessive-compulsive disorder was the French doctor Legrand du Saulle. In *La folie du doute* from 1875, du Saulle describes what he calls the madness of doubt. He takes pains to point out that patients suffering from this affliction do not possess the conviction of delusion. They know that what they are worried about is unlikely, and yet they cannot shake their concerns:

> These strange and unhappy patients are fully aware of their condition. They assess the situation in which they find themselves with striking clarity and lament it with even greater bitterness... they openly confess that their fears are absurd, and they say: "I know there is no sense in any of this, but it still preoccupies me, and I cannot help it."[10]

As many have since noted, "madness of doubt" is a misleading term, because even du Saulle's patients wanted to be rid of their doubts. In reality, they suffered more from a "madness of assurance," and one expression of this was that they were constantly seeking du Saulle's comforting words. The source of their worry was almost exclusively failings in their Christian faith.

What du Saulle calls *les scrupules religieux* – religious scruples – took many strange forms. One young woman lamented that she had laughed during her first church service, that she had not been in a state of grace, and that she had kept back sins from her confessor. She fretted over what sacrilege really was, and whether she was guilty of it. Only ever eating lean meals was one of several punishments she subjected herself to.

Though du Saulle assured her that she had not sinned, her doubts remained. She became so afraid that she would not have time to confess before she took her last breath that she kept vigil at night in order to avoid the risk of dying in her sleep. This – remembering, immediately after confession, something one should have brought up – appeared in several of du Saulle's patient notes. Even more common was the worry of not having prayed well enough.[11]

A forty-five-year-old man wrote in a letter that even as a child, he'd had the sense that his prayers didn't measure up:

> I found myself starting over three or four times; I often fell asleep on my knees in the evening, and stayed like that all night. Since I wasn't always entirely honest in my confessions, it seemed to me that I hadn't accounted for all of my sins, and I accused myself of things I hadn't done.

From this doubt, he would develop a number of obsessive-compulsive thoughts that du Saulle, in his own words, cured with bromine, cold baths, and exercise.[12]

Like the doctor Jean-Étienne Esquirol and the "monomania" that became a fashionable diagnosis in nineteenth-century France, du Saulle considered his "madness of doubt" a "pathology of intelligence." Those affected were not stupid; they all possessed a solid intellect. Like most psychiatrists, however, he provided no institutional analysis of why Christianity might foster doubt. Du Saulle was likely unaware that even the theologically versed could suffer these crises of conscience.

The most widely discussed example of this is Martin Luther, who, in his younger years, was racked with doubt with regards to the inadequacy of his prayers. Luther also struggled with what psychiatrists have since described as obsessive-compulsive thoughts about the Devil's behind and cursing God and Jesus. Others around him – his confessor, for example – were irritated by his detailed confessions because he had no sins to confess. His self-accusations simply did not cease.[13]

One of the first Christians to analyse the problem in more psychological terms was the Anglican bishop John Moore, who in 1691 wrote a short text about what he termed "religious melancholy." Moore had noticed that "unhappy persons" could have "naughty, and sometimes blasphemous thoughts start in their minds, while they are exercised in the worship of God, which makes them ready to charge themselves with the sin against the Holy Ghost."[14]

Moore argued, however, that these thoughts had nothing to do with blasphemy because "they are mostly good people, who are exercised with them," whereas "bad men... rarely know anything of these kind of thoughts." His advice was therefore to simply let them happen: "When you find these thoughts creeping upon you, be not mightily dejected ... Neither violently struggle with them; since experience doth teach that they increase and swell by vehement opposition."[15]

Obsessive-compulsive thoughts involving religion – also known as *scrupulosity* – are not unique to Christians; they have been documented in all major religions. As a rule, those affected tend to be the most devout, and the more devout they are, the harder they find it to simply accept their intrusive thoughts. Since the thought is seen as being linked to who they are (an idea that can also take root among Buddhists, despite so much in their religion coming from the opposite starting point) the thought has to be counteracted, at which point – as Moore pointed out – it grows. For someone who is not religious, or who is religious but attaches less weight to the purity of thoughts, it is much easier to allow words such as "I hate God" to drift through their mind, and they feel no need to subject themselves to the impossible task of not thinking about a white bear.

Unsurprisingly, the more religious a country is, the more likely a person is to suffer from religious obsessive-compulsive thoughts. While American studies have shown that between five and ten percent of patients with OCD are preoccupied with religious themes, studies from more devout countries like Saudi Arabia and Egypt show figures of fifty and sixty percent respectively. In all likelihood, the total share of religious obsessive-compulsive thoughts is even higher there because the devout have communities other than psychiatry to turn to. Among Muslims, obsessive-compulsive thoughts can fall under the banner of something known as "satanic whispering" (*Al-Waswas* in Arabic). These people then become part of a religious model of explanation that replaces the diagnostic and treatment apparatus of western medicine.[16]

Worry, in all its expressions, is fraught with cultural fears. Religion need not become a territory of risk for an individual – obsessive-compulsive thoughts of a religious nature seem relatively unusual among Hindus, for example. It is also possible to remain alert to sins, immorality, impurity and blasphemy without allowing the worry of doing wrong to grow into a compulsion. The problem arises when the individual believes that life (and the afterlife) is determined by the slightest deviation – even if this is in the form of a thought.

Sometimes this may be the result of an inverted interpretation of a particular teaching, but religions can also be more or less encouraging depending on how harshly deviation is condemned. In this respect, there is definitely something in Max Weber's analysis of Calvinism – with its doctrine of predestination – as being particularly conducive to doubt. According to this doctrine, not only is there a clear line between the chosen and the lost, but God has already decided which group every single person belongs to, and the only way to still one's doubts is through "restless activity," "inner-worldly asceticism," "conscientiousness" and other traits that would also be found in any diagnostic manual for obsessive-compulsive disorder.[17]

Today, there are those who argue that devout Protestants are most at risk of religious obsessive-compulsive thoughts, while others claim that Protestantism's emphasis on *sola fide* – the idea that salvation is found in "faith alone" – is a good foundation for managing uncertainty and resisting neutralisations.[18]

Territory of Risk 2: Sexuality

Sexuality is, perhaps, the territory of risk that most closely corresponds to religion within secular society. There are few other areas in which a person can become quite so impure, lost and condemned. The worry does not need to be linked to shame – it could take root in the fear of being ostracised, of not being true to one's self and of living a false life. In Knausgård's budding obsession with the idea that, deep down, he might actually be gay – the same obsessive thought Daniel suffered from in the first chapter of this book – we can see the Freudian idea of a psychological resistance so strong that sexual desire is unable to make itself known. As we will see, this can go both ways: homosexual people can also worry that, deep down, they are actually heterosexual. And this same *deep down* can also apply to a person's lack of feelings, to the fear that they don't really love their partner, despite on a conscious level understanding that they do.

Present here is the fear of *living inauthentically*, of denying something within us. Sometimes, however, this anxiety can be compounded by something else: the idea that the sexuality within us is disgusting or evil. The fear of *the perverse* raises the stakes because the thing we might be denying is seen as terrible.[19]

When Isaac first began to worry that he was gay during his teens, he couldn't imagine anything worse. Unlike Knausgård, Isaac was plagued by both disgust and shame, as well as a fear of being teased by his classmates. His worry was homophobic. Not only did he worry about inauthenticity, he also saw homosexuality as a perversion.

If he felt aroused by an attractive girl in his class, he would quickly decide that it was actually the boy sitting beside her that he was attracted to. If he saw an attractive man at the gym, he would turn his attention to his own body in an attempt to check whether he felt even the slightest hint of sexual arousal. Could he feel the tingling that might be the first sign of an erection? By focusing all his attention on his crotch, it wasn't hard to sensitise the area and feel *something*. What he couldn't work out was whether that *something* was also a sign of sexual attraction.

For a couple of years, Isaac was depressed. He came home, lay down on his bed, and contemplated suicide. In his head, he pictured nightmare scenarios in which his friends discovered the truth and outed him as a closet gay. The turning point came when Isaac learned that a couple of his friends were actually gay themselves. In an instant, it no longer mattered whether he was teased or hung out to dry. Isaac believes that his obsessive thoughts about whether he was gay disappeared because he stopped seeing homosexuality as "the worst thing."

But what Isaac's story highlights is just how easy it is to switch the object of our anxiety. With a sufficiently strong aversion to risk, a new looming catastrophe will present itself soon enough – and sometimes this will be a catastrophe we never thought possible.

In Isaac's case, he soon became increasingly obsessed with bestiality as "the worst thing." For as long as he could remember, he had loved animals, and the very thought of someone taking advantage of an innocent creature made him sick. Didn't it?

He began to feel uncomfortable the minute he saw a cat or a dog walk by. A wagging tail was all it took for him to start testing himself in order to neutralise the thought. Was he attracted to the animal? He forced himself to look at the dog's anus and tried to imagine having sex with it. Was he attracted to it? He had just thought about it, so of course he must be. "Why in the world," he asked himself, "should looking at a dog or cat on the streets lead me to stare at their private parts or trigger these thoughts about having sex with them, unless that is what I really want?"[20]

Unwelcome, intrusive thoughts about sexual or violent themes represent the most common type of compulsion today – more common than excessive cleaning. In the general surveys that have been carried out, the results are relatively unambiguous in showing that almost all (ninety-four percent, to be precise) respondents occasionally have intrusive thoughts of some kind. Not necessarily about bestiality, but about some sort of topic that they perceive to be disgusting, frightening, or anxiety-provoking. The compulsion does not derive from the thought itself, however. The problem arises from the desire to get rid of the thought.[21]

One of the most vibrant depictions of this issue can be found in Rose Bretécher's book *Pure*, the title of which alludes to the idea of an obsessive-compulsive disorder that is "pure" in the sense that it only results in compulsive mental rituals. The first time an image "flickered" through her mind, she was only a child, just fourteen years of age, and yet the thought immediately took root.

"I mouthed the words slowly to the dark, slamming my hands against my mouth, 'What if I'm a paedo?'"[22]

For the next decade, she would torture herself with this very question from morning until night, all the while managing to live a normal teenage life centred on having fun and meeting boys. "*Am I a paedophile? Am I a paedophile? Am I a paedophile?*" After a while, she also developed a fear that she might have abused someone as a child, an assault she had repressed, but which, through self-interrogation, she tried to get to the bottom of:

Did I commit paedophilia when I was a kid?
Will I ever do it again?
Will the children remember what I did and tell the police?
Will I get taken away from my family and locked up?
Will my picture be in the paper?
How could I have done those things?
...
No.
No.
No.
It disgusts me.
I'd rather die.
I could never.
I would never.
I have never.[23]

Also present in her self-interrogation is a kind of double punishment, when on yet another metalevel, she accuses herself of being too preoccupied with the idea:

Am I enjoying these thoughts?
No.
No.
No.
Then why can't I stop thinking them?
What do they mean?
They must mean something.[24]

With a great deal of insight, Bretécher reflects on the questions' psychoanalytical framing and the way she identifies with the thoughts: "I'd always presumed that my thoughts spoke from some deep, unconscious part of me, like they were some repressed Freudian yearning trying to breach the surface. I'd always thought that I *was* my thoughts."[25]

As a modern territory of risk, however, sexuality cannot be explained by Freud alone. Sociologists have long been investigating how sexuality could have been elevated to a blueprint for who we are. After all, discovering a sexual desire is not like discovering a new type of music; engaging in sexual behaviour carries much greater meaning than trying out a new sport. Sexuality wants to get at our very essence, and its claims stretch right to the heart of the self. To some extent, everyone – whether compulsively or not – feels compelled to study, dissect and confess to this sexuality.[26]

What is new here is not that sexuality is regulated by society – even in the most permissive of cultures, there is some form of social regulation. What is new is that this regulation takes place through the self to such a high degree.

In pre-industrial Europe, there was an extensive list of sexual practices that were considered sinful. But sin is and always will be something one *does*, rather than *is*. With the idea of a distinct "sexuality" (a concept that, in its current meaning, first appeared in both Swedish and English in the late nineteenth century), a shift took place. This shift can be traced back to the origins of sexology at the turn of the previous century.

Driven by the growing interest of nation-states in managing the risks of heredity, prostitution, and venereal disease, the "science of sexuality" began to emerge. This science quickly out-competed the various sins with its medical categories of physical and mental illness (fetishism, sadomasochism, necrophilia and zoophilia, to name a few early examples), several of which would later be de-pathologised. The British sociologist Jeffrey Weeks summarises this development as follows: "Sexology was simultaneously inventing and exploring a new continent of knowledge, assigning thereby a new significance to the 'sexual'."[27]

In his historical analysis of western sexuality, Michel Foucault estimates that no society has ever created so many sexual categories in such a short period. Since the emergence of sexology, sexuality has not been repressed; "it may well be that we talk about sex more than anything else," writes Foucault, one of many hard-to-prove hypotheses in his work. There is every likelihood that Isaac would have struggled to worry about unwittingly harbouring zoophilia within him before the German psychiatrist Richard von Krafft-Ebing coined the concept in 1886, with the publication of his influential work *Psychopathia Sexualis*. In the same vein, Bretécher would have struggled to interrogate herself were it not for another of his diagnoses: *paedophilia erotica*.[28]

The fact that obsessive thoughts revolving around paedophilia seem more common than, say, zoophilia – so common that they have been given their own acronym, paedophilia-themed OCD, or P-OCD – can be partly explained by the fact that paedophilia represents an exceptionally severe form of assault. But paedophilia also holds a unique position in our culture. As a symbol of pure evil, it has, since the 1980s, become increasingly popular as a theme in both literature and film. Sexual assaults of children have also gained news traction, and the more violent and twisted the details (networks of paedophiles, satanic rituals, famous people), the more these cases are reported. As a result, the idea of the paedophile as an ever-present risk has been cultivated for decades. The paradoxical result is what the sociologist Frank Furedi describes as the *normalisation* of paedophilia.[29]

In a study in which participants were asked to interpret a photograph of a man hugging a child, the majority said that the image depicted a paedophile rather than a loving father. Furedi argues that warnings and rules intended to counteract paedophilia all contribute to this normalisation. One much-debated phenomenon are the so-called "no-touch" rules originating in the United Kingdom. Implemented in nurseries, schools, and youth sports clubs, teachers are banned from touching children. Through these rules, simple acts like giving a comforting hug or correcting a movement in gymnastics have become increasingly complicated, resulting in absurd situations – union representatives advising teachers not to apply sun cream to their students' faces during a heatwave, for example, as it may arouse suspision.[30]

The authors of a study into the ways teachers deal with this decline in trust found that many respondents were "fearful of being seen as physically or sexually abusive. Many behaved as though they did not trust themselves ... they did not trust others (adults and children) to judge their actions as innocent and appropriate."[31]

As Furedi writes, this means that adults are forced to act as though they do not deserve trust. The basest, most grotesque of acts, "the unthinkable," therefore become remarkably present in the way we view others – and in how we imagine other people view us. Instead of trusting others, guilty until proven innocent becomes the norm. Add to this a little Freudian self-suspicion, and Bretécher's compulsive thoughts suddenly seem much less exotic.[32]

Territory of Risk 3: Aggression

Just as the conscious self can repress sexuality, we know – from Dr. Jekyll and Mr. Hyde, as well as proverbs such as "still waters run deep" – that aggression can also be stowed away in the filing cabinet of our subconscious. When this happens, the aggression risks being warped and perverted into something monstrous. There are cases, for example, of people murdering in their sleep.

One person who knows a little about this is Maria. When I meet her, her hands are red and chapped. She washes them frequently, ideally in hot water.

"I've had periods where I've scalded myself all over, because I told myself that it's like doing the dishes: the hotter the water, the cleaner the plates will be. For a while, I kept dropping things, almost like I'd lost my grip. I think I must have damaged the nerves by scalding myself so much."

Maria is less afraid of catching something herself than she is of passing on some sort of disease – HIV, aids, hepatitis – to the people around her. She is afraid of causing harm to others in general. No risk seems too small. In her last job, she was a personal assistant to a woman with paralysis. The risks were endless. *What if* after *what if* stacked up in her mind.

What if I break my duty of confidentiality and tell someone about her? What if I forget to give her the medication she needs?

What if I accidentally suffocate her while I'm lifting her into bed?

What if I forget to put the side of her bed up, and she falls and breaks her back?

What if I forget to strap her into her wheelchair, and she falls out and hits her head and cracks her skull?

What if I spill poison in her water bottle?

What if I touch her inappropriately while I'm washing her?

What if she swallows some of the shampoo and it poisons her?

These thoughts made her wonder whether she wasn't a psychopath, deep down.

During a shower one day, the soap ran into the woman's mouth and she licked her lips and swallowed. Maria's heart immediately started racing. She fainted.

When she woke up, she was on the bathroom floor. Above her, the woman was still lying on the shower trolley, frail and helpless. Maria's first thought was: what if I tried to kill her when I lost consciousness?

The event simply reinforced her fears.

"I'm afraid of all sorts of unconscious states. Even psychosis. That has to be the worst thing that can happen to a person: transforming into something else."

Right now, Maria has real trouble spending time with her nieces and nephews. Ahead of every visit, she has to weigh up the guilt she would feel if she happened to kill them against her desire to be around them.

"I could find a pillow and smother them, I could decide to grab a knife and stab them to death. All in my sleep, of course. It could happen without me being conscious of it."

"Have you told your siblings about these thoughts?" I ask.

"I don't think I've ever come out and said 'I'm afraid I'll kill your kids.' I wouldn't dare."

Even though the children are oblivious to her fears, it upsets her to think that her obsessive thoughts have seeped into her relationship with them.

"I've been in therapy for fourteen years, and it hasn't helped."

"Doesn't it help to know that the thoughts themselves are harmless?"

"Yeah, but the thing is that I worry about things that could happen. And all the thoughts I have could happen."

Maria knows that none of the scenarios she imagines are *likely*, but the fact that they *could* happen is enough. It may even be that she could run over someone in an unconscious state and then forget all about it.

"I once saw on the local news that someone had been run over outside the supermarket, and I got it into my head that I was the one who'd done it. But it has to be realistic. For something like that to take root, it has to be nearby. There have been several occasions where I've come close to calling the police to confess."

"Because you thought you really had done it?"

"No, not really. I guess what I wanted was for them to tell me I didn't. But the problem is that I'm not sure about anything, so if they asked me, do you know where you were at seven o'clock that day, I'd say: no? No, well, it could have been you, then. Yes!"

She laughs.

"Reporting myself probably isn't the best idea."

The stamp of shame inherent in obsessive thoughts – celebrities often talk about their bipolar disorder, drug addiction or depression, but so far no one has confessed to having obsessive thoughts about harming others – encourages reflection. We frequently read about people who really are paedophiles, child killers, and psychopaths, but the majority of us have never heard of anyone who plagues themselves with thoughts that, deep down, they belong to one of those categories.

There are plenty of stories about the small number of people who really do harm others, but we lack any real understanding of the vast majority who harm themselves.

The idea that thoughts of this kind are harmless is only partly true. We don't need to turn to the team around the "serial killer" Thomas Quick to see that imaginative interpretations of thoughts and their possible meanings can be shared by people who are, strictly speaking, "healthy."

To say "I can't stop thinking that I might want to strangle my son" naturally puts the recipient of the message in a tight spot. Is it really responsible to try to dissect the semantics behind "can't stop thinking" and "want to strangle," or is it better to calmly move towards the door and, with your hand behind your back, call the police?

In this hypothetical situation, we catch a glimpse of the cultural aversion to risk that makes obsessive thoughts about violence so potentially catastrophic. Though it is usually a good idea to share one's problems with someone else, it can also have devastating consequences.

According to Bill Blundell, a psychotherapist specialising in obsessive-compulsive disorder in children, things sometimes go wrong when high school students tell their friends about their obsessive thoughts. Their friends tend to "freak out, it spreads like wildfire, and the teenager becomes an outcast."[33]

The writer Olivia Loving knows all about this. Loving had long been irritated that obsessive-compulsive disorders relating to sexuality and violence were practically unknown to the majority of people, despite them being among the most common. She herself had avoided knives for several years, terrified that she might stab her mother to death. Her obsessive thoughts about potentially assaulting children began when she was just thirteen, and when she was given the opportunity to write anonymously about her problems in the school paper, the counsellor sent a report of concern to her teachers and the principal. Because the counsellor concluded that her thoughts had nothing to do with OCD, she was suspended from school for being a "threat to the other students."[34]

Loving calls this the "darker side of OCD": Living in a culture in which it is taboo to talk about one's obsessive thoughts, and where people are much too keen to push the emergency button the minute anything seems suspicious. Despite the therapeutic community recommending – for good reason – that people seek professional help as soon as they can, this can complicate matters.

When Samuel watched the violent film *City of God* with his wife, he began to imagine slicing her stomach open with a knife. His first reaction was to go to their bedroom and curl up in the foetal position. As he lay there, he tried to make the violent images go away, but they just grew stronger and stronger. After a long period of angst and confusion, he eventually sought help from a psychotherapist. But this professional help was no help at all. Samuel's therapist belonged to the Freudian school, and he got the impression that even she was afraid of his thoughts.

"I think, in a way, she was kind of scared of what I was seeing – you know, the images that I was having of, you know, the killing, the raping, the maiming. And I kind of got that she may think that I would be a danger."

After four visits, she stopped returning his calls.[35]

Fred Penzel, an American researcher in clinical psychology, has written about the trouble some new mothers find themselves getting into. One woman who eventually ended up in his care had been reported to social services by her third therapist, after sharing her worries about harming her child. Another patient had to call Penzel from the maternity ward, having had her child taken from her shortly after birth. She had attempted to tell the staff about her obsessive thoughts, but all they seemed to hear was "harm my child."[36]

Thoughts of harming one's child are such a common part of postnatal depression that they are occasionally listed as one of the key diagnostic criteria. In one study, for example, forty-one percent of mothers with postnatal depression reported that they were struggling with thoughts about harming their baby, and yet surprisingly few people are aware of this. With this in mind, the courtroom scenarios that sometimes form part of these obsessive thoughts, with the person worrying about having their child taken away from them and eventually ending up on the front pages, suddenly seem much less fantastical.[37]

Catastrophes such as these may be caused by someone acting with the best of intentions. Interpreting a person's thoughts as an indication of inner will has, through a long series of material and cultural societal transformations, become commonplace. But distinguishing between those who are unusually cautious and those who are unusually aggressive is not particularly hard. Psychotherapists typically ask not only what their patients are *thinking* about, but how they *feel* about murdering their child, and whether they have previously acted violently. Our emotions do not define who we are, but they do give a better indication of what is going on inside us than our thoughts.[38]

None of this is particularly advanced. What these misunderstandings demonstrate is that it seems possible to live in the most violence-obsessed culture in history while also being historically ignorant of what real violence is like. Graphic depictions of violence that previous generations would have had difficulty processing or even enduring now attract more readers and viewers than any other genre.

Within literature, crime fiction dominates sales. It is often argued that the genre shines a light on the dark sides of life and that it therefore plays a socially critical function, but the few studies that have been carried out in this area have emphatically rejected this notion. The killers we read about or watch on film bear very little resemblance to real-life killers, and since murder has become so tired a trope, the stories we consume have become increasingly removed from reality as writers and filmmakers seek the spectacular.[39]

While it is difficult to argue that violent entertainment creates aggressive individuals, there is a real consensus among researchers that it does encourage a so-called "mean world syndrome." We believe that the world is more violent than it really is, and therefore also develop a paranoid notion that violence could be lurking in anyone. The repetitive nature of crime novels – "who is the killer?" – takes on a sort of ghostly parallel life. In these circumstances, even the slightest indication that someone could, possibly, turn violent is enough for suspicion to take root – or self-suspicion, for that matter.[40]

But thinking violent thoughts is something everyone does, sometimes with the support of our emotions. Driving during rush hour is enough for "homicidal impulses" to raise their heads, for example. The idea that a person's panicked fear of murdering their own child would actually lead to them doing so is an impossibility. Lee Bauer, a clinical psychologist who regularly treats patients with obsessive thoughts about murdering their own children, describes in detail what happens when genuinely homicidal parents commit infanticide. If it isn't simply a cold-blooded way of getting rid of a problem individual, then uncontrollable rage, drug-related aggression or certain types of hallucination are all warning signs that should be taken seriously. One woman suffering from postnatal psychosis saw, for example, yellow smoke coming from her baby's nostrils, something she interpreted as a sign that the baby came from the devil. She concluded that it would be best to throw the baby in the rubbish bin, where her husband later found the infant.[41]

To the extent that any scientific "markers" for violence can be found, they are all incredibly simple – verging on trivial. But the violence we consume as part of popular culture is shrouded in an aura of mystery. Dr. Jekyll and Mr. Hyde are the prototypes here, if not as a cat-and-mouse game between the conscious and the subconscious, then between the killer and his surroundings.

The idea of an innate violence in certain individuals has an even longer history than that of die-cast sexuality. For over 250 years, medical science has attempted to determine how to recognise a violent "nature." The eighteenth-century doctor Franz Joseph Gall believed he could see all manner of characteristics in the shape of the human skull, and his phrenological theories were updated in the nineteenth century by Cesare Lombroso, one of the founders of criminology – and a pioneer of race biology. Lombroso gave huge weight to the size and shape of the cranium, and he also showed that born criminals – so-called *delinquente nato* – lacked the "higher nervous centres" that distinguished civilised man from the savage. In his view, those who were violent lived closer to nature than their law-abiding counterparts, and should therefore be considered more animal than human.[42]

Much of this research lives on today, albeit in a form less focused on the shape of the skull and more on the brain and our genes. In his much-discussed book, *The Anatomy of Violence*, the psychologist Adrian Raine introduces the "Lombroso Program" as a thought experiment in which all men are scanned upon turning eighteen, in order to see which of them possess the brain of a killer.

Raine is refreshingly open about the fact that he believes Lombroso has been treated unfairly by posterity. He concedes that science has found nothing but minor correlations for what may be biological markers of violence, but like anyone with a field of research to defend, he remains convinced that we will get there eventually – providing the research funding remains in place. Even now, Raine argues, we can predict which infants are at risk of becoming violent in later life.[43]

Raine and others involved in the research of biological causes of violence suggest a disposition model in which a person can only ever be "predisposed" to violence, never "pre-determined." The idea is that "triggering" factors in a person's surroundings will make some individuals more violent than others. This theory has, to an extent, calmed the trench warfare between "nature and nurture" within the field of behavioural science, but it has also reinforced the idea of an inner nature that *precedes* the social – a mechanist "nature + environment = individual" model in which the only choice a person may have left is whether to affirm or contest the hand fate has dealt them. This idea was also present in the works of Marquis de Sade who, unsurprisingly, sang the praises of following one's nature. Several centuries later, when Josef Fritzl was discovered to have imprisoned, abused and raped his own daughter over a period of twenty-four years, he explained – well aware of the disposition model – that his actions had, in fact, been restrained, given he was a "born rapist."[44]

In an attempt to refute the idea that innate violence would give the less conscientious of us a carte blanche to commit all sorts of atrocities, Raine has been open about the fact that he too shares the abnormal brain structure and low resting heart rate of a serial killer. This type of thesis-driven confession attracted real media interest when the neuroscientist James Fallon wrote a book about the chance discovery that his own brain structure was identical to that seen in psychopaths. In his book, Fallon writes about how – high on his discovery – he realised that he had actually behaved like a psychopath on many occasions, with a thirst for revenge, secret love affairs, constant lies and a life-long lack of warmth in his family relations. Like Raine, Fallon had a field of research to defend, and unfortunately he also failed to address whether it was even possible to say what a brain scan of psychopathy even looked like – other than on an extremely weak correlation basis.[45]

As I have suggested elsewhere, there is good reason to view the idea of innate psychopathy as inherently psychopathic, because it presupposes psychopathy's mechanist view of humanity. By regarding a psychopath as a *thing*, a broken machine that cannot be fixed (psychopaths are consistently described as being immune to therapy), we show as little empathy for the psychopath as the psychopath is assumed to show to the world around them. That there is variation in whether people are guilty of a "grandiose sense of self-worth," "lack of remorse or guilt," "irresponsibility," "many short-term relationships," and the other twenty criteria used in diagnosis of psychopathy is nevertheless likely. Also likely is that those who exhibit the least evidence of psychopathic traits are those who will worry most that, deep down, they are psychopaths.[46]

Territory of Risk 4: Relationships

"An unhappy day can be used by your brain as evidence that your obsession is true, but so can happiness. In my experience the very act of laughing can trigger an instantaneous obsessive question: am I really happy?"

Bretécher's awareness of the fluctuating nature of happiness indicates a worry that, at first glance, seems fundamentally different to her self-accusations regarding her sexual orientation. To stop in the middle of a great moment to question whether you really are happy, deep down, seems like a luxury. As a question, "Am I really *really* happy now?" sounds almost provocative.

But the object of a person's worry does not determine its strength. Assessing one's happiness is an effective way of distancing oneself from the moment and becoming unhappy. A particularly thorny question on this theme is: *is this really the right relationship for me?*

This question has become so commonplace that it has actually given rise to its own field of research within the wider umbrella of OCD research. Relationship-obsessive compulsive disorder, or R-OCD, takes "what if this is wrong?" as a recurring obsessive thought. In one of the first articles on the concept, two cases are presented in detail. David, a thirty-two-year-old consultant, describes his problem as follows:

> I've been in a relationship for a year, but I can't stop thinking about whether this is the right relationship for me. I see other women on the street or on Facebook and I can't stop thinking whether I will be happier with them, or feel more in love with them. I ask my friends what they think. I check what I feel for her over and over again, whether I remember her face, whether I think about her enough. I know I love my partner, but I have to check and recheck. I feel depressed.[47]

Jane, a twenty-eight-year-old academic, has more specific concerns on the same theme:

> I love my partner, I know I can't live without him, but I can't stop thinking about his body. He does not have the right body proportions. I know I love him, and I know these thoughts are not rational, he looks good. I hate myself for having these thoughts, I don't think looks are all that important in a relationship, but I just can't get it out of my head. The fact that I look at other men also drives me crazy. I feel I can't marry him like this.[48]

It would be difficult to classify these musings as pathological, but the intensity and space such thoughts take up may well excuse widening the psychiatric diagnosis further.

When Laura was asked by her therapist to describe her flow of thoughts over the course of one day, she felt exhausted after three hours of dwelling on her relationship. In the following passage, she offers up a number of questions about whether she is "actually" heterosexual – questions of the type we have already seen – but the overshadowing concern is something else entirely:

> Who do I want to be with? What if she isn't the right person? What if I should be with a guy? But, wait, I have been with guys… How did I feel? Is that who I see myself with? Was it different from this? Should I try again? It's expected of me. How should I feel? What if I doubt this and can't commit? Does this feel right? Am I sexually attracted? But emotional means more to me…but you just doubted sexually so what about

> that?... What makes me happy? Should I move or try to go out more? No but that's not who I am, but who am I? But wait, I want to be with her but do I need to explore myself more before committing? How do I know? I want to be with her. I had never acted this way with anyone else: losing track of time or had 7 hours feel like 1, sharing as much as I did with someone, yet my brain kept fighting me! I wasn't used to this feeling. Comfort, calm, connection, and oh wait love–no, never! With a girl...was this right? Did I really feel this way? What if I am wrong?[49]

Laura estimates that roughly ninety-five percent of her day is dominated by this kind of back and forth.

And yet the question remains: don't we all think along these lines at regular intervals? In what way could these thoughts have something in common with the torment of whether you want to suffocate your child, or whether you're actually a paedophile? While the self-help books give little in the way of advice for people attempting to make sense of these questions, they are packed full of information for those who are wondering whether their relationship is "the right one." From a vast pool of titles, we can find books such as:

Should I Stay or Should I Go?
A Guide to Knowing if Your Relationship
Can – and Should – Be Saved

Too Good to Leave, Too Bad to Stay
A Step-by-Step Guide to Help You Decide Whether to Stay In
or Get Out of Your Relationship

Should I Try to Work It Out?
A Guidebook for Individuals and Couples at the Crossroads
of Divorce

What these books want to help us understand is whether there is any point in giving a relationship another chance. How to make the relationship work going forward opens up another world of self-help books, with the titles numbering in the thousands.

Asking whether we are right for our partner seems perfectly normal. Among people with generalized anxiety disorder, there is even evidence that the most widespread worry is about family and interpersonal issues. But that isn't to say that it is something natural or existentially inevitable. Just a few hundred years ago, many of these questions would have seemed incomprehensible. One reason for this is that a person's choice of partner was, for a long time, transactional, and the decision was made through collective negotiation. Historically, it was almost never down to the two individuals alone.[50]

Deciding to end a relationship is also relatively new. In the nineteenth century, just 15,000 divorces were granted in Sweden, a figure lower than the number granted in a single year now. It wasn't until 1915 that it became possible to divorce for no other reason than "fundamental incompatibility" here. In Germany and France, it would be the mid-70s before the law was liberalised in this way, and in many countries – India, for example – laws and standards continue to function as a real brake on those considering divorce.[51]

Emotions have always existed, but we have historically – for better or worse – given little weight to them. The concerned parties have long attached importance to the spouses' affection for each other, but there is plenty to suggest that as late as the nineteenth century marriage remained a largely loveless affair. Not that the dream of a loving duality was new, but because marriage fulfilled other – not least financial – functions.[52]

Newest is the imagined dividing line between actual and illusory emotions. On this point, the similarity with the worry of "repressed desire" is clear, but where religion and science have for centuries fuelled the fear of *forbidden lust*, the fears in a sexually liberal consumer society also focus on *insufficient lust.*

Mats is afraid that, deep down, he doesn't feel enough. Looks-wise, with his greyish-blue eyes, his defined jaw, and curly blond hair, he would probably have plenty of choice if he uploaded his picture to a dating site. But Mats is already in a relationship, and that is precisely what he cannot make sense of: whether he is doing the right thing by shutting down the counterfactual possibility of endless passion in order to be in that relationship.

When Mats was a child, he suffered from more pronounced compulsions. It started with him connecting his thoughts to spatial boundaries. If he crossed a threshold and thought that his family was going to die in a horrible accident, he had to back up and "think back" the thought. This neutralisation strategy was tricky to get just right, and he occasionally found himself standing in doorways at both school and at home.

When he got to high school, his obsessive thoughts became more intense, with fears of infection – particularly those spread through needles. If he sat down on a bench outside, he might decide to search the entire park for discarded drug users' needles. Through this fear of needles, he became afraid of himself. His mother realised that something was wrong, and Mats went through exposure therapy, where he learned to challenge his anxieties.

The fact that his thoughts would eventually encroach on his relationship isn't so strange. Mats realised from an early age that he was a romantic, that reciprocated love was more important to him than for many others his age. While his friends were busy preparing for their next training camp or LAN party, Mats was longing to be an adult and find the love of his life.

Things didn't work out how he imagined.

"Even before I met my partner, I spent a lot of time thinking about relationships. Is this right? Am I really in love, or do I just want to be in love? Is it morally right to be with someone even though I have so many doubts?"

Some sociologists have argued that these questions derive from late modernity's cult of authentic living. But authenticity is a complex concept. In this context, it doesn't relate to Martin Heidegger's figure living with full knowledge of death, nor Jean-Paul Sartre's non-reflexive combatant, realising his freedom and never blaming any failures on his "nature." The authenticity referred to here is more about seeking an inner nature – an inner nature that a person can use to offload decisions and shape the rest of their life around. Only once the emotional "core" – am I really in love? – has been separated from the obscuring tissue of this inner self can life take its course.[53]

As Mats points out, this is not necessarily a case of hedonistic self-examination. He has such a great sense of responsibility towards his partner that – simply because of his doubts – he also feels guilty, almost as though he has cheated on her. Doesn't she have the right to live with someone who actually knows what he wants?

"I've told her some of this, and it never ends very well, it obviously causes upset. And it's painful, when it's about relationships in my own life. So when I realised that these thoughts were taking up all my waking time, I had to do something about it. I started having therapy again. But during that time, I began doubting whether it was really a case of obsessive thoughts. I started wondering: who am I?"

Not long later, Mats' partner got pregnant.

"The therapy was pretty weird, because I started with my doubts about our relationship. Then I found out about the pregnancy and everything, so that was pretty ... Things got much more serious then, because the whole family thing is a life-long commitment. Then it's like, more than imagining you staying together a few months."

From the tidal wave of self-help books on the theme of *should I stay or should I go*, several would likely have pushed Mats in the direction of breaking up with his partner. Obsession or not, doubt and romance barely go hand in hand. And yet: How can any thinking person who has seen a deep love affair transform into a marital balance of terror and then something even more unpleasant do anything but doubt?

What patients with various anxiety disorders occasionally learn from their therapists is that the sense of security that healthy people experience in relation to the world around them is also a kind of illusion. After all, it is impossible to escape uncertainty. It *may* be that Freud was right and we repress all sorts of perversions within us. We *could* also have a psychotic episode and kill someone we love. Much further along the scale of probability, we might even get divorced one day, end up in a custody battle, and see what was once a powerful love for someone transform into an even more powerful hatred.

To deny these risks is to deny that our knowledge of the world can ever be anything but incomplete. And yet love ballads and romantic adventures on film seem to suggest that the sphere of unity between two people can endow us with an ethereal certainty. The barrage of images and stories tell us that of course we can find a fixed point in life. This is where disenchantment really stems from. Alienation, anxiety, depression – no sorrow is too great to be drowned out by "the right one."[54]

And as though to put yet another spin on our confusion, the tools we are offered to sift out "the right one" also reveal a rationalised process with little room for what is written in the stars. How is it, for example, that the same "love" depicted as boundless and mysterious is so bad at uniting rich with poor, uneducated with highly educated, or fat with fit?

As early as the 1950s, the German psychoanalyst Erich Fromm described how our choice of partner reflected the rationality of the market. When we choose a partner, we do so on the basis of various "capital" considerations – how attractive we are, how successful we are, how interesting we are – that should either match or be surpassed by the other person. The process is similar to a financial transaction aiming to maximise profits, and love can often be translated as just that: the sense of having made a catch.[55]

Fifty years before online dating consolidated these sorting mechanisms, Fromm warned of what he saw as consumer culture's passivisation of love. "To love" (as an active verb) gave way to "to fall in love" (the passive form). Standing firm through hard times was replaced by anxiously keeping watch over the spinning compass needle of our emotional lives.

This is one of Fromm's few analyses not built on a revelation of unconscious processes. Many would openly admit that by love, they mean little more than lust or infatuation. And despite his appearance as a highly moral love guru, Fromm is reported to have cheated on each of his wives.[56]

Even in Mats, love's promise of merging and ego death lives on. The same passion that Plato, Spinoza, and the majority of Western philosophy condemned as unworthy of enlightened reason symbolises, in Mats' world, the highest experience a person can have. The fact that his ability to relive that rush has now been stymied by life as a young father is a sorrow that makes his obsessive thoughts about eternal unhappiness so much more realistic.

"There were reasons for my doubts, and that changes things. With the compulsion to wash or the fear of needles, you know it's not real. You know that. But when it comes to relationships, it's such a complex area. Love, that kind of deep love I felt in high school, I'm never going to experience that again. I know that."

With love as a guiding star, it is hardly surprising that sexual attraction is a key criteria in couple building. As the Israeli sociologist Eva Illouz has shown, this is another young phenomenon. As late as the nineteenth century, beauty was associated with both body and spirit. The love affair between the poets Robert Browning and Elizabeth Barrett is an example of this: that she was paralysed and bedbound the first time they met did not stop him from falling in love with the inner beauty he had seen in her poetry. Her physical body does not seem to have had any impact on his love. The physical aspect may well have influenced many other relationships, but sexual attraction was not considered an acceptable reason to enter into marriage. Today, however, physical attraction is typically ranked higher than both education and intelligence in surveys, and in a longitudinal study in the United States, researchers have shown how this criteria has grown in importance over the past fifty years.[57]

This tendency can be seen in both men and women, but within heterosexual relationships the nature of this follows a gendered pattern. In the book *Dataclysm*, Christian Rudder, one of the founders of the dating site OkCupid, presents some of the findings that emerge when studying the vast amount of data provided by the site's users. According to Rudder, men value physical appearance to a much higher degree than women. Or rather: A certain type of appearance. While heterosexual women using online dating platforms tend to set their preferences so that the ideal age of their desired partner reflects their own age, heterosexual men – regardless of whether they are thirty or fifty themselves – have a more limited age range for when they think women look their best: between twenty and twenty-three.[58]

This male fixation on appearances can have troubling consequences. In my own limited study of online dating behaviours, I was struck by just how badly women who might be categorised as overweight were treated. They were repeatedly contacted by men who initially behaved civilly, only to suddenly write things like "PIG" or laugh at them. Some men even went so far as to tell them to delete their accounts and quit online dating altogether.

I am still to find a single man who has been treated in the same way by women.

"They're embarrassed to be in a relationship with anyone who is a little bigger," one woman told me. "But we're still good enough for sex."[59]

This was something several people attested to. Sexually, men would seek them out, often with an explicit desire to get close to a large pair of breasts, but when it came to holding hands, they suddenly seemed much more anxious. How "sexual" – i.e. bodily rooted – the preoccupation with physical attraction is, is up for discussion. There is also a sense of social pressure to maximise returns – so similar to the protestant work ethic Weber once described, now with the body as work and love the dream of salvation.

"I've been on paternity leave since our son was born, and during that time I've noticed I've been avoiding certain people," says Mats. "Because I've been so ashamed of my doubts."

The guilt he felt towards his partner has, however, lightened since telling her how he felt.

"There were so many problems during the pregnancy, all sorts of uncertainties. I was unemployed, didn't know what I wanted to do. She was a student. We were living in this apartment, which is pretty shabby, and we got in touch with a couple's therapist. That's been a good tool. One thing you do there is to talk more about ambivalence instead of compulsion. And I can relate to that. It's another way of expressing how I feel in relationships. Is this right? Is there anything better out there? And I can also say it to her, that I feel ambivalent about you."

These days, Mats is no longer quite so plagued by thoughts of being in the wrong relationship. Talking about it has played down the question, and though he feels bad about having upset his partner, he no longer feels like he is hiding any kind of essential truth from her.

"Something I've started thinking instead is: what if I'm a paedophile? It's been a recurring thought for a long time now, but since I became a father it's gotten worse. Because when you've got someone so fragile and dependent on you, it triggers that kind of thing: what's the worst I could do to this person? And abusing a child really is the worst thing you could do. But that's something I haven't been able to share because things could really go wrong then."

The Courage Not to Interpret

If we analyse worry as though it were an iceberg in cross section, visible from top to bottom, it reveals very little other than the things that concern us. As one treatment manual puts it: "It is no coincidence that we typically see harming obsessions among gentle people, religious obsessions among religious people, thoughts about sexuality among highly moral people, and thoughts about mistakes among careful people: the more important something is, the worse it seems to have a bad thought about it."[60]

But why do we so frequently interpret our thoughts – obsessive or not – as being more than simply thoughts?

This question is crucial to all types of anxiety. In the type of dissertation on anxiety disorders often seen within the field of cognitive science, the fundamental problem stems from "catastrophic misinterpretations." With panic disorders, this happens in sudden jolts: interpretations of bodily sensations create fears of doom that manifest in the form of a panic attack. In obsessive-compulsive disorders, this happens constantly: intrusive, uneasy thoughts that feel ever-present are interpreted as a risk of ruin and reinforce, the more they are fought, the sense of risk. But can this wild zeal for interpretation really be seen as historically independent?[61]

In the first chapter, I mentioned that epidemiological estimates in the 1970s put the spread of obsessive-compulsive disorder at a tiny fraction of the population, whereas today the figure is somewhere between two and three percent. This type of comparison is likely complicated by differences in the design of questionnaires. A more important observation we can now make is that all these questions and self-suspicions require a cultural framework in order to concern the individual at all. Precisely dating this framework is difficult, but we can be relatively sure that it has not always existed.

This is particularly relevant with regards to the specific territories of risk that I have discussed. There are, of course, more territories of risk that can be mapped out in relation to other obsessive-compulsive and anxiety disorders, but the key thing is not the risks themselves, but how they are used by our "inner critic." In his historical analysis of the growth of obsessive compulsion, the disability researcher Lennard Davis writes: "People in the past may well have had these feelings and sensations, but there does seem to be something uniquely contemporary about the litany of self-accusations."[62]

Though the few epidemiological studies carried out in the area show significant variation between countries, there continues to be a basic assumption within clinical research that there is a genetic constant in the number of people affected by this complex form of anxiety. From time to time, researchers will announce that they have found a combination of genes that predispose a person to the various types of anxiety, but what these studies are unable to explain is how the variation between geographic areas arises, and why those who do not possess the specific set of genes also develop the "disorder" in question.[63]

One of the most hollow attempts to consolidate the idea of a genetic constant is the historical re-writing that occasionally rears its head in psychological textbooks, describing anxiety disorder as something that has been affecting people since time immemorial. As Davis points out:

> In such books, there are only cursory references to 10th-century Persians, Paracelus, medieval and Renaissance physicians, Lady Macbeth and Dr. Johnson, Catholic Church concerns with religious scrupulosity, and a smattering of other examples. So based on this slimmest of evidence, the claim remains that OCD has always been around and further that it is found in all cultures. Each book that is published – whether clinical or self-help – repeats these snippets of proof in an introductory paragraph or two. Yet the actual historical evidence for the existence of a clinical disease of OCD is scant and would not stand up to the scrutiny in a freshman history class.[64]

Even researchers within clinical psychology have queried whether OCD is a meaningful or valid clinical category in all cultures, and this question is not only relevant for our sociological understanding of anxiety.[65]

If we believe that the problem is in the brain, it will be the brain that is treated. Brain surgery has long been used in "complex" cases of obsessive-compulsive disorder, and one of the most prominent research nations in this field is Sweden, where operations have been carried out since the 1950s.

One procedure developed in Sweden is known as a "capsulotomy." That the word resembles "lobotomy" is no coincidence. A capsulotomy involves cutting into the internal capsule, a deep-set cluster of nerve fibres in the brain, and from a medical point of view, doctors have been keen to emphasise just how effective the method is. A few years ago, the Karolinska Institute in Stockholm sent out a press release with the headline "Half of patients relieved of obsessive-compulsive disorder after brain surgery." The paper the press release referred to showed a different story, however. Among the twenty-five patients operated on between 1988 and 2000, twelve saw a reduction in their compulsions by at least thirty-five percent – a far cry from liberation. Seven patients also attempted to take their own lives following the operation, and one was successful. Other "side effects" included drastic weight gain, urinary incontinence, apathy, and memory problems.[66]

Since 2007, no further capsulotomies have been carried out in Sweden. Today, instead, many pin their hopes on "deep brain stimulation," a procedure in which electrodes are implanted into the brain in order to deliver continuous electrical stimulation. Despite the brutal nature of these interventions, the majority of specialists are open about their lack of knowledge about the root cause of obsessive-compulsive disorder. In an article about deep brain stimulation, a Swedish neurosurgeon was asked about what he believed to be the cause of OCD. He replied:

"I don't know what causes it, but I have a good idea which parts of the brain are involved and where the signals that give rise to the obsessions pass through and how we can dampen them."[67]

Far removed from this experimental sphere, there is a form of therapy it is difficult to feel anything but the deepest respect for. One of the most fascinating aspects of OCD are the treatment methods that aim to expose patients to their fears. Take the following two examples:

A woman who was afraid she might push someone onto the tracks and therefore stopped taking the metro eventually learned to live with the risk, through a period of gradual habituation: First, by simply going down to the platform, then standing there for a while, watching all her potential victims. As a final exercise, she was told to stand right by the rails with her therapist at the very edge of the platform. As the train raced by, the woman stood so closely behind her therapist that she could have pushed him over the edge with minimal effort.[68]

Following the same basic principle, a man who was afraid of stabbing the first person he saw whenever he was near a knife was given a sharpened machete-like blade to hold against his therapist's neck as the final stage of his exposure.[69]

But how could these therapists know that their patients wouldn't murder them? They cannot possibly have been 100 percent sure, yet they chose trust over suspicion, and that trust had a healing power.

Notes

1 Karl Ove Knausgård, *Dancing in the Dark*, London: Vintage, 2015, p. 234
2 Rachel Cusk, *A Life's Work: On Becoming a Mother,* London: Faber and Faber, 2008, p. 51.
3 Cusk, *A Life's Work: On Becoming a Mother*, p. 108.
4 Cusk, *A Life's Work: On Becoming a Mother*, p. 105.
5 See e.g. Ulrich Beck and Elisabeth Beck-Gernsheim, *The Normal Chaos of Love*, Cambridge: Polity Press, 2002, pp. 75–76. According to the authors, the idea that having children is the greatest thing a person can do is fuelled by the fact that the relationship between parent and child is enduring, the only constant, while other relationships – not least romantic relationships – have become ephemeral.
6 Horwitz, *Anxiety: A Short History*, pp. 42–43; Joel Gold and Ian Gold, *Suspicious Minds: How Culture Shapes Madness,* New York: Free Press, 2014.
7 For a report on OCD relating to infection during the coronavirus pandemic, see Katherine Rosman, "For those with OCD, a threat that is both heightened and familiar", *New York Times,* ¾, 2020.
8 Padmal de Silva, "Culture and obsessive–compulsive disorder", *Psychiatry*, vol. 5, nr. 11, 2006, p. 403; Judith L. Rapoport, *The Boy Who Couldn't Stop Washing: The Experience & Treatment of Obsessive-Compulsive Disorder*, New York: Signet, 1991.
9 L. Silva et al., "Koro syndrome in an obsessive-compulsive disorder patient", *European Psychiatry*, vol. 33, 2016; Sheung-Tak Cheng, "A critical review of Chinese koro", *Culture, Medicine and Psychiatry*, vol. 20, nr. 1, 1996.
10 Legrand du Saulle, *La folie du doute (avec délire du toucher),* Paris: Adrien Delahaye, 1875, p. 11.
11 du Saulle, *La folie du doute (avec délire du toucher)*, p. 13.
12 du Saulle, *La folie du doute (avec délire du toucher)*, p. 30.
13 See Lee Baer, *The Imp of the Mind: Exploring the Silent Epidemic of Obsessive Bad Thoughts*, New York: Plume, 2014, p. 106.
14 R. A. Hunter and Ida Macalpine, *Three Hundred Years of Psychiatry, 1535-1860*, London; New York: Oxford University Press, 1970, p. 252.
15 Ibid, p. 253.
16 Chris H. Miller and Dawson W. Hedges, "Scrupulosity disorder: An overview and introductory analysis", *Journal of Anxiety Disorders*, vol. 22, nr. 6, 2008.
17 Weber, *The Protestant Ethic and the Spirit of Capitalism.*
18 Douglas Staley and R. Roxburgh Wand, "Obsessive-compulsive disorder: A review of the cross-cultural epidemiological literature", *Transcultural Psychiatric Research Review*, vol. 32, nr. 2, 1995; Jennifer L. Fleissner, "Obsessional modernity: The 'institutionalization of doubt'", *Critical Inquiry*, vol. 34, nr. 1, 2007;

Jonathan S. Abramowitz et al, "Association between Protestant religiosity and obsessive–compulsive symptoms and cognitions", *Depression And Anxiety*, vol. 20, nr. 2, 2004; Theodore F. Witzig Jr. och C. Alec Pollard, "Obsessional beliefs, religious beliefs, and scrupulosity among fundamental Protestant Christians", *Journal of Obsessive-Compulsive and Related Disorders*, vol. 2, nr. 3, 2013; Ian Osborn, *Can Christianity Cure Obsessive-Compulsive Disorder?: A Psychiatrist Explores the Role of Faith in Treatment*, Grand Rapids: Brazos Press, 2008.

19 For the most vivid description of this type of compulsion, see Rose Bretécher, *Pure*, 2015. Compare with Guy Doron, Danny S. Derby and Ohad Szepsenwol, "Relationship obsessive compulsive disorder (ROCD): A conceptual framework", *Journal of Obsessive-Compulsive and Related Disorders*, vol. 3, nr. 2, 2014.

20 Baer, *The Imp of the Mind: Exploring the Silent Epidemic of Obsessive Bad Thoughts*.

21 See Baer, *The Imp of the Mind: Exploring the Silent Epidemic of Obsessive Bad Thoughts*. David J. Castle, Alicia Deale and Isaac M. Marks, "Gender differences in obsessive compulsive disorder", *Australian & New Zealand Journal of Psychiatry*, vol. 29, nr. 1, 1995. In this survey study, 94 percent report troublesome, intrusive thoughts, which, given social desirability, is likely misleadingly low: Adam S. Radomsky et al., "Part 1—you can run but you can't hide: Intrusive thoughts on six continents", *Journal of Obsessive-Compulsive and Related Disorders*, vol. 3, nr. 3, 2014.

22 Bretécher, *Pure*, p. 22.

23 Bretécher, *Pure*, p. 34.

24 Bretécher, *Pure*, pp. 46–47.

25 Bretécher, *Pure*, p. 84.

26 Kenneth Plummer, *Telling Sexual S tories:Power, Change and Social Worlds*, London: Routledge, 2004.

27 Jeffrey Weeks, *Sex, Politics and Society: The Regulation of Sexuality Since 1800*, London: Routledge, 2018.

28 Michel Foucault, *The History of Sexuality vol.1*, New York: Pantheon Books, 1978, p. 33; Richard von Krafft-Ebing, *Psychopathia Sexualis: The Case Histories*, Washington, DC: Solar Books, 2011 [1886].

29 See e.g. Simone Leavell Bruce, Terence H. W. Ching and Monnica T. Williams, "Pedophilia-themed obsessive–compulsive disorder: Assessment, differential diagnosis, and treatment with exposure and response prevention", *Archives of Sexual Behavior*, vol. 47, nr. 2, 2018; Ross E. Cheit, Yael Shavit and Zachary Reiss-Davis, "Magazine coverage of child sexual abuse, 1992–2004", *Journal of Child Sexual Abuse*, vol. 19, nr. 1, 2010; Frank Furedi, *Culture of Fear Revisited*, London: A&C Black, 2006.

30 Frank Furedi, "Good, bad or none of our business", *The Australian*, 9/4, 2011. See also Jacqui Gabb, "Embodying risk: Managing father–child intimacy and the display of nudity in families", *Sociology*, vol. 47, nr. 4, 2013.

31 Heather Piper and Ian Stronach, *Don't Touch! The Educational Story of a Panic*, London: Routledge, 2008, s. x.

32 Frank Furedi, *Moral Crusades in an Age of Mistrust: The Jimmy Savile Scandal*, Basingstoke, Hampshire: Palgrave Macmillan, 2013, p. 51.

33 Olivia Loving, "Obsessive thoughts: A darker side of OCD", *The Atlantic*, 8/11, 2013.

34 Loving, "Obsessive thoughts: A darker side of OCD".

35 Alix Spiegel, "Dark thoughts," *NPR*, 8/1, 2015.

36 Loving, "Obsessive thoughts: A darker side of OCD".

37 Kay Donahue Jennings et al., "Thoughts of harming infants in depressed and nondepressed mothers", *Journal of Affective Disorders*, vol. 54, nr. 1–2, 1999.
38 Baer, *The Imp of the Mind: Exploring the Silent Epidemic of Obsessive Bad Thoughts.*
39 Karl Berglund, *Mordens marknad: Litteratursociologiska studier i det tidiga 2000-talets svenska kriminallitteratur*, Uppsala: Uppsala universitet, Litteraturvetenskapliga institutionen, 2017; Karl Berglund, *Död och dagishämtningar: En kvantitativ analys av det tidiga 2000-talets svenska kriminallitteratur*, Skrifter utgivna av Avdelningen för litteratursociologi vid Litteraturvetenskapliga institutionen i Uppsala (del 73): Uppsala universitet, 2017.
40 Jeffrey Jensen Arnett, "High hopes in a grim world: Emerging adults' views of their futures and'Generation X'", *Youth & Society*, vol. 31, nr. 3, 2000; Margaret Vandiver and David Giacopassi, "One million and counting: Students' estimates of the annual number of homicides in the US", *Journal of Criminal Justice Education*, vol. 8, nr. 2, 1997; Sven Jöckel and Hannah Früh, "'The world ain't all sunshine': Investigating the relationship between mean world beliefs, conservatism and crime TV exposure", De Gruyter Mouton, 2016.
41 Baer, *The Imp of the Mind: Exploring the Silent Epidemic of Obsessive Bad Thoughts.*
42 See Paulsen, "Mediated psychopathy – a critical discourse analysis of newspaper representations of aggression" for summary.
43 Adrian Raine, *The Anatomy of Violence: The Biological Roots of Crime*, New York: Vintage, 2014. When Raine was interviewed by Svenska Dagbladet, under the headline "Ondskan sitter i pannloben" [Evil Resides in the Frontal Lobe] readers were also given the opportunity to conduct their own test, in which "lines across the palm," a "clear line on the tongue," "ears lower than eyes" and other phrenological indicators were ticked off. The article was criticised by several of Sweden's leading neuroscientists, who argued that Adrian Raine's conclusions were too far-reaching. Henrik Ennart, "Ondskan sitter i pannloben", *Svenska Dagbladet*, 4/5, 2013; Jenny Stiernstedt och Lena Hennel, "Hjärnscanning ifrågasätts", Svenska Dagbladet, 5/5, 2013.
44 Tony Paterson, "Fritzl describes himself as 'born rapist'", *Independent*, 22/9, 2008.
45 James H. Fallon, *The Psychopath Inside: A Neuroscientist's Personal Journey Into the Dark Side of the Brain*, New York: Current, 2014.
46 Paulsen, "Mediated psychopathy – a critical discourse analysis of newspaper representations of aggression"; Ronson, *The Psychopath Test: A Journey through the Madness Industry.*
47 Doron et al., "Relationship Obsessive Compulsive Disorder (ROCD): A Conceptual Framework", p. 169.
48 Doron et al., "Relationship Obsessive Compulsive Disorder (ROCD): A Conceptual Framework".
49 Laura, "Lessons learned from relationship focused OCD", 2017, https://theocdstories.com/stories/lessons-learned-from-relationship-focused-ocd/, [2019-11-21].
50 For details on worries associated with generalized anxiety disorder, see Jason Schnittker, *Unnerved: Anxiety, Social Change, and the Transformation of Modern Mental Health*, New York: Columbia University Press, 2021, p. 96.
51 Marja Taussi Sjöberd, *Skiljas*, Stockholm: Författarförlaget, 1988.
52 Stephanie Coontz, *Marriage, A History: How Love Conquered Marriage*, New York: Penguin, 2006.

53 Compare Eva Illouz, *Why Love Hurts: A Sociological Explanation*, London: Polity, 2012; Beck and Beck-Gernsheim, *The Normal Chaos of Love.*
54 For an analysis of this promise, see esp. Zygmunt Bauman, *Liquid Love: On the Frailty of Human Bonds*, Cambridge, UK; Malden, MA: Polity Press, 2003; Beck and Beck-Gernsheim, *The Normal Chaos of Love.*
55 Erich Fromm, *Kärlekens konst,* Stockholm: Månpocket, 1988 [1956], p. 13.
56 Lawrence Jacob Friedman, *Lives of Erich Fromm: Love's Prophet*, New York: Columbia University, 2014.
57 Julia Markus, *Dared and Done: The Marriage of Elizabeth Barrett and Robert Browning*, London: Bloomsbury, 1995; Illouz, *Why Love Hurts: A Sociological Explanation.*
58 Christian Rudder, *Dataclysm: Who We Are (When We Think No One's Looking)*, London: Random House Canada, 2014, pp. 33–34.
59 Roland Paulsen, "Den kroppsliga differentieringens praktik: Övervikt och internetdejting på intimitetens marknad", *Sociologisk Forskning*, nr. 1, 2010, p. 20.
60 V. E. Caballo, *International Handbook of Cognitive and Behavioural Treatments For Psychological Disorders*, Amsterdam: Elsevier, 2007, p. 141.
61 Stanley Rachman, *The Treatment of Obsessions,* Oxford: Oxford University Press, 2003, p. 14.
62 Davis, *Obsession: A History*, p. 15.
63 On the variation between countries: M. M. Weisman et al., "The cross national epidemiology of obsessive-compulsive disorder", *Journal of Clinical Psychiatry*, vol. 55, nr. 3 Suppl., 1994.
64 Davis, *Obsession: A History*, p. 27.
65 Staley and Wand, "Obsessive-compulsive disorder: A review of the cross-cultural epidemiological literature", p. 128.
66 Sabina Bossi, "Hälften befriades från tvångssyndrom efter hjärnoperation", *Karolinska Institutet, pressmeddelande*: https://nyheter.ki.se/ halften-befriades-fran-tvangssyndrom-efter-hjarnoperation, 26/11, 2013, [2019-11-21]; Christian Rück et al., "Capsulotomy for obsessive-compulsive disorder: Long-term follow-up of 25 patients", *Archives of General Psychiatry*, vol. 65, nr. 8, 2008; Sara Rörbecker, "Riskabel hjärnkirurgi i Umeå", *Expressen*, 23/9, 2010.
67 Maria Carling, "Elektroder i hjärnan mildrar tvångstankarna", *Svenska Dagbladet*, 18/3, 2013.
68 Mantosh J. Dewan, Brett N. Steenbarger and Roger P. Greenberg, *The Art and Science of Brief Psychotherapies: A Practitioner's Guide*, 2018, p. 76.
69 Spiegel, "Dark Thoughts".

PART 3

Action in Our Time

11

QUIETING WORRY

"My problem is that I intellectualise things too much. I'm constantly thinking and trying to interpret things instead of just switching off."

This is a problem Samira shares with many others. But her story isn't about thinking away thoughts with thoughts; Samira has found a far more radical way of quieting her worries. She knows how to stop her intellectualising and "switch off" her brain, because she has done so several times.

Sitting cross-legged, she tells me about her breakdown. Looking back now, it feels like another life. She wanted to settle down in Norrland and create the life she had always dreamed of living. She was married and had been working as a doctor for several years – a job she had sacrificed a lot to achieve. They had found a stone house with incredibly high ceilings, and planned to live there while she continued her studies. Escaping the city, just the two of them. Enjoying the peace and quiet.

But after only three years, they got a divorce.

Now in her mid-thirties, she returned to Stockholm. It was like moving to a ghost town. Unfamiliar and exclusionary, with a healthcare system in disarray. Her friends had long since moved away or wrapped themselves up in the cocoon of family life. The one thing her hopes had been pinned on for years – a comfortable life in Norrland – was gone, and she wasn't doing well.

"I've always been depressed," she says. "I've been depressed ever since I was a child."

But this was something other than depression. This time, increasing the dosage of her antidepressants or booking in a few sessions of conversational therapy wouldn't work.

"I felt like *I have to do something, otherwise I'll kill myself.*"

DOI: 10.4324/9781003514930-14

The idea came from an acquaintance, who told her about a drink that had changed his life. It was a bit like a tea, he explained. Shamanic tea. Psychedelic.

"You take it to face up to your demons, he said. It sounded perfect to me. I really wanted to face up to my demons."

"What kind of demons?" I ask.

Samira thinks for a moment.

"I remember that things were already tough during the war. Not because we didn't have enough food or anything, but other things. My dad used to beat my mum and my siblings."

Back then, Samira's father was an alcoholic and an opium addict. When she was seven, they fled from Lebanon to Sweden, and he overcame his addiction. Instead, a new threat emerged: Swedish society.

Samira had the sense that if they weren't careful, they would be kicked out. At first, that was the reality, and Samira shouldered the burden herself. Being granted residence permits hinged on her; she couldn't afford to make any mistakes.

But even after the family were given their permits, that heavy burden of responsibility lingered. She grew up with it. Since her parents never learned any more than basic Swedish, she became their link to society. In meetings with the social services or the health system, she tagged along as the family's unofficial interpreter.

Her guilt became mixed up with shame. She was ashamed that her parents didn't work, that they didn't cook, that they were so old. Every year, she avoided the parent-teacher meetings at school, giving new excuses every time.

She says that the emotional issues – the guilt and the shame – caused far more problems than their lack of money, or growing up on welfare. It would have been far easier if she hated her parents, but Samira has always loved them, even when living with them was at its most painful. Like the time her father hit her in public, for example. It happened at the entrance to the swimming pool, when Samira tried to buy some juice from a vending machine – a special treat, given they had so little money. But the flap wouldn't open, and she didn't get her juice. Her father slapped her on the mouth.

"I completely lost it, I cried so much. But it wasn't because of the pain. I was crying because I was ashamed, because he'd let the others see, because we were so weird and, you know, because of the stereotype of immigrants hitting their kids."

Perhaps Samira's father was her demon? Or maybe it was the high school classmate who, without warning, decided to freeze her out? Or her husband, whose criticism and need to be in control eventually became too much for her? Samira didn't know, but whatever it was, she wanted to face up to it. She wanted to get to the bottom of herself.

And so, Samira began reading. The psychedelic brew her friend had mentioned was as good as harmless, near impossible to overdose on or become addicted to. Some people occasionally became anxious after taking it, but she was already so anxious that it wouldn't make any difference. She got in touch with a shady retreat company in Spain, quickly phased out her antidepressants, and flew down there.

The minute they picked her up from the airport, she began to doubt herself. What was she doing? Why had she put herself in this situation? Apparently she was expected to face up to her demons in a shed. There were candles and flowers on the floor, and they had built a pretty altar and hung colourful fabric on the walls. Beside her mattress, there was a roll of toilet paper and a plastic bucket in case she needed to throw up. There were thirty or so other people taking part, and they had all been instructed to dress in white before the ceremony. Samira, wearing white herself, snorted when she saw them.

"I thought, shit, have I joined a cult?"

She hugged her soft toy – a rabbit without any legs – to her chest. That was the one personal object she had chosen to take with her, as per the instructions. After an introductory presentation in which they each talked about their intentions, the brew was passed around the group. It tasted bitter, yeasty, metallic. Not good at all. And once they had each drunk from the cup, she lay down on her mattress and closed her eyes.

That was when the nausea hit her. It was a different kind of nausea than she had expected. Raw and merciless. She felt explosions in her brain, and opened her eyes. Her toy rabbit was covered in snake-like patterns. It looked like it always had, she didn't see anything that wasn't really there, but suddenly she noticed new details. They looked like eyes. So many eyes.

Samira panicked and started shouting, despite having been told to keep quiet. An assistant came over, and Samira explained that she couldn't cope. She must have taken too much, it felt so much more powerful than she had thought it would.

They left the shed together, and the assistant told her it would help if she pressed her hand to the grass. That if she just pressed her hand to the grass, the earth would absorb a little of the energy. Drenched in cold sweat, Samira bent down and did as she was told.

It helped, and before long she was back on her mattress. The drug found its way in to her consciousness, and she tried to keep up, to "give up," but didn't know how. When she reached the turning point, she thought: if I die now, I die now. And then she disappeared.

Wordless stretches, deafening silence, lightyears of grief and space.

She was finally there. She was ready to face her demons.

As the memories raced through her, she felt no fear. She studied them, each memory in turn. Even the very worst recollections filled her with warmth. A man appeared before her, the son of a shop owner in the town they had fled. The one who had sexually abused her as a girl.

"Of everything I'd expected to turn up, he wasn't even on the list," she says.

It wasn't that she had forgotten the man, he hadn't sprung up from her subconscious. It was just that she hadn't given him much thought. The entire story was so disgusting and shameful – perhaps most of all because she had continued going to the shop, despite knowing what awaited her. Wasn't that just typical of her? So unbelievably stupid, she thought. Continuing to expose herself, time and time again.

Yet suddenly she saw it in a different light. She saw the Samira she was back then. She was in young Samira's body, and she felt her boredom, her fears, how desperately she wanted to be seen. But the inconceivable thing was that she could also see her perpetrator. His life was laid out like a map in front of her, lying side by side with her own, joining hers, becoming a part of it.

Empathy is too weak a word for what she felt in that moment. She saw where he was when he abused her, where he was coming from, and how his assault would forever live on in both of them.

"It's impossible to explain now, outside of it," she says, "but right there and then, what I felt for him was love."

After three hours, she sat up. She was back on earth. Everything was the same as ever, yet it was also completely different. The strangers in the barn had become her fellow men and women. The providence she had seen running through her life was also in them. They were part of the thousand-voice chorus of fear and trust, they were part of the mystery that lay hidden beneath their own countless shapes, each one of them a masterpiece. She watched in astonishment as they each returned from their journeys.

Everything was clear, her thoughts still. Her mind had fallen silent.

Moments of Silence

Making an effort not to think about a particular subject is, as we have seen several times now, a difficult task. The thought keeps returning to us whether we want it to or not.

"Aren't we always lost in thought?" That was the most frequent comment I received on telling others about this book.

White bears aside, the answer to that question is no.

Being deep in thought is not our only conscious state. Whether we like it or not, a significant chunk of our lives is spent free from thought. At night we explore several thoughtless states of consciousness: deep sleep and dream sleep, sometimes even sleepwalking and lucid dreaming. In the Hindu and Buddhist traditions, there has long been a vocabulary for different types of waking thoughtlessness. One such shared concept is *samadhi*, which has been described as "a soundless state of breathlessness," among other things. *Samadhi* can have a transformative impact on meditators, lasting for a long time, but it can also be limited to a few seconds of complete focus. Similar concepts appear in other mystic traditions. Within Sufism, it is known as *fana*, and within Christian mysticism, *gezucket*.[1]

In secular contexts, waking thoughtlessness is often practised within art and sport. Thinking of all sorts – negative, positive, commentary and analytical – often leads to devastation in these fields. We see this when authors suffer from writers' cramp, in tennis players' unforced errors and in chess players' analysis paralysis. Opera singers, dancers, footballers and pole-vaulters all share a method in the sense that they practise so that their skills will become part of them, transformed into unconscious actions.

Once something has taken root in this way, the intrusion of thoughts can be ruinous, and yet our thoughts insist on butting in. In finals in particular, it is a recurring phenomenon that sportsmen and women suffer from "the choke," making mistakes they wouldn't normally make. In an analysis of 30,000 darts matches, for example, researchers found that players became considerably worse at throwing at decisive moments. The social pressure seeped in, via their thoughts, to the movement of their arms.[2]

Even in everyday life, we can relate to the problems caused by thoughts. We know that self-criticism won't help us to relax at a party, that hesitation rarely makes the sparks fly in a romantic encounter and that dwelling on things will stop us from getting to sleep. So what do we do when the thoughts insist on barging in?

I have already discussed the impossible task of trying to think away the thoughts that trouble us most, but there are other things we can do. We could, for example, go to a psychotherapist and talk through our difficult experiences. We can exhaust the body through physical exertion. We can drink alcohol. We can watch TV. We can meditate. We can read.

The need to focus on something other than our thoughts has created enduring institutions of human activity. It would be hasty to call all such activities a distraction, but there is no denying that nowadays, we distract ourselves more than ever.

Since the 1980s, the amount of information the average person takes in has increased fivefold. Just a century ago, it was unusual for a person to have read more than 50 books in their lifetime. Nowadays, it is common for a child to have seen over 200 films. Close to half of American teens report that they are "almost constantly" online.[3]

It is this increased amount of time spent online that has led many psychologists to introduce "internet addiction" as a new diagnosis. The ongoing global debate about screen time has, among other things, led the WHO to recommend that children under the age of five should spend no more than an hour a day looking at a screen.[4]

The forces that encourage addiction are both strong and real. Computer games and social media are not alone in being programmed to catch our attention; news sites, streaming services, online shops, and web forums all share the same aim: for us to give them as much of our time as possible.

Many argue that this is one of the factors behind the past decade's rising levels of ill health among the young. The argument takes its basis in the rapid increase in anxiety and depression among teenagers in the 2010s, the same period in which mobile phone usage among the young rocketed and social media gained billions of new users. According to psychologists Jean Twenge and Jonathan Haidt, the connection is clear cut, and they argue that screens have created new forms of addiction that isolate young people from the world.[5]

As mentioned earlier, however, it is difficult to draw such simplistic, x leads to y connections when it comes to human well-being.

For one thing, the sharp rise in mental health issues among children in Sweden started well before the advent of smartphones. Screen time may well have an effect, but on the other hand, there are a lot of things that have an effect on how we are feeling. An article published in the journal *Nature* compared screen time with other variables from the databases Twenge used as the basis of her research, and found that the correlation between lower well-being and high levels of screen time was as weak as the correlation between lower well-being and regularly eating potatoes. Wearing glasses was, statistically speaking, even more strongly correlated with feeling bad.[6]

And yet the question remains: why do so many people want to devote so much time to their screens? Do we feel bad because we spend so much time online, or do we go online because we feel bad?

Within the field of addiction research, this question has been formulated in countless ways. It can be asked in relation to all kinds of addiction: why do people take up certain activities to the extent that it has negative consequences on them and their surroundings?

The world of screens is not our only retreat. Many live in a world of cocaine, alcohol, gambling, working out, and so on. More people than ever are living in some kind of addictive world, and for each of these worlds, there is a debate between addiction researchers. What they cannot agree on is whether it is enough to restrict access to certain drugs, or whether the addiction is a societal phenomenon in which the drug itself is relatively irrelevant.[7]

From Distraction to Addiction

The concoction Samira drank is called ayahuasca, a psychedelic brew made from plants containing the active substance DMT. In its pure form, DMT can also be smoked, resulting in an intense trip lasting around fifteen minutes. An ayahuasca trip typically lasts around four hours. It is more gradual and considered slightly easier to navigate.

Alongside LSD, mescaline, and psilocybin (magic mushrooms), ayahuasca is the most commonly taken psychedelic drug, not least in countries like Peru and Brazil, where it is legal and has been a part of shamanic rituals for thousands of years. The drug is now responsible for a healthy tourist trade around the Amazon, and many who have taken ayahuasca describe the experience as a kind of rebirth.[8]

On Samira's trip to Spain, she took ayahuasca five days in a row, and by the time she got home she was a different person. It wasn't that she felt euphoric, nor that she saw and understood everything around her. But her constant intellectualising had stopped. Her *what if* questions no longer bothered her so much. She began to re-establish contact with her father, who, by that point, was an old man full of regrets. She felt sadder than before, but she was also happy to be sad – and happy to feel the emotions streaming through her.

On her first day back at work, however, she felt the cold sting of anxiety.

"I noticed that I was becoming increasingly bitter. I saw the stress, the politics, the competition, the pointless admin, and I thought: let them play that game."

After another few days, she had joined the game herself.

A month or so after that, she was reminded that there were a whole host of unresolved problems in her life. That she was single, for example. Why was that?

"It was like ploughing furrows of negative thoughts into my brain," she says.

The clarity she had felt earlier seemed to cloud over, and before long the anxiety reappeared as a series of "emotional electric shocks." She was back at square one, though she was now aware that there was something beyond the whirr of thoughts, a garden of Eden that was just one ayahuasca trip away.

As the amount of screen time exploded in the 2010s, several countries also found themselves in the midst of a so-called opioid crisis. This crisis was so severe that in countries like the United States and the United Kingdom, average life expectancy actually fell. One explanation for this is that strong opioids were made widely available as pain medication, but that isn't the only explanation.[9]

Opioids have similar effects to morphine and are particularly effective at dulling pain. In any discussion of just how strong opioids are, an experiment from the 1960s is often brought up. In the experiment, a number of rats were fitted with catheters and given a button that would secrete the drug into their bloodstream if they pressed it. In certain cases, the rats pressed the button so frantically that they eventually died.

Even now, these experiments are considered clear-cut evidence that there are certain drugs that can fell their victims with a single high – drugs that create an immediate addiction, taking happy, healthy individuals and turning them into addicts.

What is rarely mentioned is that these experiments were also carried out in so-called "Skinner boxes" – cages so small that the rats could barely turn around. In a now-classic study, researchers repeated the experiment, but in a new context. Several of the rats were placed in a larger box, a "rat park" in which they could move freely, socialise with other rats and access a station where they could choose between sweetened morphine and water. Another group of rats were placed into Skinner boxes in which they were given the same choice.

When the researchers compared the results, they found that the rats in the Skinner boxes consumed nineteen times more morphine than those in the rat park. Several variations were made to the experiment. Among other things, the researchers studied what happened when caged rats that had been forced to drink the morphine solution for two months were released into the rat park. Even these rats chose water over morphine.[10]

The experiment proved the starting shot for a larger discussion: is it the drug or the situation that makes an individual develop an addiction?

Right before the American opioid crisis began to escalate and we turned to smartphone screens to rest our eyes, a summary of almost 100 epidemiological studies into addiction in the USA was carried out. The most common forms of addiction were found to be:

Cigarettes:	fifteen percent of the population
Alcohol:	ten percent
Work:	ten percent
Shopping:	six percent
Illegal drugs:	five percent
Working out:	three percent
Food:	two percent
Gambling:	two percent
Internet:	two percent
Sex:	two percent

Since many people may be addicted to more than one of these things, the percentages cannot simply be added together to determine how large a proportion of the population has an addiction of some kind. But taking any such overlaps into consideration, the researchers estimated that forty-seven percent of people suffered from at least one addiction.[11]

If, by addiction, we mean that a certain activity has such an impact on a person's life that it becomes damaging to them or their surroundings, then it seems that many of us either are or have been addicts, long before the drugs that dominate today's debates ever came into the picture. It also seems that illegal drugs have only a tiny bearing on the overall problem of addiction.

If addiction can be extended to work, physical exercise and sex, then we may question how important the object of the addiction really is. The majority of people who drink alcohol do not become addicted. Similarly, the majority of those taking painkillers do not become addicted. Howard Shaffer, the Harvard professor of psychology who specialises in gambling addictions, notes that we rarely talk about "addictive dice." In his opinion, it is "magical thinking to imagine that drugs have this power." So why is the problem of addiction so frequently reduced to a question of drugs?[12]

It is true that drugs vary in how addictive they are, but even in relation to heroin we may question whether it is the drug itself or its relatively low cost and accessibility that makes it so lethal. In a study that had an explosive impact upon publication, two Harvard researchers in clinical psychology documented fifty-four cases of people who, over a long period of time (between two and twenty-three years), injected heroine without developing the habitual patterns generally associated with addiction. These so-called "chippers" used the drug regularly without any self-destructive behaviour – in other words, without it having any impact on their working or social life. What separated the chippers from typical addicts wasn't the level of access they had to the drug, but the life situation the heroin formed a part of.[13]

The point of such studies is not to market heroin as a safe drug – it isn't – but to examine the degree to which a drug's "pharmacological power" can explain addiction. According to the Canadian psychologist Bruce Alexander (who was involved in the above "rat park" experiment), one problem with the older research into addiction is that the focus on drugs and individuals typically downplayed the importance of societal context. In Alexander's analysis, epidemic explosions of addiction would not occur without the problem of widespread feelings of exclusion, emptiness, loneliness, or repression. This is why we are seeing a global increase in addiction right now because these feelings are becoming increasingly widespread.[14]

When researchers from the old school are confronted with the question of why so many people are able to exercise, have sex, eat, and drink without becoming addicted, the answer has often been that some people are simply more vulnerable than others. Despite decades of researching and documenting our genes, it remains unclear precisely which these vulnerability genes are, yet there is still a strong belief that we will one day discover them.

Another field of addiction research that has many adherents, even today, touches upon the supposed genetic susceptibility to alcoholism of Native American populations. Since indigenous Americans show statistically disproportionate rates of alcohol dependency, many have assumed that the problem must be in their genes. As Alexander points out, however, there are higher frequencies of virtually all kinds of addiction in that particular societal group. Should we therefore draw the conclusion that they are simply genetically more sensitive to drugs in general?

History would suggest otherwise. Addiction does not seem to have been an issue among Native Americans before the European colonisers arrived and destroyed their society. That isn't to say that the time before this was some kind of golden age – there are plenty of historical relics that show that average lifespans were short, that brutal war and torture took place, and that individuals occasionally murdered one another. But what there is no evidence of is widespread addiction.

This cannot be explained away by a lack of drugs. Thanks to European trade, the Innu people of northern Québec had, for example, access to whisky for several centuries. They lived like nomads with their reindeer and had plenty of resources to buy whatever they needed, yet they did not develop an addiction to alcohol. The same is true of the indigenous peoples of South America: no pre-colonial problems of alcoholism have been documented, despite the fact that they produced their own alcoholic drinks long before the Europeans arrived.[15]

Even in Europe, there are few signs of alcohol addiction further back in history. Within philosophy and religion, there have certainly been many discussions around whether alcohol is good or bad. In the Middle Ages, there was no shortage of critics of drunkenness and the social disorder that arose when people drank too much. But drinking excessively represented more of a moral issue than anything – it was seen a case of giving in to something evil.

In the United Kingdom, it wasn't until the eighteenth century – when the industrial revolution took hold – that the country first began to suffer an epidemic of gin consumption, and addiction became widespread among the population. This was also the same period in which British doctors began to warn about the epidemic spread of nervousness.[16]

It is possible that both a genetic predisposition and the appeal of a drug play a role in whether we develop an addiction or not. That view does not necessarily have to be false. But what *is* false is failing to take other factors into consideration.

The idea that addiction "fills a hole" is a common idiomatic expression these days – simple to understand and likely adequate. But where does this "hole" come from? If the drug isn't responsible for digging it, then it seems unlikely that eliminating the drug will solve the problem.

Alexander, who has worked in the field of drug addiction in a clinical setting for over forty years, admits that treatment clinics could be given limitless resources, but it still wouldn't solve the problem. The abundance of different treatment methods hasn't done much to improve the situation. If anything, it is striking how little has been achieved:

> Neither legal prohibition, moral medicine, scientific medicine, psychoanalysis, Alcoholics Anonymous, counselling, compassionate love, tough love, behavioural management, acupuncture, case management, therapeutic communities, civil commitment, eastern meditation, behavioural genetics, neuroscience, sophisticated advertising, antagonist drugs, psychedelic drugs, motivational interviewing, community reinforcement, treatment matching, harm reduction, nor any combination of these techniques has come close to overcoming alcoholism or any other type of addiction.[17]

To be sure, these methods do help some people, but it is difficult to say why, and which method is best suited to whom. The same could be said of all psychiatric treatment.[18]

New Findings in the Therapy Factory

After her divorce, Samira clutched at any straws she could find. She managed to get hold of a CBT psychologist who, despite being younger than her, made a good impression.

When Samira told the psychologist about her ayahuasca trip, she got no response from the younger woman. The great sense of love she had brought back from her trip made no impression at all. The woman's blue Swedish eyes blinked robotically. Other than a concerned frown that Samira read as irritation, her face remained blank.

"If it was so good, maybe you should keep doing it?" said the psychologist.

She probably meant it as a cutting remark, perhaps even sarcastic. Samira had already told the woman about her childhood, about their escape to Sweden, about their poverty, her guilt and shame. Again, none of these things had made an impression on the woman. What mattered was how Samira was going to change her behaviour. Frustration gripped the room. Samira had forgotten to do her homework. She hadn't filled in the log book like she was meant to, and if they couldn't map out her anxiety, what caused it and how she reacted to it, how were they ever going to get to grips with her thoughts?

"I don't actually think I can help you," said the psychologist.

"What do you mean?" asked Samira.

"I don't think we're going to get any further here."

As Samira left that day, she couldn't decide whether the psychologist had been serious about continuing down the psychedelic path. On the train home, she pulled out her phone and searched "Peru."

At the edges of the psychedelic wave currently sweeping through clinical psychology, we can see hints of failure. This has been called the "crisis of psychotherapy" by some.

We don't hear much about this crisis – there is a shortage of psychotherapy in relation to demand, after all. Psychiatric care is under great strain, and for many clinics the focus is often on putting out fires. In such a strained situation, delving into methodological questions about how much psychotherapy really helps may seem absurd.

And yet, among researchers, a lively debate is underway. In 2015, the so-called "replication crisis" rocked the world of psychology. It was triggered by the decision of 270 researchers to test whether 100 of the most-cited experimental studies could be replicated in a so-called meta-study. The basic idea of an experiment is that it should be replicable, yielding similar results, but before this study took place it was rare for researchers to actually check whether or not this was the case. When it did eventually happen, the outcomes were disappointing: statistically, the results held up in just four in ten repetitions.[19]

Although these experiments did not belong to clinical psychology, the debate has raged over methodological problems there, too, focusing on issues such as: undersized experiment groups, skewed recruitment of participants, poor control of participants dropping out of studies, poor randomisation of which people are placed in which experiment group, and a lack of interest in long-term effects.[20]

Yet another problem that has been increasingly debated in relation to the evaluation of drugs is the fact that studies which do not yield positive results tend to end up in the "filing cabinet." They are never published, in other words. This leads to a "publishing bias," since the only studies we get to read are those that show that the treatment was effective.

Within clinical psychology, this problem is one that has only recently gained attention. In a meta-study of fifty-five studies financed by the American National Institute of Health, researchers requested the data from thirteen research projects that never led to publication. Overall, the effectiveness of various psychotherapies fell by twenty-five percent. Suddenly, the likelihood of achieving better results from psychotherapy than talking to a regular doctor was vanishingly small.[21]

Some, such as the British psychologist Paul Moloney, have argued that such studies show that what little benefits exist are all in the mind: "there is little reason to believe that the claimed benefits of psychotherapy amount to more than placebo therapy."[22]

If we look beyond the tangled world of experimental studies, it is peculiar that the Western world, which spends far more (an almost incomparable amount more) on the treatment of mental illness also has the biggest problems with mental illness. In terms of somatic health, average lifespans differ by over twenty years between high and low-income countries, yet in terms of mental health, the level of care a country is able to provide seems not to have any real effect.[23]

Some have gone so far as to suggest that psychotherapy can actually have a negative impact on how we are feeling – impacts that are not always visible in experimental studies. The form of therapy offered in studies may differ from the type of therapy typically offered by our healthcare systems. How would things look if we attempted to measure the benefits of the more widespread forms of therapy?

In a German study, researchers compared people's responses to a survey on two separate occasions to see how their mental state had changed. They chose 5,000 participants who scored highly on things such as "depression" and low on things like "life satisfaction." Four years later, the same individuals were asked to fill in the survey again, enabling the researchers to compare the responses of those who had undergone psychotherapy in the intervening years with those who had not. The results showed that those who had been in therapy felt worse. This came as a surprise, given the majority of studies into psychotherapy show positive results. There are several possible explanations for this, but one hypothesis made by the authors of the study is that the kind of psychotherapy available to people in real life is of a lower quality than that involved in studies.[24]

The discussion of psychotherapy's lack of benefits, and the fact that more and more people are feeling worse and worse, has created fertile ground for new forms of therapy. Right now, psychotherapy using psychedelic drugs is one of the most-discussed forms of therapy. After forty years of being relegated to the sidelines after the wild experiments of the 1960s, funding for psychedelic research has begun to flood in.

These days, researchers are testing the use of psychedelic drugs in combination with conversational therapy for various anxiety disorders, obsessive-compulsive disorder, depression, alcohol and nicotine addiction, with positive results. There is nothing to say that these studies should be spared from the methodological issues already mentioned, but what sets the psychedelic approach apart is that it does not simply aim to *cure* a symptom. It also promises re-enchantment, a religious experience, and to widen the consciousness beyond the limits of oneself.[25]

The psychedelic drugs are also known as hallucinogens, but those who have just come down from a psychedelic high often emphasise the opposite: that the world seems more real than ever. Not infrequently, they talk about a mystical contact, a sense of having been led by an unknown being.[26]

How the psychedelic experience affects us is not clear. On the one hand, there are those who emphasise neurological changes such as increased blood flow, electrical activity, and plasticity in the brain. But on the other, there are those who leave the door to mystery wide open. The American psychiatrist Roland Griffiths, who led the early psilocybin experiments on dying cancer patients at the Johns Hopkins Hospital, has given several interviews in which he suggests that psychedelic drugs act as something more than a reset button for the brain. Perhaps the drugs give us a taste of life after death, he suggests.

"Western materialism says the switch gets turned off and that's it. But there are so many other descriptions. It could be a beginning!"[27]

On this point, Griffiths is far more outspoken than many others in the field, who – in order to avoid the mistakes of the first wave – have tried to stick to a strictly scientific vocabulary. Yet what supports his view are the many witness statements claiming that the psychedelic experience allows us to dip a toe into a world far greater than this life.

"The phenomenology of these experiences is so profoundly reorganising and profoundly compelling that I'm willing to hold there's a mystery here we can't understand."[28]

Faced with this mystery, of course, it isn't so strange that thought is silenced – if only for a while.

Wanting to Be Knocked Out

In Peru, Samira underwent nine ayahuasca ceremonies in total. She came home a different person, and this time it lasted. For several weeks. Then life at work caught up with her again, along with questions about how others really see her, how she wanted to live, and the accompanying dejection and anxiety.

Enthusiasts often like to emphasise that it is impossible to become addicted to psychedelic drugs. Having a bad trip is a well-known risk that may involve feelings of death and panic – not something to do for fun, in other words. As a result, most people cannot handle more than a few "trips" per year.

But for Samira, there have been far more trips than that – both physically and spiritually. After twenty flights to Spain, where she typically undergoes three to five ayahuasca trips in a row, she stopped counting.

She says that it follows a pattern.

"Every time I go, I'm bitter and annoyed with everyone. But when I come home, I feel so much love. The ayahuasca helps me break out of those patterns of thought."

"Would you say you're addicted to tripping?" I ask her.

"It depends what you mean by addicted. It's not like I isolate myself or can't work. I don't feel any physical withdrawal symptoms, either. But sometimes I do feel like I'm escaping to the ayahuasca. That I, unlike most people, actually enjoy the rush itself, though obviously I like the calmness and the insights afterwards more."

Samira doesn't see it as the usual type of escapism. If it came out that she was combining her work as a doctor with regular highs, she would risk losing her job. That is a risk she takes very seriously. Her colleagues see her as diligent, not least because she doesn't drink and avoids social media. That type of escapism simply dulls things, she says. With every ayahuasca trip, she learns new things. If she hadn't discovered the drug, she probably wouldn't have been able to keep working.

During her years in this psychedelic world, she has seen several examples of "spiritual bypassing" – people who adopt new, enlightened identities without being particularly enlightened. But, she points out, this is also a phenomenon among people who meditate and, for that matter, doctors.

"Once you're back in the real world, it's up to you. You might have an insight for one to three weeks, when you realise the importance of change, but you have to actually follow through on it."

"And do you?"

"I'm bad at this. I can do some things, like managing jobs and diets, without a problem. I understand people better, too. I get less annoyed. I have insights, but I don't think I've done everything I should have."

Samira's ambitions go way beyond the boundaries of normality. Given her start in life, she is close to the definition of a Swedish success story: integrated and hardworking, in a high status job. But the most important things in life remain. What is the most important?

"I feel like I want to be knocked out so hard that all I can do is feel. Just feel and understand. I need to shut off my thoughts, that's my problem. And that's why I want to try ibogaine, because with ibogaine you lose control completely."

What psychedelic research may yet show is that it isn't so hard to treat anxiety and depression after all, that we can "treat the disease" over and over again – in the very same person.

British psychiatrist Robin Carhart-Harris describes seeing this happen several times in his psilocybin experiments. In one case, a woman who worked as a receptionist experienced a powerful sense of awakening. She felt like material possessions no longer mattered, that everyone was equal, that differences in status were hollow. But when she got back to work, she was forced to accept the principle that material things are all that matter, that we are anything but equal, and that status is all important. Before long, she was depressed again.[29]

Considering there are no known side effects or somatic diseases linked to psilocybin and DMT, there are worse fates to fall victim to than ingesting these substances and going on a trip from time to time. What the phenomenon makes clear is somewhat more important than whether psychedelics are a good treatment method or not – namely, the difficulty in our society of "switching off" our thoughts, as Samira puts it.

In his book on the psychedelic world, journalist Michael Pollan describes how, after his psilocybin sessions, he saw the effects weaken until they seemed like distant memories, perhaps even illusions. Whenever he tries to write about his own trips, he hears a doubting voice in his head attempting to tone down his powerful experiences. "Fool, you were on drugs!"[30]

He is struck by the fact that those who have devoted decades to psychedelics never seem to have arrived, that they are still talking about the next trip, using this substance or that, this dosage or that. The language occasionally resembles that used to describe Prozac when it was first introduced – take a pill and you'll be fine – only in the murky tones of new spiritualism.

The enthusiasm shown towards the therapeutic benefits of psychedelics is, in Pollen's view, at least partly down to the fact that their advocates see it as the first step in legalising the drugs for personal use. First, emphasise the medical need – that seems to be the strategy, as when cannabis was legalised in Canada and various American states.

One problem with this therapeutic approach, however, is that the goal of harmonious adaption to society is not being challenged.

The shamanic practice of taking psychedelics has never been about helping people to endure a life travelling back and forth between home and work. Even during the first wave in the 1950s and 60s, the ambition went further than that. The reason LSD became such an important part of 1960s counter culture was precisely because of the lurch between clarity and thoughtfulness experienced by Samira and others like her. Industrial capitalism seemed to stand in opposition to the reality that psychedelic drugs allowed people to see. Timothy Leary , the clinical psychologist who conducted some of the first experiments using psilocybin at Harvard University, became so radicalised by this insight that Richard Nixon went on to call him "the most dangerous man in America."

Turn on, tune in, drop out, that was Leary's message to the world. What Ram Dass, Allen Ginsberg, and the other "psychonauts" of 1960s counter culture wanted to achieve was not simply to get high. Once they got high, there was only one conclusion to draw: that society as a whole needed a psychedelic trip.

The Worry that Remains

Focusing one's attention on something other than one's thoughts is not necessarily a bad thing. In many cases, distraction is actually preferable to constantly dwelling on the same old concerns. Yet not even the most grandiose of visions can change the fact that we live in a society where we are forced to relate to a future full of risks and choices. No matter how far we float away, that worry is always lurking in the background. This chapter was about different methods for dampening that worry. The next will focus on methods of living with worry.

Notes

1 Paramahansa Yogananda, *Autobiography of a Yogi*, Washington: Ancient wisdom publication, 2019, p. 123. See also Etzel Cardena and Michael Winkelman, *Altering Consciousness. Multidisciplinary Perspectives: History, Culture, and The Humanities Vol. 1*, Santa Barbara, CA: Praeger, 2011.

2 Roy F. Baumeister, "Choking under pressure: Self-consciousness and paradoxical effects of incentives on skilful performance", Journal Of Personality and Social Psychology, vol. 46, nr. 3, 1984. On darts performance: Bouke Klein Teeselink et al, "Incentives, performance and choking in darts", *Journal of Economic Behavior and Organization*, Forthcoming, 2019.

3 Martin Hilbert, "How much information is there in the 'information society'?" *Significance*, vol. 9, nr. 4, 2012. Monica Anderson and Jingjing Jiang, "Teens, social media & technology 2018", *Pew Research Center,* 2018.

4 World Health Organization, *Guidelines on Physical Activity, Sedentary Behaviour and Sleep for Children Under 5 Years of Age*, World Health Organization, 2019.

5 Twenge, *iGen: Why Today's Super-Connected Kids Are Growing Up Less Rebellious, More Tolerant, Less Happy.* See also Jean M. Twenge, "Stop debating whether too much smartphone time can hurt teens, and start protecting them", *TIME*, 21/3, 2019, and Haidt, *The Anxious Generation: How the Great Rewiring of Childhood Is Causing an Epidemic of Mental Illness.*

6 Amy Orben and Andrew K. Przybylski, "The association between adolescent well-being and digital technology use", *Nature Human Behaviour*, vol. 3, nr. 2, 2019.

7 Bruce Alexander, *The Globalization of Addiction: A Study in Poverty of the Spirit*, Oxford: Oxford University Press, 2010.

8 See Rick Strassman, *DMT: The spirit Molecule: A Doctor's Revolutionary Research into the Biology of Near-Death and Mystical Experiences*, Rochester,Vermont:Park Street Press, 2001.

9 See Sonia Sequiera, "Longer term influences driving lower life expectancy projections", *Institute and Faculty of Actuaries*, 7/3, 2019 and Janet Adamy, "Life

expectancy rises in U.S. For first time in four years", *The Wall Street Journal*, 30/1, 2020.

10 See Patricia F. Hadaway et al., "The effect of housing and gender on preference for morphine-sucrose solutions in rats", *Psychopharmacology*, vol. 66, nr. 1, 1979; Bruce K Alexander et al, "Effect of early and later colony housing on oral ingestion of morphine in rats", *Pharmacology Biochemistry and Behavior*, vol. 15, nr. 4, 1981.

11 Steve Sussman, Nadra Lisha and Mark Griffiths, "Prevalence of the addictions: A problem of the majority or the minority?" *Evaluation & The Health Professions*, vol. 34, nr. 1, 2011.

12 Craig Lambert, "Deep Cravings", *Harvard Magazine,* 3/1-2000, 2010.

13 Norman E. Zinberg and Richard C. Jacobson, "The natural history of 'chipping'", *The American Journal of Psychiatry*, vol. 133, nr. 1, 1976.

14 Alexander, *The Globalization of Addiction: A Study in Poverty of the Spirit.*

15 Alexander, *The Globalization of Addiction: A Study in Poverty of the Spirit*, pp. 11–20.

16 In 1819, the term "dipsomania" was used for recurring drunkenness, something that would now be referred to as intermittent alcoholic behaviour. See also: Friedrich-Wilhelm Kielhorn, "The history of alcoholism: Brühl-Cramer's concepts and observations", *Addiction*, vol. 91, nr. 1, 1996 and Richard J. Rosenthal and Suzanne B. Faris, "The etymology and early history of 'addiction'", *Addiction Research & Theory*, vol. 27, nr. 5, 2019.

17 Alexander, *The Globalization of Addiction: A Study in Poverty of the Spirit*, p. 11.

18 Paul Moloney, *The Therapy Industry: The Irresistible Rise of the Talking Cure and Why it Doesn't Work*, 2013, pp. 79–85.

19 OSC, "Estimating the reproducibility of psychological science", *Science*, vol. 349, nr. 6251, 2015. It should be said that this experiment led to a re-evaluation and a new discussion in which more and more researchers have begun to register their results before they have had time to analyse them. The requirements of such transparency reforms may well lead to higher reliability.

20 For summary, see William M. Epstein, *Psychotherapy As Religion: The Civil Divine in America*, Reno, Nev.: University of Nevada Press, 2006; Norbert Schwarz, "Self-reports: How the questions shape the answers", *American Psychologist*, vol. 54, nr. 2, 1999; Arthur C. Bohart," The client is the most important common factor: Clients' self-healing capacities and psychotherapy", *Journal of Psychotherapy Integration*, vol. 10, nr. 2, 2000.

21 Ellen Driessen et al, "Does publication bias inflate the apparent efficacy of psychological treatment for major depressive disorder? A systematic review and meta-analysis of US National Institutes of health-funded trials", *PLOS One*, vol. 10, nr. 9, 2015.

22 Paul Moloney, *The Therapy Industry: The Irresistible Rise of the Talking Cure and Why it Doesn't Work*, p. 79.

23 John F. Helliwell, Richard Layard and Jeffrey Sachs, *World Happiness Report 2013*, New York: Sustainable Development Solutions Network, 2013, pp. 42–46. The countries that spend most on treating anxiety and depression are also the countries with the greatest issues of spread. It is unlikely there is a causal relationship here, but it remains a bad sign that twice the treatment levels have no discernible effect.

24 Philip I. Chow et al., "Therapy experience in naturalistic observational studies is associated with negative changes in personality", *Journal of Research in Personality*, vol. 68, 2017.

25 For summary, see Jeremy Daniel and Margaret Haberman, "Clinical potential of psilocybin as a treatment for mental health conditions", *Mental Health Clinician*, vol. 7, nr. 1, 2017 and David Nutt, "Psychedelic drugs – A new era in psychiatry?" *Dialogues In Clinical Neuroscience*, vol. 21, nr. 2, 2019.
26 Rich Strassman, *DMT: The spirit Molecule: A Doctor's Revolutionary Research into the Biology of Near-Death and Mystical Experiences.*
27 For the neuroscience in this area, see e.g. Robin L. Carhart-Harris et al., "Neural correlates of the LSD experience revealed by multimodal neuroimaging", *Proceedings of the National Academy of Sciences*, vol. 113, nr. 17, 2016.
28 Michael Pollan, *How To Change Your Mind: What The New Science of Psychedelics Teaches Us About Consciousness, Dying, Addiction, Depression, and Transcendence*, New York: Penguin, 2019, p. 79.
29 Interview in Johann Hari, *Lost Connections: Why You're Depressed and How to Find Hope*, London: Bloomsbury publishing, 2019, p. 290.
30 Pollan, *How To Change Your Mind: What The New Science of Psychedelics Teaches Us About Consciousness, Dying, Addiction, Depression, and Transcendence*, p. 269.

12

LIVING WITH WORRY

One of the least-planned interviews for this book takes place in a cathedral during an avant-garde organ concert. I haven't managed to arrange a quiet space where we can talk – usually a prerequisite for people being willing to share their niggling thoughts – but Sanne insists she is happy to meet there. She is almost seventy, with a pair of kind eyes behind her small glasses. We head into the church, where the music bounces off the vaulted ceiling. At the far end of the transept, we find a secluded spot where we don't need to shout to make ourselves heard.

All I know about Sanne is that she has been diagnosed with generalised anxiety disorder. The almost atonal organ works surprisingly well as background music to the rest of her story.

It started in school. The pressure of having her work assessed and graded was just too much. Sanne built up an anxiety around being found out – for what, she never knew; she just had the feeling that someone might see through her at any moment. Speaking in front of a group made her panic. Long before a presentation, she would find herself getting lost in thoughts of becoming dizzy and fainting. Whenever she got up in front of her classmates' searching eyes, it was almost as though her thoughts came true. This dread of being judged stayed with her into adulthood, forcing her to give up on both her studies and her work. And with time, she found herself daydreaming more and more.

"When I'm not dwelling on something, I daydream a lot, watching whatever is going on, searching for patterns. I can do it for half a day sometimes – a whole Sunday can pass with me doing nothing but daydreaming. And then I wake up, look around and think, what, how is it so late already?"

DOI: 10.4324/9781003514930-15

Putting up with queues or having to wait is easy for Sanne. She just disappears into her thoughts and the time quickly passes. The less positive aspect of this ability is that she is unable to switch it off.

"I often find my thoughts swinging between what I could have done differently and what actually happened. I end up in an unreality where I almost forget that it's happened. Like, am I in a dream now? Everything seems to slow down, and I can't get anything done. Nothing matters any more. That strikes me sometimes. Who am I without my thoughts, if I'm not thinking? Do I even exist without my thoughts?"

Her eyes drift out across the empty pews as she speaks. She was first given her diagnosis while she worked in a group home for people with severe autism. One of her adult sons was struggling. She was exhausted. Given that she was worrying so much, and "excessive worries" is the most common description of generalised anxiety disorder, the psychologist thought it was a fitting diagnosis. But were her worries excessive?

Sanne's son soon developed such bad depression that he began to self-medicate and she became the over-protective mother. She helped him get psychiatric help and wanted to be with him all the time. Not just to check that he was OK but because they had fun when they hung out, and they enjoyed philosophising together.

"You have this idea of what life will be like once you have kids, and you think you've got it all under control," she says.

"You think that maybe if you've got enough love, you're protected. But many of the things I used to believe have come crashing down. It's not a lack of love that makes someone struggle. Or it can be, of course. But there are so many other things that have an impact."

When her son went missing, she reported it to the police that same evening. But since his disappearance seemed voluntary, the police told her there wasn't much they could do. Sanne had no idea where to turn.

"I know it would've been impossible, like looking for a needle in a haystack, but I even dream about this sometimes, and in my dreams I often find him."

In another part of the church, the organ has started roaring in a threatening disharmony. I worry that the organist must have heard us talking and become annoyed. This was probably a bad place to conduct an interview, though Sanne barely seems to have noticed the angry soundscape.

"I didn't want to think the worst, and when I heard the knock on the door I thought, that must be him, even though I already knew. In my daydreams, I'm always replaying those steps down the hallway, to the door. I repeat them over and over again, that moment when everything changed."

Even now, no one knows whether Sanne's son overdosed because he wanted to die or whether it was an accident. Her friends say it was an accident.

The world grew pale. For a time, it barely existed outside her worrying thoughts. When she goes out shopping today, she occasionally finds herself stopping, astounded that everything still looks the same.

"Does the world just go on out here? How is that possible? It's like living in a nightmare."

At first, the anxiety she had been living with for so long lightened. Since the worst had already happened, grief made her less afraid. But then her thoughts began to reappear. Rather than counter-factual thoughts about what might happen in the future, she became preoccupied by the other type of counter-factual thought: what *could have been* if only she had done things differently.

"It's almost like a compulsion. I can't stop thinking about him, it would be a betrayal. In some strange sense, there's a certain comfort in clinging on to destructive things. You know what's what. It's familiar ground."

The organ music fades, and it feels like we're alone in the church. I say something about understanding that she has a lot to think about. Sanne continues to stare out over the pews, and I get the impression that she has long since had enough of meaningless comforts like that.

"He doesn't exist in that brooding," she says. "I have good memories too, but it's like they're overshadowed by what happened. And I know that it wouldn't have helped me or anyone else if I'd worried more."

Sanne's other son recently announced that he had decided to go abroad to act as a human shield in a protest movement. Catastrophic thoughts immediately came marching in like an army, making so much noise that she struggled to sleep. And yet, she held back. She steeled herself against influencing his decision and watched him leave. There was a risk he too would die. There's always a risk, she points out.

"I see that as the price of love."

Illness and Situation

Sanne has experienced loss. First, a few subtle losses that fall within the bounds of normality, followed by the undeniable loss of losing her child. Is it really so surprising that she was worried? If not, is it reasonable that she was given a diagnosis of excessive worry and anxiety?

Sanne herself admits that her worry hasn't helped her, that she wished she had been more present, less preoccupied with her thoughts. In that sense, her worry has been "excessive." But her catastrophic thoughts about something happening to her son weren't imagined. There was good reason for them – they were proved true.

Even with regards to more severe forms of worry, the same question has been asked on a number of occasions: Wouldn't it make more sense to diagnose *situations* rather than *individuals*?[1]

In Sanne's case, the worry was not just in her head. It involved at least one other person: her depressed son. She and her son also existed within a societal context, and for a more substantial analysis of their situation we would have to take into context the historical period in which they lived, including what type of familial model was dominant, the prevailing norms about parental responsibility, how people with addiction problems were treated, how people with psychological problems were treated, how people without a job were treated – not to mention the long development of the importance of time, disenchantment and calculation of risk described in this book.

In such a situational analysis, "generalised anxiety disorder" would act as a description of a host of interconnected factors that led a person to experience significant anxiety. Some psychiatrists have promoted the theory that *all* diagnoses describe situations of this kind, that mental illness does not arise in a vacuum, and that we should therefore give up the idea of "mental illness."

The question of whether mental illness is a valid category continues to sit at the heart of much criticism of psychiatry. It has been in circulation since the 1950s, when the Hungarian-American psychiatrist Thomas Szasz began to argue against it. I met him a year before his death, when he was ninety-one and in good humour. He repeated his theory "there is no such thing as mental illness" – no fewer than five times.

One of his arguments related to the function of the psyche. We know how a healthy brain, thyroid gland or small intestine should work, but we do not know how a human psyche should work. What is considered dysfunctional human behaviour cannot be separated from situation or society. If, by functionality, we mean only adaptation to a certain society, then this raises the question of whether societal adaptation is a good thing under all circumstances.

By asking such questions, Szasz argued that we are doing people a disservice when we convince them they are mentally ill. The very idea of mental illness gains a performative effect: we become depressed by our depression, we have obsessive thoughts about our obsessive-compulsive disorder, we feel anxiety towards our anxiety disorder and panicked by our panic disorder. In Szasz's view, psychiatry creates many of the problems it is supposed to correct.[2]

Despite his criticism, Szasz himself was active as a psychotherapist. He disliked being associated with the so-called anti-psychiatry movement, and was keen for people to be given help. But with what? If not mental illness, what can a psychotherapist really help with?

When I asked him, he answered as follows: "I help them with problems."[3]

Mental health problems is the term I have tried to use in this book, because there is a distinction between *being mentally ill* and *having a problem*. Believing that one is mentally ill and that there is something inside one that needs to be repaired in order to be healthy is as futile a project as deciding not to think about white bears. If a single thought or feeling associated with the illness passes through one's mind, then we are right back at square one – still "ill." The spiral of worry about worry and dejection over dejection are reinforced by this model of sickness. To learn to break these spirals is to unlearn the idea of mental illness.[4]

If we can manage to do away with this idea – and all its linguistic variants, including "disorder," "syndrome," "sickness" and "neuroses" – then it would have radical consequences. Without a concept of mental illness, it would be difficult to talk about the treatment of patients. We do not treat people with problems, after all. But what we can do – as people have understood for centuries – is help them to live dignified lives. There are several historical examples of what this help might look like.

In the Belgian city of Geel, for example, the community has been taking care of people who do not fit the mould since the thirteenth century. The city's simple approach is to place individuals with mental health problems with host families who, even today, are not informed of their specific psychiatric diagnoses. The idea is *not* to treat them as ill, but to allow them to live and move around as though they were any other member of the family. The Geel model has long attracted interest. In 1845, for example, the French psychiatrist Jacques-Joseph Moreau wrote that Geel was one of few places where those who would otherwise be locked up "have not completely lost their dignity as reasonable human beings."[5]

The history of psychiatry also contains more subversive attempts to help people without providing treatment. In the 1960s, the Scottish psychiatrist R. D. Laing opened a treatment centre in London's Kingsley Hall, where the staff lived alongside people diagnosed with schizophrenia. In film footage, it is almost impossible to tell who is the schizophrenic and who is the psychiatrist. The idea was to do away with the usual roles and to cease all treatment – particularly medication and electro-shock therapy – and take LSD together.[6]

A more offensive experiment was initiated in Germany at around the same time, under the leadership of the psychiatrist Wolfgang Huber. Huber founded the Socialist Patients' Collective, and carried out his psychiatric work from a base at the University of Heidelberg. His basic idea was that people who had been diagnosed with schizophrenia should rebel against the capitalism he believed to be responsible for their suffering.

"Turn illness into a weapon!" was the motto – and the title of a book by the collective, in which Jean-Paul Sartre's foreword asserted that mental illness is "indissolubly tied to the capitalist system which turns working power to a commodity."[7]

Precisely what it meant to turn "illness" into a weapon remained unclear. The group grew and radicalised and was eventually barred from the university campus. Huber himself was arrested just one year after the experiment began. Some members of his patient collective began to collaborate with the Baader-Meinhof group, and participated in the occupation of Sweden's West German embassy in 1975. Siegfried Hausner, who accidentally detonated a bomb and died from his injuries, was one of the Socialist Patients' Collective's first members.[8]

This is where a pattern begins to emerge: the moment the notion of mental suffering as an illness met resistance, the problem of action arose. The question of "what should we do?" remains unanswered.

Following the daring experiments of the 1960s, the discussion around whether a person really must be ill in order to feel bad faded away somewhat. Even in the more exploratory areas – such as the current psychedelic experiments – the focus has been on effectiveness and adaptation to society: make it so that people can quickly feel better, or at least well enough to be able to work.

But over the past few years, the question has regained new life. Yet again, a large number of psychologists are questioning whether the model of "healthy doctor treats sick patient" is really so desirable. This time, the criticism is not coming from socialists aiming to overthrow capitalist society, but from cognitive behavioural therapists interested in Buddhist philosophy and meditation. Their answer to what should be done is even more complex.

Acceptance

Steven Hayes had his first panic attack when he was thirty, and a newly qualified lecturer in clinical psychology. This attack, to which he often returns in interviews, took place when he raised his hand to ask for the floor during an institutional meeting. When he tried to speak, no words would come out. Fifteen seconds of silence and confused faces passed. Steven couldn't manage a single word, and he left the meeting upset by what he suspected was the beginning of some sort of panic disorder.[9]

In his role as a psychologist, Hayes knew a lot about the treatment methods for panic disorders, and he tried various things in an attempt to get better. But over the next two years, his panic continued to worsen. He avoided situations that might trigger his anxiety. He passed off his teaching duties to PhD students, or else simply put on a film and left the lecture theatre. For a while he also developed obsessive thoughts, about throwing his newborn son out of the window "like a frisbee," for example, to "see how far he would go." Relaxation techniques, medication, drinking, humour and exposure therapy – none of it worked.[10]

"The problem," he says, "was that the foundational message my mind was sending me was toxic: anxiety is my opponent and I have to defeat it."[11]

These days, Hayes is best known for having founded the rapidly growing form of therapy known as ACT: Acceptance and Commitment Therapy. ACT is part of the third wave of cognitive behavioural therapy, and stands out in that its aim is not to cure anyone.

Having struggled with panic anxiety for some time, Hayes came to the conclusion that anxiety grows the more we attempt to get rid of it. Even when we expose ourselves to it – the basic approach of CBT – there is a white bear effect because the end goal is to shake off the anxiety. The *real* exposure is therefore to learn to live with anxiety.

Hayes is not as controversial as Szasz once was. Like many other CBT psychologists, he has been careful to test out his methods in controlled experiments and has stayed within the framework of evidence-based psychology. And yet in his view of mental health, he reminds me of Szasz.

"The truth about mental health," he writes, "is that the causes of all the mental conditions you hear about are unknown, and the idea that 'hidden diseases' lurk behind human suffering is an out-and-out failure."[12]

Today, this view is less controversial than it has been in a long time. This is partly because it links to the core of CBT, namely that behaviour and thoughts are all we can know anything about. That so little progress has been made, both in terms of genetic mapping and neuropsychiatric research regarding the biological processes assumed to cause mental illness, has only added to this criticism. According to Hayes and many others – including Allen Frances, editor of the fourth edition of the Diagnostic and Statistical Manual of Mental Disorders – medicine has, despite hundreds of years of well-financed research and increasingly advanced technology, failed to discover a single mental illness. With the exception of a few obvious neurological disorders, the psychiatric diagnoses remain descriptions of different behaviours. Neither blood tests nor brain scans can come anywhere close to telling us who is suffering from what.[13]

The acceptance Hayes tries to teach his patients stems from the idea that painful experiences are an inevitable part of human life. Since they are inevitable, acceptance is the only reasonable approach to dealing with them.

But what does acceptance mean here? That we should accept all suffering that comes our way?

It is possible to interpret the concept of acceptance as a radical exercise in societal adjustment. Hayes criticises societal factors that contribute to poor mental health – not least psychiatry, a field in which he himself works – but his societal analysis doesn't cut particularly deep. This has likely contributed to the gospel of acceptance occasionally being used as a weapon to silence dissatisfaction. One study has shown, for example, that an ACT workshop for employees of the National Health Service in the UK became an ideological exercise in accepting unacceptable working conditions.[14]

As almost all preachers of acceptance typically emphasise, however, acceptance should not be understood as resigning oneself to the state of the world. Acceptance involves letting our thoughts, feelings and impressions exist as they are. Refraining from neutralising them. The fundamental approach, taken from Buddhism, is that we are neither our thoughts nor our feelings; that the movements of the mind pass through us, depending on impressions and experiences that we do not control. All we can control are our actions, and therefore our ability to act in a "valued direction" – i.e. doing what we want to do – is what matters.

Sanne could, for example, have chosen to forbid her remaining son from going to join the protest. She could have made him feel guilty and told him that she couldn't handle worrying about losing another child. If, after all that, he still left, she could have consoled herself with the knowledge that she did what she could. She could have quieted her worry. Instead, she accepted her worry. She decided not to get involved in his decision. Her valued direction was to accept his autonomy, and she chose to prioritise that over her own mental wellbeing.

"Kill yourself every day," is Hayes' incisive advice. After enough times, the voices we so easily associate with our "self" will give up. Once we are no longer fighting our worry, it will disappear – according to the theory. In essence, there is a hope that by accepting how we feel, we are also liberating ourselves from feeling bad.[15]

Uncertain Wisdom

But if we accept worry in the hope that acceptance will liberate us from it, have we really accepted it?

Accepting uncertainty is an ancient technique practised by people belonging to all manner of religions, but when this technique is adopted as part of psychotherapy, it is forced into a new context. In therapy, the aim becomes to free people from the problems they are seeking treatment for. This leads to the same type of problem seen by Hayes and others in classic CBT.

If Sanne turned to an ordinary CBT psychologist and announced that she was petrified of her remaining son dying in an accident, the treatment would likely hone in on two things. One would involve her mapping out the types of situation that trigger her anxiety. The second would see her gradually exposing herself to that anxiety by actively thinking that there is a risk something may happen to her son.

The aim of exposure is to get used to thinking about a certain risk, making the thought seem less threatening. This type of "habituation" therefore reduces anxiety – or is supposed to – by actively exposing us to anxiety.

What Hayes and other critics of exposure therapy argue is that the aim of freeing a person from anxiety throws a spanner in the works. If Sanne exposes herself to anxiety in the aim of getting rid of that anxiety, the idea that anxiety is her enemy will constantly be lurking at the back of her mind. It will prevent her from ever truly exposing herself to her anxiety.[16]

The same objections can also be levelled at acceptance therapy. If Sanne attempts to accept her anxiety with the aim of escaping it, she isn't *really* accepting it at all. She may well think "I accept my thoughts and everything I feel, including my anxiety," carrying out various thought exercises in acceptance. But acceptance is not about thinking in a certain way. Acceptance involves achieving distance from our thoughts, really *realising* that the stream of impressions, feelings and thoughts is not who we are.

This is where the explicit aim of psychotherapy to reduce anxiety gets in the way of accepting it. From the very first meeting, it shapes the direction of the therapy. It is also on this basis that psychotherapies are assessed, in order to gain "evidence."

Within the religions and philosophies that accept uncertainty, the aim of acceptance is not primarily to reduce anxiety. The aim is not even to feel good. The aim is to see the world as it really is: fundamentally uncertain.

Through worry and anxiety, we come into contact with the uncertainty of existence. This uncertainty is not just to do with the infinite risk that something might go wrong. Uncertainty goes to the very heart of who we are, present in the most ingrained notions of ourselves and the world around us. This means that accepting uncertainty is valuable in and of itself, because through uncertainty, we come closer to the truth.

This basic premise is particularly evident in Buddhism, which not only affirms the acceptance of uncertainty, but of suffering in general. From a Buddhist perspective, acceptance is an exercise in *insight*, it is recognising what Buddha said in his first teaching: "birth is suffering, ageing is suffering, illness is suffering, death is suffering; union with what is displeasing is suffering, separation from what is pleasing is suffering, not to get what one wants is suffering." In other words, suffering is part of life.[17]

In the same teaching, Buddha points to two more conditions of life that are relevant to human worry. The first is our "non-self," or the idea that there is no unchanging self. The second is *anicca*, the impermanence of all things.

Anicca lies beyond the realm of thought. It is an incomprehensible reality that the majority of people experience for only brief moments. The point of *anicca* is not simply that everything we care about will one day be lost. The point is that everything *is* lost, all of the time, because everything is in a state of flux. A flame is created and ceases to exist in a flickering process, but through the abstraction of thought it appears as a constant. It is only by moving beyond thought and everything we think we know about how the world is made that we can get a sense of its transience.

This esoteric ambition snakes like a vein through several philosophical and mystical traditions. In Western philosophy, we can see it in Heraclitus and his metaphor of no man being able to step into the same river twice. In Plato's *Apology of Socrates,* he describes – in what was probably his first dialogue – the way Socrates defended himself during his trial by explaining his philosophy of insecurity. Socrates' starting point is that the human condition is uncertainty, and that through reason, we can deepen this uncertainty.

It is in this same speech that Socrates also expresses what we continue to learn about him in school, namely that wisdom does not come from memorising a set of facts and opinions, but from understanding one's ignorance. This understanding is not empty; it is itself a form of knowledge. Armed with this understanding, one could, for example – as Socrates does in Plato's dialogues – enlighten others about their ignorance.

In the four schools of thought that took over after Plato and Aristotle – Pyrrhonism, Stoicism, Epicureanism, and Cynicism – different aspects of the Socratic understanding that nothing can be known with certainty are emphasised. The Cynics took this line of reasoning furthest by rejecting everything seen by convention as being safe and right – everything from national borders to washing.[18]

But the acceptance of uncertainty has played the greatest role with regards to the biggest question of all: the existence of God. Agnosticism, or the notion that we lack any certainty about the divine, dates back much further than 1869, when it was given a name by the biologist T. H. Huxley. Agnostic ideas can be found in the work of many Christians, among them Søren Kierkegaard, who saw doubt as a prerequisite of faith, because doubt guarantees that believers live on faith alone.

Some Christians have also promoted the theory that we can never understand God through the categorisation of thought; that we can only get closer to God by understanding what God *is not*. This "apophatic" – i.e. negative – theology echoes the thirteenth century Christian mystic Meister Eckehart's words about every image of God being a step *from* God, and that the only way to love God is as "a non-God, a non-spirit, a non-person, a non-image."[19]

Meister Eckehart is one of the mystics who, through their respective religions, attempted to free people from frightening patterns of thought. He was, unsurprisingly, accused of heresy.

Certain religious teachers have placed so much emphasis on acknowledging uncertainty that it has become more important to them than professing their respective religions. The scholar Linji Yixuan, for example, wrote in the ninth century that we must learn to "kill" (metaphorically speaking) everything we hold true, even Buddha himself: "Kill anything that you happen on. Kill the Buddha if you happen to meet him. Kill a Patriarch or an arhat (saint) if you happen to meet him. Kill your parents or relatives if you happen to meet them. Only then can you be free."[20]

By affirming uncertainty, we can see that in every fear there is a grain of truth, an opening for mystery, for an understanding of how little we know, and an opportunity to see that the real madness is in believing that we know what is going on.

What We Are Doing When We Live with Worry – Or Why the Problem of Action Remains

In what is likely the oldest preserved distinction between pain and suffering, Buddha describes how, when we feel pain on being struck by an arrow, we have a tendency to shoot another arrow into ourselves by counterfactually wishing the pain away. With the second arrow comes suffering.

For a person who finds themselves in a situation in which catastrophe is looming, it is of little comfort to know that anxiety helps us to understand the uncertainty of being. Acceptance can liberate us from what Buddha referred to as the second arrow, but it cannot alter the fact that we have already been hit by one.

This distinction is key. Accepting what we currently think, feel or experience does not mean we must also accept the situation we find ourselves in. We can accept "life" – or what we are experiencing in the moment – without accepting the conditions in which we are living. If, for example, we find ourselves on a sinking ship, it is reasonable to accept the justified fear of dying, but we do not have to accept the situation. We can accept that we are afraid and still try to find a lifeboat.

When this distinction is forgotten – as it often is – acceptance becomes total. No matter what happens to us, we have to accept it. This can be seen in the neoliberal mutations within Buddhism: the mindfulness exercises often imposed on people, employed and unemployed alike, to help them breathe through the exploitation, chaos and humiliation. These exercises have long been questioned by Buddhists who embrace the idea of social critique as part of their ethical practice. According to these critics, developments in society cannot be reduced to a question of the right meditation technique.

During the Vietnam war, some – including voices from the monastic ranks – began to argue that Buddhist practice was out of touch with society. The monk Thích Nhất Hạnh proposed a form of "socially engaged" buddhism. Thích Nhất Hạnh was himself accused of being too conservative, and the discussion on what a socially-engaged Buddhism actually looks like is still ongoing.[21]

Like natural science, the philosophy of acceptance offers no answers to the problem of action. The question of what we should do while we accept our worry remains. Choosing a "valued direction" and then pursuing it is of little help. How do we go about choosing that direction? Shouldn't the endeavour that is life be based on more than arbitrariness in order to be worth the effort? What else do we have to go on?

This is where looking inward cannot help us. In order to find the act that makes a difference, we need to look outward. It requires societal analysis, an understanding of the historical context we find ourselves in – what we can do something about, and what we need to learn to live with. Understanding why so many people feel bad today is a good place to start.[22]

Notes

1 See George W. Brown, James L.T. Birley och John K. Wing, "Influence of family life on the course of schizophrenic disorders: A replication", *The British Journal of Psychiatry*, vol. 121, nr. 562, 1972 and Gregory Bateson et al, "Toward a theory of schizophrenia", *Behavioral Science*, vol. 1, nr. 4, 1956.

2 See e.g. Thomas Szasz, *The Medicalization of Everyday Life: Selected Essays*, Syracuse: Syracuse University Press, 2007.

3 I met him after a seminar at Cornell University, where I was a visiting PhD student. The seminar, which took place in Malot Hall on 13 April 2011 had the title "The Insanity Defense: The Case for Abolition".

4 For an investigation of the many definitions of mental illness that have been presented through the years, see Kaj Håkanson, *Psykisk sjukdom: Illusioner och realiteter*, Stockholm: Prisma; Verdandi, 1973.

5 Eugeen Roosens and Lieve van de Walle, *Geel Revisited: After Centuries of Mental Rehabilitation*, Antwerp; Philadelphia, PA: Garant, 2007, p. 27.

6 R. D. Laing and Aaron Esterson, *Sanity, Madness and the Family: Families of Schizophrenics*, New York: Routledge, 2017.

7 Sozialistisches Patientenkollektiv, *SPK – Turn Illness into a Weapon*, Heidelberg: KRRIM, 1993, p. 2.

8 Gianfranco Sanguinetti, Barker John and Scribner Charity, *Red Army Faction. Red Brigades, Angry Brigade. The Spectacle of Terror in Post War Europe*, London: Bread and Circuses, 2015.

9 Hayes, *A Liberated Mind: The Essential Guide to ACT*, p. 16.

10 Stuart Ralph, "Dr Steven Hayes on ACT, OCD and living a meaningful life", 2016, https://theocdstories.com/podcast/dr-steven-hayes-on-act- ocd-and-living-a-meaningful-life/, [2019-11-21].

11 Hayes, *A Liberated Mind: The Essential Guide to ACT*, p. 31.

12 Hayes, *A Liberated Mind: The Essential Guide to ACT*, p. 14.

13 Allen Frances, *Saving Normal: An Insider's Revolt Against Out-Of-Control Psychi- Atric Diagnosis, DSM-5, Big Pharma, and the Medicalization of*

Ordinary Life; Steven C. Hayes, *The ACT In Context: The Canonical Papers of Steven C. Hayes*, New York: Routledge, 2016, pp. 172–173.

14 Moloney, *The Therapy Industry: The Irresistible Rise of the Talking Cure and Why it Doesn't Work*, p. 164.

15 Hayes, *The ACT In Context: The Canonical Papers of Steven C. Hayes*, pp. 244–245.

16 See e.g. Hayes, *The ACT In Context: The Canonical Papers of Steven C. Hayes*, p. 227.

17 For the Buddhist body of thought within ACT, see Hayes, *The ACT In Context: The Canonical Papers of Steven C. Hayes.*

18 James Miller, *Examined Lives: From Socrates to Nietzsche*, NewYork: Farrar, Straus and Giroux, 2011, p. 80.

19 Meister Eckhart, *The Complete Mystical Works of Meister Eckhart*, New York: Herder and Herder Crossroad, 2009, p. 465.

20 Peter Marshall, *Demanding the Impossible: A History of Anarchism,* Oakland, CA: PM Press, 2010, p. 63.

21 See e.g. this interview with Bikkhu Bodhi, Joshua Eaton, "American Buddhism: Beyond the search for inner peace", *Religion Dispatches*, 20/2, 2013 and Vietnam: *Lotus in a Sea of Fire*, New York: Hill and Wang, 1968.

22 Plato, *Skrifter bok 1*, Stockholm: Atlantis, 2016.

13

BEYOND TREATMENT

When I was a child, other people's fears were a mystery to me. I never saw anything but glimpses. Whenever that happened, I felt giddy that something so well hidden could be so big. I just couldn't understand it. Late at night, when we were supposed to be sleeping, a rainbow of worries – doubt, uncertainty, ambivalence and guilt – would start streaming from the adults' mouths, and I would sneak out of my bedroom to eavesdrop.

I never suspected any anxieties among my peers until I found out that one of them took antidepressants. Dan, as I'll call him, had always found school easy. He was one of those students who was ahead of everyone else, and had to wait for the rest of us to catch up. But when we got to high school, he lost his advantage. He started sitting at the back of the classroom, skipped lessons, handed in blank exams.

I remember how big Dan's pupils were sometimes, his irises shrinking to a narrow ring around them. They gave him all sorts of pills, and tricky names like selective serotonin reuptake inhibitors, MAO inhibitors and tricyclic antidepressants all became part of Dan's vocabulary from an early age. The SSRIs were, according to Dan, rat poison. During the introductory period, he felt more anxious than ever. Almost nothing helped with it, not even lithium or Atarax (an allergy medication that his doctor tried out on him). The "benzo," however, cleared his mind.

So many of Dan's fears were my fears, too. The reason he didn't finish his exams was not because he didn't care about them, he just couldn't handle sitting still and being interrogated. He couldn't think, he said. It was like a nightmare. It *was* a nightmare. The blank space beneath each question was such a normalised form of violence that our heads ached with unarticulated grief. With every hoop they demanded we jump through, yet another

DOI: 10.4324/9781003514930-16

shadow fell over the future. I did everything they asked of me. Dan did almost nothing.

We stayed in touch through different high school programmes and into adult life. Dan would go on to collect a number of diagnoses: social anxiety, bipolar disorder, panic disorder. He went through CBT and conversation therapy. One psychologist told him he was probably "a bit psychotic" and that the best thing would be for him to find a woman to have sex with. The psychologist then went on to tell him about all the women he had slept with at Dan's age.

I always assumed that Dan's anxiety was to do with being rejected, about ending up on the wrong side when society sorts children into winners and losers. He continued to live at home – for a long time – and he was also admitted to a psychiatric ward on several occasions. While our classmates took out mortgages and started families, Dan and I spoke about LSD therapy, primal screams and Lacanian psychoanalysis, but also about benzos and SSRIs and the crazy fact that the health system pushes so much medication onto people without also helping them to phase the drugs out.

Dan read up on how to kick the benzo online. He ground up the tablets and diluted each dose with water, increased it again, diluted it, year after year. After fifteen years in the comforting embrace of psychiatry, Dan's life revolved around two competing, sometimes conspiring poles: anxiety and benzodiazepines.

We were both in our thirties when I went to visit him at his childhood home. His mother opened the door to their house like always – her face didn't give anything away. She was kind, Dan's mum, and had previously told me that she was glad Dan got visitors from time to time. I popped my head into the living room to say hello to his dad. His eyes didn't leave the sudoku he was busy working on, but his mouth did move in reply, his lips blue and puffy. One of his eyes was swollen shut.

Still, of everything I saw during that visit, nothing was more remarkable than the painting Dan had set up on the easel in his room. It was so big that it took up almost half the space. With his bed and his desk, there wasn't much room for anything else. I sat down on the bed and stared at it. Dan's paintings were usually monotone Mark Rothkoesque canvases I didn't understand, but this one actually depicted something. I could see human-like veins of light and golden yellow trees, painted so thickly that the detail was lost in the oil paint.

It was a painting full of warmth, confidence, belief. As I sat there and looked at it, it seemed to grow before my eyes. It contained a state of mind I must have forgotten, a nameless feeling of disappointment and jubilation.

Dan had painted it while his life was in freefall.

The police had come to the house the night before. His father had been drinking and started shouting at Dan and his mother. Dan had hit him over the head with a guitar-shaped game controller, then he had locked himself in his room and called the police.

It wasn't the first time he had hit his father, he told me. And it probably wouldn't be the last. The aftermath was always the same: his father emptied the bottles of wine into the sink and said he was going to kill himself. His mother comforted him in his humiliation.

Going through all that was better than the alternative. Ever since Dan had started "getting in between them," his father hadn't hit her. But it also meant that Dan was a prisoner in his own home.

When the police showed up, his parents had apologised and said that Dan had mental health problems.

It wasn't until that moment, seventeen years into our friendship, that I really understood Dan's situation.

I asked whether any of his psychologists knew that he had grown up in an abusive household. They didn't. To them, he was simply one of many patients with "therapy resistant" anxiety disorder. Untreatable.

I asked whether he understood that he didn't owe it to his parents to stay at home. He said he did. I told him that he had every right to report his father and let the law decide his parents' fate. He understood that, too, but he also had the right not to report him. They were clearly willing to let him suffer for their misery, so why not leave them to suffer on their own?

Dan turned to his painting, used the paintbrush to point.

"I know," he said.

The key thing now was that he cut back on his dose and got his life in order. Until then, there wasn't much he could do, he said.

We sat in silence for a while. Yet again, I found myself being drawn to Dan's painting, which seemed to possess a reality so much greater than our own. Whatever I said, I knew Dan would have already thought about it. There was no repressed trauma, no knot of nerves to untangle in his brain. The situation was as simple as his options were awful.

Dan wasn't looking to defend his rights or even to abide by imposed morals. He didn't want to condemn his parents to an old age spent in separate apartments. Nor did he want his mother to fall apart in their continued life together. He wanted to find a solution. Unfortunately that solution was something that no primal screams, no psychedelic dissolution of the self, no enlightened state of nirvana could bring him.

Dan was in a difficult situation, and that situation was in him.

It would be easy to point to a story like Dan's and claim that the modern intolerance of uncertainty is irrelevant, that all we should be interested in are concrete examples of repression. There may well be good strategic reasons for this kind of approach, but it does nothing to help us understand worry. In Dan's case, there was one thing that – all other things being equal – would have helped him: if he had stopped viewing his worry as a sign of ill health.

He needed to take his worry for what it was: A reasonable reaction to an unreasonable situation. He should have been given help understanding that it wasn't *his* worry, *his* problem; that it was, in some sense, admirable that he was taking such responsibility for his family but that he was not the only individual to analyse or treat in the context. For over fifteen years, Dan had been taught the opposite. The psychiatry that had failed to create an honest relationship with him had invested considerable resources into uncovering him one limb at a time, until all that remained was a cardboard cut-out with zero context.

That isn't to say that Dan was a defenceless victim in all this. He could have shared his situation with the people who were tasked with helping him, and he could have refused treatment. Instead, he chose the dizzying path that I – before I began working on this book – thought was unique to him. He chose Christ-like suffering – albeit without the satisfaction of feeling like a Christ-figure. His story remained hidden from the world (even now, anonymised as he is), buried beneath colossal assumptions about genetic predisposition, serotonin, dopamine, stress, and so on.

One confusing circumstance is that Dan developed a number of independent anxiety problems – all of which fulfilled the criteria for several diagnoses – while he was undergoing various psychiatric treatments. As a result, calling his case an example of medicalisation obscures rather than clarifies. In some ways, his situation was less complicated than many others', because it involved such a concrete concern. But Dan's mental health problems were very real. He belonged to the broad group of people who have spotted a risk, attempted to neutralise it, and seen their worry sprout more worry in the process.

The usual approach here is to explain this awareness of risk through human evolution and a survival instinct. I have suggested several other explanations.

Like other sociologists and anthropologists, I have taken our *expanding time horizon* as my starting point. The reason is simple: a person who is not thinking about tomorrow is a person who is not worrying. The Buddhist mantra about being present in the here and now is an effective technique for derailing worry. No matter which world religion we turn to, we see the same basic message in different forms. "Therefore take no thought, saying, What shall we eat? or, What shall we drink? or, Wherewithal shall we be clothed?" urged Jesus. "For your heavenly Father knoweth that ye have need of all these things."[1]

What neither Jesus nor Buddha said was that the earliest people in history seem to have survived perfectly well without these questions about tomorrow. The relatively young age of clock time only tells half the story. What matters more is the time shift that took place when mankind began to farm the land and plan for future harvests. The social structures that emerged once agriculture became the dominant means of production cannot be overstated. Among those who continued to hunt and gather, attentiveness remained an inherent part of life. It wasn't something they had to achieve. They lived lives full of danger and suffering, but they didn't live their lives lost in thought.

When the ticking clock became the model for the universe, with plants and animals seen as *mechanical machines* rather than organisms, that left man as the only autonomous being – like a puppet master with countless strings of cause and effect in his hands. Manipulating the world to our own advantage became modern mankind's project, but it also became a way to manage the *risks* we created in the process. Society emerged as an external object whose inherent risks began to preoccupy both science and politics. From having occupied a relatively obscure space in public life, risk became the weapon politicians used to win elections.

A more risk-focused politics would have been an easy burden to bear if the logic of risk had stopped there. A collective risk is a shared risk, after all, something we can talk and worry about together. But the most severe worry does not stop on the surface. The most severe worries want to get to the very heart of us.

I have sketched out no more than an outline of the awareness of time and the development of mechanist philosophy, but there is much to be said about *the creation of the self-aware individual.* I cannot emphasise enough that individuals have, in a certain sense, always existed. What we sociologists mean when we speak about individualisation is that we have become increasingly *preoccupied by ourselves* as individuals. While there were once frameworks that were of more importance than the individual – from the family to the village community, religion to class, gender to profession – these have, for better or worse, fallen away, and what has emerged in their place is a job market, a welfare system, an education system and a justice system in which the individual is expected to take responsibility for themselves. Where the individual ends up in these systems' catalogues of success or failure is down to the individual themselves.

This autonomy is associated with ambivalence and self-examination. While social systems are based on a unified, independent individual, science has long been preoccupied with splitting the individual into opposing forces. Predisposition, nerves, subconscious desires, repressed trauma, selfish genes and labile neurotransmitters are all present within the individual, like foreign bodies with the power to deceive and undermine the supervisory authority we call our self. Which of these is thought to be pulling the levers of the machine has varied over history, but each has contributed to alienating the individual from their own experiences. One consequence of this is that we no longer simply have to navigate an exterior world full of all sorts of risks. There is also an inner world – of thoughts, feelings and amalgamations of the two – and it too provides a rich source of worry.

When we worry, these external and internal risks come together. Worry is not simply a statement of risk. Worry is also a desire to shake off the internal tension that is the worry itself. There are countless variations in the type of worry affecting us, but it also follows patterns.

There are *territories of risk* in which individuals are particularly preoccupied with searching themselves. These territories of risk are historic, and can have both long and short lifespans. There is, for example, nothing natural about a religious person questioning whether they "believe" in the right way, just as there is nothing natural about a person questioning whether they have the right sexuality or love in the right way. These territories of risk rest on notions and practices that, for previous generations, would seem as incomprehensible as the seventeenth century frenzy over witches does today.

The uncertainty of these territories of risk is also surrounded by an expectation of rationality and certainty. Though we cannot possibly make the many life choices we are faced with on rational grounds, we expect that both of others and of ourselves.

To remain in uncertainty is to lower one's guard. It is to risk catastrophe, and it is also to risk being blamed for acting "thoughtlessly."

None of this crossed my mind as I sat on Dan's bed that day, studying his painting. What I thought about were the lightyears of wordless distance separating him from me, and both of us from our surroundings. Right there and then, I think we both would have welcomed an alarm warning of the imminent end of the world. Breaking the spirals of lonely thought and becoming part of a community of destiny would, at least initially, have been liberating.

This highlights the inconsistency of worry: boundlessly responsible on the inside, almost indifferent on the outside; megalomaniacal in the counterfactual world of thought, passive in the actual world of action. Self-sacrificing but egotistical. Rational to the point of absurdity.

Straightening out the contradictions of worry is one of its favourite thought exercises.

Anyone who has ever tried to think away worries will also have experienced their elasticity and white bear-like stubbornness. Even on a purely theoretical basis, it can be hard to see a way out. Focusing on individual variables like inequality or screen time has the benefit of allowing us to mechanically imagine how, by doing away with evil at one end, we can achieve relief at the other. But if worry is grounded in modernity itself, what are Dan and all the rest of us supposed to do?

Meditate, accept and medicate?

If the great worry is rooted in a society that is really just the sum total of how we, as individuals, live together, is there nothing we can do to change that society?

Our age is often described as the age of cynicism. We believe in neither God nor utopia. We look truth in the eye and are under no illusions. But if we take a closer look at that cynicism, it is directed primarily at the possibility of making social progress. When it comes to individual happiness, we are anything but cynical. Society may be screwed, but as an individual I can still forge my own path to happiness. What if this cynicism could be inverted? What if, instead, we said: my happiness may be screwed, but the idea that this society – the only one in history – cannot be changed seems unlikely.

In a speculative break with the rest of this book, I would like to end by shifting from facts to counter-facts with regards to the world, not as it is but as it could be. What I am suggesting are opportunities: fragile, surreal and, to varying degrees, improbable openings to something else. Going back in time is not an option. The many choices and risks we are faced with today are here to stay, but the way in which we approach them is not set in stone. What I have in mind is not a certain world.

What if we abandoned the promise of peace of mind? While collective well-being is strangely absent from public discourse, the societal decree that I, as an individual, should be happy hangs like a millstone around my neck.

In the harmonious smile of Buddha, in the magical images of weekend ads, the newspapers' heart-warming "at home with" reports, the message is always the same: be happy!

In the face of this ideological bombardment, acceptance – living life as it is – is a powerful antidote. But if worry and other "negative feelings" are only accepted in the hopes of making them go away, this acceptance is nothing but an illusion. With the promise of eternal peace of mind looming, acceptance becomes yet another move in the game of getting rid of thoughts through thoughts. The transcendence of acceptance does not come from the paradoxical reward that may arrive when we stop expecting a reward. Transcendence comes from choosing the truth over our feelings.

The truth of worry is that the world is uncertain. This truth lives in even the most obscure compulsive thoughts, and what such compulsive thoughts exemplify is that uncertainty is eternal. Only our imagination can set limits on the number of risks a person can worry about. As a result, worry contains a microscopic insight. The microscopic nature of this insight may well prevent us from realising that the entire world is uncertain and that no matter what we do, we take risks in our everyday lives that other people would regard as unacceptable. But it is only by approaching our own fear that we can come to really know the nature of the world. In this sense, courage is neither a feeling nor a virtue. Courage is an act, and the promise of courage is not to make us experience the world in a certain way, but to bring us closer to it.

What if our worries about the bad gave way to a longing for the good? The aversion to risk has, throughout history, paid few dividends in terms of social development. It has played no part in any reforms of historical significance. In fact, in the abolitionists' demands for the end of slavery, in the suffragettes' fight for universal voting rights, in the union movement's first health and unemployment schemes, the logic was the opposite: taking a risk for a greater good.

The demand for rational calculation fuels the irrationality of risk-based politics. Those risks that win votes are rarely the most likely or damaging. So far, no one has won an election on the promise of fighting global warming, despite the fact that its consequences are already catastrophic, with melting glaciers and the most rapid mass extinction of species in sixty-five million years. On the other hand, several elections have been won on the promise of taking a harder line against supposedly violent and sexually deviant immigrant groups.[2]

Pictures and narratives, not likelihood or damage: These are the hard currency of the politics of risk, and the overarching message is always one of neutralisation – that we need to neutralise that which frightens us. Risk management is built into modern technology, and is therefore unavoidable. It is reasonable that bridges, power stations and dams are maintained, that they are preserved for the future. But when that same logic is applied to society, it only benefits a type of conservatism based on the premise that society is fine as it is.

Breaking with the politics of risk involves swapping downward counterfactuals for upward ones, allowing our worries to be challenged by the longing for better things. This also means refraining from invoking external necessity as a political argument – no longer lying, in other words. Neither the arms race, international terrorism nor global warming can force society in any direction. It is always possible to choose vulnerability over the minimisation of risk, and it is often the more ethical option, too. Which vision we choose to build our politics on can, of course, be informed by the risks we face. But when faced with global warming, for example, there is a difference between laying the foundations for an economy that is not built on constant growth and finding the solution in geoengineering, electric vehicles and an expansion of nuclear power. When faced with gang violence on the fringes of our cities, there is a difference between pursuing policies that aim to reduce inequality and introducing stricter borders and expanding the police force. The centring of risk is not an either or. There are degrees, and there is always a possibility that the worry will cling on, no matter what we do. The choice isn't between worry or peace of mind, it is about the principles our politics are built upon.

What if our understanding of time can still be reshaped? Setting off on mental journeys through time, to futures we have never seen and pasts that will never come back, is a natural human ability. But when we go on these journeys through time so often that we feel alienated from the world that is right before our eyes, that is not natural.

It is true that, as individuals, we can learn to be more attentive through all sorts of methods, but it is also true that there was a time when attentiveness was not something that needed to be practised, it simply was, as natural as hearing and seeing. The prerequisite for this attentiveness was the natural abundance, the fact that the earth provided us with enough food that we didn't have to plan so much, nor calculate the likelihood of future catastrophes.

That natural surplus is never coming back. We are never going to be able to leave our cities and go picking fruit in our billions. That isn't to say that we are living in a time of shortages. During the twentieth century alone, industrialised societies increased their productivity levels by tenfold on average. We are now producing more than ever, with less and less labour, and since the "affluent society" of the 1970s was criticised for its unsustainability, productivity among OECD countries has doubled. According to the UN Food and Agriculture Organization, we currently produce enough food to feed the global population – and half again. Surplus is a fact, but it is unevenly distributed, not just in terms of food but all production.[3]

We can continue to produce more and more – if not indefinitely, then at least for the foreseeable future. We can allow sea levels to rise, the deserts to grow, possibly even mine for ore on other planets. Nature is not going to force us to stop.

But we can also choose another path. How this is done – through increasingly shorter working hours, universal basic income or the democratisation of production, in which we 3D print the majority of what we want ourselves – is of less importance. What matters is that the question is not just one of social justice or environmental sustainability. Something else is at stake, namely the opportunity to forge a new principle of living by, in the words of Hartmut Rosa, creating a "secure baseline or floor in a system of *steep and slippery declines*".[4] Ultimately, this would imply shaking off "the economic problem," as John Maynard Keynes put it – having to work to survive – which, without exaggeration, would represent the greatest transformation of human existence since we began to farm the earth.[5]

What if our thoughts become increasingly ineffective? A person can have murderous thoughts about her neighbour while, in reality, helping her. A person can also have fond thoughts about her neighbour while, in reality, murdering her. Thinking is a means of abstracting and understanding the world. Our thoughts themselves are as real as the numbers on a calculator.

The purpose of observing our own thoughts without engaging with them – a practice most major meditative traditions make use of – is to get a glimpse of this unreality. That applies to *all* thinking, not just the anxious or "negative" thoughts. Pleasurable, intelligent, altruistic, well-meaning thoughts are just as illusory.

Over and above this eternal condition, we see a historic tendency in which the *communicative* thought – the thought that has left a person's silent consciousness – loses meaning in the same way as a currency in inflationary decline. Nailing one's thesis to a church door – or sharing it on social media, in a newspaper, in a book – represents, at most, one distraction among many. This can also be seen in scientific advances, with the number per published study falling – at the time of writing, a new scientific article is published every twenty seconds, with the emergence of between two and three hundred new scientific journals every year. [6]

Using the analogy of an individual's many thoughts, we have created a maelstrom of opinion in which the most radical ideas and profound analyses are promoted and shot down without making the slightest bit of difference to our lives.

What if the idea of a social critique that mobilises collective outrage and drives society towards eternal development rests on assumptions that have no basis in reality?

In an analysis of eleven million posts on social media in China, a group of researchers managed to map out which posts were removed by the state censorship machine. When they investigated what the censored posts had in common, they were surprised by their findings. The pattern ran contrary to Orwellian notions of a dictatorial thought police. Posts accusing the government of being "shameless with greed," of trading dignity for power, of "having no limits on immorality" or of providing its ministers with mistresses, for example, were not censored. Nor were intellectual arguments about the party betraying its Maoist legacy.

The censorship was focused on something else: action. Anything touching upon or encouraging collective action was quickly taken down. In this, the censors were remarkably effective. These posts were typically almost completely eliminated within twenty-four hours. And not just those explicitly calling for protests or resistance – comments about demonstrators and terrorist attacks also disappeared, as did those that were more positive towards the government.

"The results are unambiguous," write the researchers, "posts are censored if they are in a topic area with collective action potential and not otherwise. Whether or not the posts are in favor of the government, its leaders, and its policies has no measurable effect on the probability of censorship."[7]

It is almost as though someone in the Chinese government has discovered that thoughts are empty, and come to the conclusion that they may as well allow people to think what they want. So long as they don't do anything about it, they are free to comfort themselves with their critical thoughts and ideas of having "seen through the system." "They don't care what you think of them or say about them," as one of the study's authors points out, "they only care what you can do."[8]

This should not surprise anyone. All power rests on action. What we think has no impact on anyone other than, perhaps, ourselves. To live a relevant life is to act in opposition to what a dictator would have wanted. If it were possible to develop a sociological self-help, this would be the overarching aim: to allow our concerns for our inner world to be transferred to our concerns for the external world.

What if catastrophe has already struck? History shows us that there are, in fact, other ways to live, but there is an idea that society as it currently exists should go on forever. This idea is so pervasive that it is often seen as neutral by social commentators and researchers. Even when the idea is challenged and, in an act of collective despair, we declare that a radical, lasting transformation of society is needed in order to address one crisis or another, action is conspicuous in its absence. United in agreement that something has to be done, we come face to face with our own impotence: *Doing* something is virtually the only thing we are unable to do.

In the proclamations of crisis that are made – something *really* must be done! – a longing is awakened. May the great crisis force us into taking the action we clearly cannot achieve on our own. But a crisis can only provoke reactions. The action is its own cause, its own explanation. It is born not from worry, hope or any other emotion. It arises by itself.

Acting means risking catastrophe. Not acting also risks catastrophe. Whether we take that risk or avoid it, the risk of catastrophe remains. But not all catastrophes belong in the future. In this book I have described the catastrophe that is our aversion to risk. That catastrophe is here and now.

Notes

1 Matthew, 6:28–33, *King James Bible.*
2 E. S. Brondizio et al., "Global assessment report on biodiversity and ecosystem services of the intergovernmental science-policy platform on biodiversity and ecosystem services", *The United Nations' Intergovernmental Science-Policy Platform on Biodiversity and Ecosystem Services* (IPBES), 2019.
3 Eric Holt-Giménez et al, "We already grow enough food for 10 billion people... and still can't end hunger", *Journal of Sustainable Agriculture*, vol. 36, nr. 6, 2012.
4 Andreas Reckwitz and Hartmut Rosa, *Late Modernity in Crisis*, Cambridge: Polity Press, 2023, p. 150.
5 John Maynard Keynes, *Essays in Persuasion,* New York: W. W. Norton & Co., 1991 [1931].

6 Mats Alvesson, Yiannis Gabriel and Roland Paulsen, *Return to Meaning: A Social Science with Something to Say*, Oxford: Oxford University Press, 2017, pp. 4–5.
7 Gary King, Jennifer Pan and Margaret E Roberts, "How censorship in China allows government criticism but silences collective expression", *American Political Science Review*, vol. 107, nr. 2, 2013; Gary King, Jennifer Pan and Margaret E Roberts, "Reverse-engineering censorship in China: Randomized experimentation and participant observation", *Science*, vol. 345, nr. 6199, 2014; Gary King, Jennifer Pan and Margaret E Roberts, "How the Chinese government fabricates social media posts for strategic distraction, not engaged argument", *American Political Science Review*, vol. 111, nr. 3, 2017.
8 Gary King, "Information control by authoritarian gover,nments", 2020, https://gking.harvard.edu/category/research-interests/applications/information-control-by-authoritarian-governments [2020/04/14].

INDEX

acceptance 222, 224
Acceptance and Commitment Therapy (ACT) 220
acrophobia 63
acting/not acting 237
action 2, 49, 54, 99, 114
affluent society 235
aggression 172–178
agnosticism 223
alcoholism 28, 204
Alexander, Bruce 203
altruistic suicide 29
ambition 2
anguish 49, 50
anicca 222–223
animal cognition 98
animism 79
Annie, Gruyer 141–144, 147, 148, 159
anthropologists 42, 74
anti-anxiety medication 135
antidepressants 135, 195, 227
anti-psychiatry movement 217
anti-suicide contract 29
anxiety 2, 6, 49, 61, 62, 72; actions 11; ambivalence inherent in 128; compulsion 11; depression and 24; disorders 10; exposure therapy 222; obsession 11; panic 106; self-reflection 11; types of 186; *what if* 5–6
arguments 4
Aristotle 95, 223
artificial intelligence 101
artistic activity 107
asceticism 92
atomic clock 82
attentiveness 235
authenticity 182
ayahuasca trips 201, 209

Barrett, Elizabeth 184
basal ganglia 8
Bauer, Lee 176
Beauvoir, Simone de 50
Being and Nothingness 49
"benzo" 227, 228
Bergwall, Sture 155–158
Bergwall's morbid claims 156
Berman, Morris 79
Bijur, Angelika 153, 154
Blundell, Bill 174
Bourdieu, Pierre 85
Boyadjian, Charly 113
"brain fag" 62
Brensing, Karsten 99
Bretécher, Rose 169
Brody, Hugh 80
Browning, Robert 184
Buddha 222, 224, 230, 233
Buddhism 222, 224
Buddhist principles 63
bureaucracy 55

Calvinism 167
cancer 4, 10, 73, 121–123, 138, 208

capitalism 86, 87, 136, 137, 218
capsulotomy 187
Carhart-Harris, Robin 210
catastrophes 3, 4, 10, 80, 237
catastrophic misinterpretations 185
catastrophic thinking 59, 123
causality 94
censorship 236
Chalmers, David 100
Chaudhary, Ajay Singh 84
chemical imbalance 25
Cheyne, George 146
childhood mental health 25
Chiles, John 27
"chippers" 203
Christianson, Sven, Å. 156
civilisation 65, 123
claustrophobia 64
climate change 10
"clinically significant suffering" 22
clinical psychology 48, 49
clinical trials 62
clock time 114
coconut clock 81
cognitive ability 55
cognitive psychology 40, 58
communicative thought 236
communism 136
comorbidity 62
concealed discontent 112
conceptual thinking 65
confession 3, 4
confidence 86
conflicting activity 5
consciousness 61, 74, 77, 79, 98, 100, 198; hard problem of 100
conversational therapy 195
Copernicus, Nicolaus 96
counterfactual thinking 40, 42, 44, 45, 58, 61, 64, 144
counter-factual thoughts 216
courage 233
craftsmanship 79, 111
criticism 1, 23, 83; of medicalisation 22
Crowe, Michael 158
cultural variation 60
culture of fear 128, 129
Cusk, Rachel 162
cynicism 233
"dark web" 5

Darwin, Charles 97
Dass, Ram 211
Davis, Lennard 186
Dawkins, Richard 101
Dawson, John 57
daydreamers 46
daydreaming 214
death 124; risk of 58, 60
debriefing 150
deep brain stimulation 187
dehumanisation 65
dejection 2
delayed dividends 75
dementia 62
Demme, Jonathan 157
depression 61, 62, 107, 149, 195, 200, 207, 209, 215
Descartes, René 96, 97, 100, 146, 147
dexterity 115
diagnostic questionnaires 23
digital evidence 6
direct dividends 75, 76
disaster 136–137
disembodied psychology 26
disenchantments 106; cause and effect 90; Homo Mechanicus 99–102; labour of animals 98; sociology 102
dispute 54
distraction to addiction 201–205
dizziness 59
"dizziness of freedom" 11
Dostoyevsky, Fyodor 47, 77, 78, 80
Durkheim, Émile 17, 29
dysfunctional connections 8

Eckehart, Meister 223
economic growth 19, 25, 137
economic uncertainty 109
education 114
Einstein, Albert 55, 56
Electra complex 148
Ellis, Bret Easton 157
emancipation, possibility of 65
emotional electric shocks 201
emotions 41, 54, 93, 176, 201, 237
empathy 198
enchantment 90–95
"ensouled" 94
environmental adaptations 98
environmental toxins 136
escapism 209
Esquirol, Jean-Étienne 166
ethereal certainty 183
"evolutionary background" 78
excessive thinking 62–64

exhaustion 105
existential philosophy 49, 50
expanding time horizon 230
experienced-based precision art 110
experience sampling 44
exposure therapy 181

Fallon, James, H. 178
false confessions 158
fatalism 102
fear of heights 59, 63
Fermat's Last Theorem 44
Fernando, Gaithri 150
"filing cabinet" 206
financial and technological development 18
financial worries 106
firearms 30
food production techniques 18
forbidden lust 181
forced mental lethargy 112
Foucault, Michel 171
Frances, Allen 220
Frankl, Viktor 102
Franklin, Benjamin 85, 114
Freud, Sigmund 8, 47, 79, 101, 142, 143, 147, 151–154, 159, 170, 182
Freudian slip 152
Frink, Horace 153–154
Fritzl, Josef 178
frustration 205
fundamental incompatibility 181

Gall, Franz Joseph 177
Gebser, Jean 78, 79
Geel model 218
gendered subordination 63
generalised anxiety disorder (GAD) 53, 180, 214, 217
genetic constant 186
genetic mapping 220
genetics 25
Gilbert, William 95
Ginsberg, Allen 211
Global Burden of Disease Study 26
global warming 134, 137
Gödel, Kurt 55, 91
Goffman, Erving 155
Goldstein, Rebecca 55
Griffiths, Roland 208
guilt 6, 58, 196; unconscious feelings of 8

habituation process 64, 222
Haidt, Jonathan 24, 25, 200
hallucinogens *see* psychedelic drugs
handwashing 164
Hanh, Thích Nhât 225
happiness: material living standards 20; meaningfulness 21; richest countries 19; younger generation 20; *see also* unhappiness
happy existence 2
Hausner, Siegfried 219
Hawking, Stephen 82
Hayes, Steven, C. 219–222
hedonistic self-examination 182
Heidegger, Martin 50, 182
Heraclitus 223
Hochschild, Arlie Russell 117, 118
Hoyle, Fred 97
Huber, Wolfgang 218, 219
humanity 9
Hume, David 96
hurting 54
Huxley, T. H. 223
Hymenoptera order 98
hypermorality 8
hypochondria 123

illness 22, 24; and Situation 216–219
imagination 44
imagined pain 31
implications 3
impossible choices 85
inauthenticity 168
incompleteness theorem 55
incomprehensible concepts 63
inconsistency 124
independent anxiety problems 230
indirect stress 71
individualisation 231
indulge 2
industrial capitalism 210
inequality 108
infant mortality 76
insight 10
insufficient lust 181
intellectual overexertion 92
intelligence 55
internet addiction 149, 200
interpersonal problems 28
interracial marriage 132
investigation 6
ironworkers 59–60

James, William 60, 92
Janet, Pierre 101
Jaspers, Karl 90
Jesus 6, 166, 230
Jung, Carl Gustav 78, 79, 151–154

Kahneman, Daniel 40
Kepler, Johannes 95, 96
Keynes, John Maynard 235
khit pen meditation techniques 63
Kierkegaard, Søren 11, 49, 50, 59, 63, 223
Knausgård, Karl-Ove 162, 163, 168
Krafft-Ebing, Richard von 171
Krishnamurti, Jiddu 65
kufungisisa ('thinking too much' in Shona) 61, 62

Lacan, Jacques 155
Lacan, Sibylle 155
Laing, R. D. 218
latent homosexual 152–154
learned inability 9
Leary, Timothy 210
life satisfaction 19, 207
Lindbergh, Charles Augustus 158
Lindbergh confessions 158
Lombroso, Cesare 177
Lombroso Program 177
loneliness 149
Loving, Olivia 174
Luria, Alexander 41–44, 46, 144–146, 150
Luther, Martin 166

magic consciousness 78
Markram, Henry 101
Martin, John Levi 151
Marx, Karl 98
mass media 129
masturbation 132, 133
maya, veil of illusion 61
"mean world syndrome" 176
mechanical clock 82
mechanical materialism 97
mechanical organisms 98
medicalisation 230
medical perspective 8
meditation techniques 61
mental health 26; childhood 25; problems 61, 218, 229; societal factors 220
mental illness 10, 24, 217, 220
mental suffering 22
metamorphoses 4
metatheoretical perspective 57
Michels, Robert 92
Miller, Alice 157
mindfulness 54
"mind wandering" 45
miscegenation 132
Mitchell, Joseph 60
modern rationality, irrational outcomes of 55
Moloney, Paul 207
Monod, Jacques 98
Montaigne, Michel de 53, 57–60
Moore, John 166, 167
Moreau, Jacques-Joseph 218
Morgenstern, Oskar 57
music 2

negative effect 18
negative feelings 233
negative thoughts 48, 49
nervous disorders 146, 147
nervousness 146
Neumann, Carl 92
neuropsychiatric research 220
neutralisation strategy 164, 181
Nikolai, Tolstoy 46, 47
"non-self" 222
"no-touch" rules 172

obsessive-compulsive disorders 7, 9, 186
obsessive thoughts 7–9
"oceanic feeling" 79
oedipal obsession 151
one-car accidents 71
Ong, Walter 80
opioids 201
orbitofrontal cortex 8
orthographic processing 126
outbursts 54
over-medication 22
overthinkers 63
"painful life circumstances" 28

Palme, Olof 158
panic disorder 106
parenthood 19
partial insanity 147
Pasteur, Louis 164
peaceful activity 2
pendulum clock 82
Penzel, Fred 175

pessimistic philosophy 48
pharmacological power 203
phenomenologists 41
philosophical notion 50
phonics-based approach 126
Pinel, Philippe 147
plagiarism 4, 5
Plato 183, 223
Pollan, Michael 210
positive thoughts 46
"post-politics" 135
poverty 9, 109, 130, 131
pre-agricultural society 73
pre-industrial societies 73
principles of aesthetics 55
prolonged stress 71
pseudo patients 23
psilocybin experiments 210
psychedelic drugs 207–209
psychedelic wave 206
psychiatric patients 73
psychiatry 23, 217; problems 9
psychoanalysis/psychoanalyst/psychoanalytical revolution 47, 141–144, 147, 148, 152, 155, 159
psychological resistance 157, 168
psychopathy 138
psychopharmaceutical drug 134, 149
psychopharmaceuticals 149, 156
psychopharmacological drugs 22
psychosis 62
"publishing bias" 206
punishment 3
"pure experience" 60
Putnam, Robert 149

Radecki, Sigismund von 83
Radin, Paul 80
Raine, Adrian 177, 178
Rapoport, Judith 164
Rasenberger, Jim 58–60
"rational soul" 97
reassurance 4
receptive stillness 80
regret 41
relationship-obsessive compulsive disorder (R-OCD) 179
relationships 178–185
religion 165–168
replication crisis 206
repressed desire 153, 181
repression 152, 229
repressive communities 149, 151
responsibility 2–4, 54, 127, 128
richest countries 19
Rickert, Heinrich 92
risk 3, 10; management, disasters of 130; of masturbation 132; morality of 127–131; rationality of 123–127; territories of 232; wrong decision 12
risk aversion 128
risk of falling 57–59
risk society 128
romantic relationship 72
Rosa, Hartmut 94, 235
Rosenhan, David, L. 22, 23
Rothko, Mark 228
Roudinesco, Élisabeth 155
Rudder, Christian 184
rumination 61

samadhi 199
Sartre, Jean-Paul 49, 50, 134, 163, 182, 219
Saulle, Legrand du 165, 166
schizophrenia 138
Schopenhauer, Arthur 48, 49
Scott, James, C. 84
scrupulosity 167
secret suicide attempts 71
self-accusations 166, 178, 186
self-analysis 144
self-awareness 79
self-castration 91
self-combustion 127
self-conservation 96
self-criticism 199
self-destructive behaviour 203
self-fulfilling risks 137–139
self-inflicted starvation 57
self-interrogation 169, 170
"selfish gene" 101
self-obsessed blindness 63
self-reflection 44, 54, 91
self-reflexivity 129
self-suspicions: homosexuality 162; obsessive-compulsive thought 164, 167; territories of risk 164–185; *what ifs* 163, 164
Semmelweis, Ignaz 164
Sennett, Richard 115
sensory information 8
sexology 171
sexual activity 113
sexuality 168–172
Shaffer, Howard 203

shame 196
shortcomings 8
Siffre, Michel 83
silence 198–200
"Skinner boxes" 202
Smith, Adam 111, 112
social anxiety 64
social desirability 22
Socialist Patients' Collective 218
social recognition 10
social regulation 171
socio-historical factors 41
sociology 17, 38, 39, 55
Socrates 223
solidarity 63
Spinoza, Baruch 183
spiritual bypassing 209
"stimulus-independent thinking" 45
stress 25, 26, 28, 105, 106, 201, 230
Strosahl, Kirk 27
subconscious fantasies 151
subsistence method 85
suffering 1, 2, 10, 22, 222, 224, 230, 231; *see also* mental suffering
suicidal patients 73
suicide 17, 18, 137, 153–155, 168; mental health issues 26; note writers 26–29; violence 27
Sullivan, Harry Stack 155
surveillance 6
Suzman, James 74
Suzuki, Daisetz Teitaro 65
syllogisms 43
Szasz, Thomas 217, 220

Taylor, Frederick Winslow 111
Terkel, Studs 112
terrorism 125, 126
thalamus 8
"therapy resistant" anxiety disorder 229
thinking too much 63
thought-filled existence 65
thoughts: absorption 61; mechanics of 63–65; sickness of 60–63
time horizon: anxiety 72; attentiveness 80; death sentence 77; hunter-gatherer society 74–76, 79, 80; indirect stress 71; intensity, of life 77–80; movement of planets 81; one-car accidents 71; prolonged stress 71; romantic relationship 72; San people's perception of time 74; secret suicide attempts 71; standardisation process 83; suicidal patients 73
"time-sickness" 84
Tolstoy, Leo 21, 46–48
transcendence 233
Turing, Alan 57
Tversky, Amos 40
Twenge, Jean, M. 24, 25, 200

uncertainty 7, 86, 110, 114, 221; acceptance of 223; territories of risk 232
underestimation 1
"underworking" 111
unemployment 9, 10, 105, 107, 109, 110, 130, 234
unhappiness 21–26; antidepressant 21; bereavement 22; depression 22, 23; medicalisation 22; psychiatric care 25; psychosomatic problems 25; survey methodology 21; *see also* happiness
Ure, Andrew 111
"valued direction" 225

violence 54, 176–178, 227, 234
vipassana 61
Vygotsky, Lev 41

Waal, Frans de 99
Wallace, David Foster 29–31
wandering mind 46
Wang, Hao 57
Warner, Charles Dudley 83
Watts, Alan 64
Weber, Marianne 91, 92
Weber, Max 86, 90, 133, 167
Weeks, Jeffrey 171
Wegner, Daniel 47
Western medicine 62
western sexuality 171
what ifs 56, 57, 60, 163; Covid-19, 9; preoccupation with 64; questions 5–6, 9, 10
working life 114
World Health Organization (WHO) 9, 23–25
worry 71, 106, 108, 146, 163–168, 224–225, 232–234; cause and effect 90; definition 39, 40; external and internal risks 232; fear 39;

inconsistency of 232; individual responsibilities 45; inner conflict 49; logical inference 44; loneliness 39; movement of thought 39; regret 49; relationships 45; self-consciousness 38; self-reinforcement 162; sensory experiences 44; *what ifs* 9–11, 39; *see also individual entries*

Yixuan, Linji 224

zazen 61

For Product Safety Concerns and Information please contact our EU
representative GPSR@taylorandfrancis.com
Taylor & Francis Verlag GmbH, Kaufingerstraße 24, 80331 München, Germany

www.ingramcontent.com/pod-product-compliance
Ingram Content Group UK Ltd.
Pitfield, Milton Keynes, MK11 3LW, UK
UKHW020147200926
475702UK00016B/2581

* 9 7 8 1 0 3 2 8 4 7 7 7 1 *